Politics of Sexuality

We live in an age when sex, gender and sexualities can no longer be presumed to be non-political, pre-political or even marginal. Political activity and activism around sexual politics have pervaded and transformed the political agenda. As a consequence, these developments have given rise to significant changes in all areas of political life, from electoral politics and local government to public policy and international relations.

This book recognises sexuality as a mainstream concept in political analysis and explores issues in the politics of sexuality that are highly salient and controversial today. These include conceptions of citizenship and nationality linked to gender and sexuality, the legislation about the age of consent, prostitution and 'trafficking in women', the international politics of population control, abortion and sexual harassment, and sexuality in the military. The international team of contributors provides a wide range of perspectives in a variety of contexts. On a national level they offer illustrative case studies from the UK, Ireland, the Netherlands, Spain and Israel, among others, and on an international plane they cover the European Union, the UN Conference on Population and Development and the role of the Vatican as an international arbiter. Moreover, the volume addresses the interaction between political discourse and the work of major theorists such as Weber, Freud, Foucault, Irigaray and Butler.

Politics of Sexuality proposes new methodological enquiries on the definition of sexuality and its role in politics, and furthers the debate on how sexual politics determines and constructs the identities of citizens. A rich and challenging addition to the literature of political science, this volume will interest all those who seek to explore the political and intellectual changes associated with the emergence of sexuality as a political issue.

Terrell Carver is Professor of Political Theory at the University of Bristol, UK. **Véronique Mottier** teaches social theory and interpretive methodologies at the University of Geneva, Switzerland.

The contributors are: Delila Amir, Mark Bell, Orly Benjamin, David Boothroyd, Terrell Carver, Alan Finlayson, John R. Gibbins, Katrina Gorjanicyn, Gail Hawkes, Stevi Jackson, Moya Lloyd, Véronique Mottier, Palena R. Neale, Joyce Outshoorn, Momin Rahman, Paul Skidmore, Celia Valiente and Matthew Waites.

ROUTLEDGE/ECPR STUDIES IN EUROPEAN POLITICAL SCIENCE

Edited by Hans Keman, *Vrije University, the Netherlands*, and Jan W. van Deth, *University of Mannheim, Germany, on behalf of the European Consortium for Political Research*

The Routledge/ECPR Studies in European Political Science Series is published in association with the European Consortium for Political Research – the leading organisation concerned with the growth and development of political science in Europe. The series presents high-quality edited volumes on topics at the leading edge of current interest in political science and related fields, with contributions from European scholars and others who have presented work at ECPR workshops or research groups.

Also available from Routledge in association with the ECPR:

Politics of sexuality

Identity, gender, citizenship

Edited by Terrell Carver and Véronique Mottier

ROUTLEDGE

London and New York

First published 1998
by Routledge
11 New Fetter Lane, London EC4P 4EE

Simultaneously published in the USA and Canada
by Routledge
29 West 35th Street, New York, NY 10001

Typeset in Baskerville by Routledge
Printed and bound in Great Britain by TJ International Ltd,
Padstow, Cornwall

British Library Cataloguing in Publication Data
A catalogue record for this book is available from the British Library

Library of Congress Cataloging in Publication Data
Politics of Sexuality / edited by Terrell Carver and Véronique Mottier.
p. cm. — (Routledge/ECPR Studies in European Political Science ; 4)
'Initially and largely the result of a workshop on The Politics of Sexuality
... at the joint sessions of the European Consortium for Political Research,
held at Oslo in the spring of 1996' - Editorial introd.
Includes bibliographical references (p.) and index.
1. Sex—Political aspects. 2. Sex and law. I. Carver, Terrell. II. Mottier,
Véronique. III. Series.
HQ23.P66 1998
306.7—dc21 98-21485

ISBN 0–415–16953–4

Contents

Contributors

Delila Amir teaches in the Department of Sociology and Anthropology at Tel-Aviv University, and she is the Coordinator of the Women's Studies Forum there. Her recent research is about 'being an immigrant and a woman', documented in research reports and articles in Hebrew and English. She is the author of *The Politics of Abortion in Israel*, and of the forthcoming book *Abortion in Israel from an International and a Feminist Perspective*. She was a member of the Israeli Government Commission on Reproductive Technologies and Surrogacy, and a Government Delegate to the UN Conference on Population and Development in Cairo in 1994.

Mark Bell is a graduate in Government and Law from the University of Ulster. Currently he is undertaking doctoral research at the European University Institute on EU policy concerned with discrimination on grounds of race and sexual orientation. He has published an article on the 1996 Intergovernmental Conference and has written a chapter on racism and the European Community for an edited volume on racism, ethnicity and Northern Ireland.

Orly Benjamin is a junior member of the faculty in the Department of Sociology at Bar-Ilan University. Her teaching and research interests are in gender relations and the sociology of emotions. She is co-author of articles on 'Abortion approval as a ritual of symbolic control' and 'The importance of difference: reconceptualizing the increased flexibility in gender relations at home'.

David Boothroyd studied philosophy at the universities of Essex and Warwick and is Course Leader for Cultural Studies at the University of Teesside. He has published articles and chapters on European philosophy and cultural theory, and is currently working on a book entitled *Culture on Drugs: Narco-Cultural Studies of High Modernity*, for Manchester University Press.

Terrell Carver is Professor of Political Theory at the University of Bristol. He has written many books and articles on Marx, Engels and Marxism, and has recently re-translated Marx's *Later Political Writings*. In the area of gender studies and sexuality he has published *Gender is Not a Synonym for Women*, a chapter 'A political theory of gender: perspectives on the universal subject' (in *Gender, Politics and the State*), and two articles: 'Theorizing men in Engels's *Origin of the Family*' and '"Public man" and the critique of masculinity'.

Alan Finlayson is Lecturer in Politics and Cultural Studies at The Queen's University of Belfast. He is author of articles on theories of nationalism and national identity, and is currently working on a study of the concept of community in Western politics and political theory.

John Gibbins is Principal Lecturer in Social Policy at the University of Teesside, and is a member of Wolfson College, Cambridge. He is co-founder of the journal *Theory, Culture and Society*, and his teaching and research are in philosophy and social theory, sexuality and politics. He is the author (with Bo Reimer) of the forthcoming book *The Politics of Postmodernity*.

Katrina Gorjanicyn is Associate Lecturer in Politics and Policy Studies at Deakin University. She has also taught at the departments of political science at the University of Melbourne, and at Swinburne University. She is currently completing her PhD dissertation, which focuses on prostitution law reform in Victoria and Queensland 1982–1992, and she has published articles and chapters on Australian and European politics.

Gail Hawkes has degrees in sociology from the Victoria University of Manchester, and is currently researching and writing on historical constructions of sexual pleasure. She is author of *A Sociology of Sex and Sexuality*.

Stevi Jackson is Professor of Women's Studies and Director of the Centre of Women's Studies at the University of York. She is the author of *Christine Delphy* and co-editor (with Sue Scott) of *Feminism and Sexuality* and (with Jackie Jones) of *Contemporary Feminist Theories*. Forthcoming books include *Concerning Heterosexuality*.

Moya Lloyd was educated at the University of Warwick and teaches politics and political theory at The Queen's University of Belfast. She has written articles and papers on Foucault and feminism, and feminism and the body. She has co-edited *The Impact of Michel Foucault on the Social Sciences and Humanities*, and is currently working on a book entitled *A Feminist Politics of Difference*.

Véronique Mottier teaches in the Department of Political Science at the University of Geneva, specialising in social theory and discourse analysis. She has degrees in sociology and political science from the University of Geneva, and a Ph.D. from the University of Cambridge. She has published on Foucault, sexual politics, and interpretative methodologies.

Palena R. Neale has recently completed her Ph.D. at the University of Wales, Aberystwyth, entitled 'Construction, Catholicism and Cairo: the Catholic construction of woman, the Holy See, and the International Conference on Population and Development (ICPD)'. She holds degrees from the University of Manitoba and the University of Hull. She has presented numerous conference papers, and has conducted interviews with UN, governmental and Vatican diplomats who were negotiators at the UN-sponsored International Conference on Population and Development in Cairo, 1994.

Joyce Outshoorn studied political science and contemporary history at the University of Amsterdam, and is currently Professor of Women's Studies at the University of Leiden. Her publications include chapters on 'The stability of compromise: abortion politics in western Europe' (in *Abortion Politics: Public Policy in Cross-cultural Perspective*), and (with J. Swiebel) 'Feminism and the state in the Netherlands' (in *Women's Movements and Public Policy in Europe, Latin America and the Caribbean*).

Momin Rahman is completing a Ph.D. at the University of Strathclyde and is currently a Teaching Fellow in Sociology at the University of Stirling. His main areas of research are the social construction of sexuality and difference, and democratic theory. His forthcoming publications include *Sexuality and Democracy: Identities and Strategies in Lesbian and Gay Politics*.

Paul Skidmore is Lecturer in the Department of Law at the University of Bristol, and is a graduate of the University of Cambridge and the European University Institute. He is currently researching legal issues that arise around gays and lesbians in the workplace, and he has published articles in the field of UK employment law.

Celia Valiente is Lecturer in Sociology at the Universidad Carlos III de Madrid. Her major area of research is comparative public policy with an analytical focus on gender. Her Ph.D. dissertation was on 'Public Policies for Women Workers in Italy and Spain 1900–1991' (in Spanish), and she has published a chapter 'The Power of Persuasion: The *Instituto de la Mujer* in Spain' in *Comparative State Feminism*.

Matthew Waites is an ESRC-funded Ph.D. student at South Bank University, having previously studied politics at the University of Bristol and gaining a Masters degree in sociology of culture from the University of Essex. His research interests are in examining the relationships between consenting sexual relations and citizenship in the UK. His publications include an article 'Lesbian and gay theory, sexuality and citizenship', in *Contemporary Politics*.

Series editor's preface

Until recently the terms 'politics' and 'sexuality' were more often than not employed to denote the complexities of sex and gender aspects of public life. More specifically sexual politics dealt with feminist issues such as the uneven (re)distribution of opportunities, representative offices, and unequal treatment of women (see for instance the title in this series *Sex Equality Policy in Western Europe* edited by Frances Gardiner). This book does not focus explicitly on this type of question, but rather on the role of sexuality as a societal phenomenon in relation to politics in a wider context, on the one hand, and the responses of the state to changing ideas about sexuality in society, on the other hand. These different angles make the volume novel and provide a new perspective on the politics of sexuality as an important topic in social discourse and political science. Taken in this sense, the contributions to this volume can be considered as an attempt to break new ground and develop new insights into 'sexual politics'.

This is particularly visible in the first part of the book. Here the contributors focus on the role of the state with regard to sexuality in a 'permissive society' in constructing categories and a discourse of sexuality. This is a very relevant debate, which has hitherto not much been elaborated on in European political science. The importance of this type of debate can perhaps be measured by pointing to the amount of public discussion in the media on, for example, the sexual behaviour of politicians (often in the tabloids), or on issues such as homosexuality (for example in the armed forces), and the role of the family as the 'cornerstone of society' (for example as presented by conservatives or Christians).

In the second part of the volume, the focus of attention is on critically reviewing existing approaches to sexuality on the basis of discourse analysis in an attempt to pin down the variable, and often contesting, usage of central concepts that figure in the 'politics of sexuality' (if not 'sexual politics').

In the final part of this volume a number of case studies are presented that range from the impact of Catholicism to the development of public policies regarding sexual issues in respect of individual rights. Although this part may appear eclectic, it serves to demonstrate to the reader the variation in the role of sexual politics across Europe and to what extent social policy has an impact on gender issues as well as on sexuality in general.

Altogether this volume, appearing in the European Political Science Series, can be seen as an important contribution to political science in that it not only shows new perspectives on sexuality as a political issue, but also offers views that can be considered as a research agenda for the future.

Hans Keman
Weesp, June 1998

Acknowledgements

The editors and contributors involved in this volume owe an overwhelming debt to the European Consortium for Political Research, which sponsored a workshop on 'The Politics of Sexuality' at the Joint Sessions held at the University of Oslo from 29 March to 3 April 1996. Not only did the impetus for the volume come from a selection of the papers presented at those meetings, but even more importantly the spirit of co-operation that developed there saw many contributors, and both editors, through an otherwise tortuous process. In professional terms the ECPR took a bit of chance in sponsoring a workshop on this topic, and it is hoped that the substantive and methodological results emerging from this volume will handsomely repay their trust.

The editors and authors listed below acknowledge the use of previously published material by kind permission of the publishers mentioned.

Mark Bell. Thanks to Professor Silvana Sciarra and Professor Colin Crouch, European University Institute, Florence, and to Professor Barry Fitzpatrick, University of Ulster, for their helpful comments and suggestions in the preparation of this chapter.

Terrell Carver. My chapter draws on material previously published in chapter 1 of my *Gender is Not a Synonym for Women*. Copyright © 1996 by Lynne Rienner Publishers, Inc. Used with permission of the Publisher. It also draws on material to be published in my chapter 'A political theory of gender: perspectives on the "universal subject"', in *Gender, Politics and the State*, edited by Vicky Randall and Georgina Waylen (London: Routledge).

Alan Finlayson. A version of this chapter was presented at the Annual Conference of the Political Studies Association of the UK at the University of Glasgow in 1996. I have drawn on material previously published as 'Discourses of nationality and discourses of sexuality', in *Contemporary Political Studies 1996*, edited by Iain Hampsher-Monk and Jeffrey Stanyer, vol. 3 (Political Studies Association of the UK, 1996), pp. 1659–66.

John Gibbins. Thanks are due to the School of Social Sciences and the Centre for Social and Policy Research at the University of Teesside for support in researching this chapter.

Katrina Gorjanicyn. I would like to thank Terrell Carver, Mark Considine, Iva Ellen Deutchman, Derek McDougall, Véronique Mottier, Joyce Outshoorn and Barbara Sullivan for their discussion and comments on this chapter.

Stevi Jackson. I have drawn on material previously published as 'Taking liberties', in *Trouble & Strife* 34 (1996): 36–43.

Véronique Mottier. I would like to thank Anthony Giddens, Max Bergman, Olaf Corry and Lorena Parini for their useful comments and criticisms. I also thank audiences at a guest lecture at the University of Teesside (January 1997) and at a Staff Seminar at the University of Geneva (May 1997) for raising pertinent issues concerning earlier drafts of my chapter. I am grateful for financial support from Clare College, Cambridge; the UK Committee of Vice-Chancellors and Principals (ORS Award); the Swiss National Science Foundation; the Schmidheiny Foundation; and the Société Académique de Genève.

Palena R. Neale. My chapter draws on material published as 'The bodies of Christ as international bodies', in the *Review of International Studies* 24 (1998): 101–18.

Joyce Outshoorn. Thanks to the civil servants of the Department of the Coordination of Equality Policy, Ministry of Social Affairs and Employment, The Hague, and to Marjan Wijers of the Foundation against Trafficking in Women, Utrecht.

Paul Skidmore. Thanks to the editors, the other participants at the Oslo workshop and colleagues at Bristol for their comments on earlier drafts. Thanks also to the SPTL Academic Purposes Fund which provided me with a grant to attend the Oslo sessions. An earlier version of this chapter was presented at the National Critical Law Groups Conference, University of Keele, February 1996.

Celia Valiente. I would like to thank Belén Barreiro, Ana Rico, Ángel J. Sánchez and Dorothy McBride Stetson for their valuable comments on earlier drafts. They were presented at: the 'II Symposium on Equality and Income Distribution', Argentaria Foundation, Madrid, 5–9 June 1995; the Tenth International Conference of Europeanists, Chicago, 14–17 March 1996; and the 92nd Annual Meeting of the American Political Science Association, San Francisco, 29 August–1 September 1996. I am grateful to the Argentaria Foundation for its financial support for my research, and also to the people interviewed who generously provided me with valuable information and insights. The names of the interviewed do not appear in the chapter but are available on request. I have drawn on material and ideas previously published as 'The regulation of sexual harassment in the workplace in Spain', in *Crossing Borders: Gender and Citizenship in Transition*, edited by Barbara Hobson and Anne Marie Berggren (Stockholm: Swedish Council for Planning and Coordination of Research), pp. 179–200 (to be reprinted by Macmillan); and 'Políticas de igualdad para las mujeres en la España democrática: la regulación del acoso sexual en el trabajo', in *Probreza, necesidad y discriminación: II simposio sobre igualdad y distribución de la renta y la requeza*, edited by Fundación Argentaria (Madrid: Fundación Argentaria and Visor), pp. 201–30.

Introduction

Terrell Carver and Véronique Mottier

This anthology explores the ways in which sexuality has moved into politics and hence into the realm of political science. Political activity and activism around sexual politics have reset the political agenda. There is a wide variety of issues, events and movements to be studied as they work through and around traditional electoral and governmental structures at all levels. Indeed there have been significant changes in electoral and government structures to accommodate these developments. Sex, gender and sexualities can no longer be presumed to be non-political, pre-political or even marginal, because electoral politics, public policy, local government and international and EU relations are all arenas in which the politics of sexuality arises. This has affected not just what is researched in political science, but the ways in which this research is constructed and carried out.

This collection of essays was initially and largely the result of a workshop on 'The Politics of Sexuality' that we co-directed at the Joint Sessions of the European Consortium for Political Research, held at Oslo in the spring of 1996, though the editorial process has engendered considerable rewriting and rethinking. Both the workshop (the first ECPR workshop ever held on sexuality) and the publication of this volume are an indication of the growing recognition of the importance of sexuality studies for political analysis. The aim of the volume is to present to a wide audience – political scientists and students of politics in the broadest sense, as well as an interdisciplinary public in law, sociology, media and cultural studies, gender and women's studies – a group of essays that address major theoretical issues in the politics of sexuality. The chapters also situate both the macro-politics of the control of citizens' sexualities and the micro-politics of regulation of the body in different geographical and institutional frameworks. Although the contributions reflect a diversity of perspectives, we feel that they share important unities of theme and approach.

In particular, these chapters have in common a post-structuralist sensitivity to the role of language in defending power relations and in creating new ones. Methodologically this is important in order to develop a political science that neither misunderstands nor ignores an important area of political activity and change. New enquiries require new concepts, and new concepts require new thinking. The terms through which the politics of sexuality are practised, whether by individuals, interest groups or pressure groups, parties or governments, and the terms through which they are understood in cognate disciplines (sociology, legal studies, cultural and media studies, women's and gender studies) must be within the vocabulary and understanding of political scientists. Otherwise emerging politics will not appear at all, and cannot be fruitfully researched. It is therefore crucial to explore the linguistic constructions and symbolic representations that underlie the politics of sexuality.

We believe that it is equally important for political analysis to avoid not only the marginalisation of sexuality but also an uncritical essentialism concerning sex. The chapters in this volume thus share a constructionist perspective on sexuality. Sexuality is not the expression of a natural identity, which 'the political' sets out to protect or control. Rather, it is the product of a complex multiplicity of social and political practices. With respect to the state, this means that sexualities and sexual identities are categorised and shaped at the same time as they are being policed through state policies. Thus the focus of the volume is both topical and methodological. Topically it proposes new enquiries that reflect a variety of views as to what sexuality is and how it appears in politics. Methodologically it aims to add political and analytical vocabularies to political science to accommodate political and intellectual change.

The contributions raise and pursue three broadly defined sets of issues that form the structure of the book. While we would not claim that these issues comprehensively 'cover the field', we do contend that they are quite broad in scope and interestingly reflective of current political problems. The first section deals with the conceptualisation of sexual 'difference' and unequal treatment. The second section examines theorisations of sexuality as a site of political agency. The final section discusses national and international public policies around women's bodies and sexuality.

Citizens' sexualities: 'difference' and unequal treatment

The state occupies a key position in the politics of sexuality. It is therefore important to analyse the policies through which national states organise and regulate citizens' sexualities, and to examine the types of political mobilisation that these policies confront. The regulation of citizens' sexualities is given prominence in Terrell Carver's essay, 'Sexual citizenship: gendered and de-gendered narratives'. Carver analyses how sexual 'difference' is constructed and policed in relation to citizenship. Citizenship, he argues, is not a simple category that is merely legal and binary (citizen/alien). Constitutional and other legalistic definitions of citizenship are linked to both gendered and de-gendered narratives. Gendered narratives establish hierarchies of citizenship that connect it with sex and sexuality. These inequalities are hidden by the egalitarian claims of de-gendered constitutional and other foundational texts of democracy. The masculinist and heterosexist character of citizenship narratives is thus overwritten with a discourse of supposed equality. Citizenship is therefore produced as a productive and disciplinary category, which is regularly deployed within formal and informal relations of power. On the basis of his analysis of how this category operates within the current politics of sexuality, Carver questions the traditional hierarchies of power that citizenship narratives construct. In particular, he raises the question of what representations of 'the citizen' the state should create and endorse.

The historically gendered nature of citizenship underlies the history of expanding citizens' rights. As a result – Matthew Waites argues in his essay, 'Sexual citizens: legislating the age of consent in Britain' – a contemporary narrative that represents age-of-consent legislation in terms of a positive endorsement of sexual citizenship is highly problematic. As his analysis of the history of age-of-consent legislation in the UK demonstrates, the emergence of an adult sexual subject who has the legal right to engage in sexual encounters is intertwined with exclusionary assumptions about citizens' sexualities and gender. For women, age-of-consent legislation has historically represented a limit on the rights of men to sexual access, rather than a recognition of women's sexual agency or right to consent. For men, the meanings that circulate in politics concerning age-of-consent legislation are conditioned by the idea of young men needing protection from preying older homosexuals. While age-of-consent campaigns represent a powerful form of egalitarian sexual politics, the basic conceptualisation is highly problematic, producing compromised subjectivities rooted in history rather than new conceptions of shared sexual citizenship.

In contrast to Carver's and Waites's focus on the macro-politics of sexual citizenship, John Gibbins's essay, 'Sexuality and the law: the body as politics', turns attention towards the micro-politics of the regulation of citizens' bodies and sexual behaviour. His contribution raises the question of whether the state should be involved in the regulation of a plurality of diverse identities. He explores how postmodern ethics could guide the state in sexual politics. In developing his argument, Gibbins discusses the ethics of sadomasochism and in particular the recent British 'Spanner Case', in which a group of forty-four adult consenting males were successfully prosecuted for 'infliction of actual bodily harm and wounds' upon one another as part of sexual activities. The interest of the Spanner Case, Gibbins believes, lies in its problematisation of a familiar liberal model of 'the individual'. It illustrates that citizens do not share a universal identity, but on the contrary hold incommensurable and often contradictory identities. Gibbins's argument is consequently that civil society should only be refereed by minimal facilitating rules that respect this diversity. The role of a postmodern state, according to Gibbins, is to protect and promote the freedom of expression of all sexual selves.

The opening essays of this volume deal with state regulation of citizens' sexualities. However, the construction of 'difference' in sexual terms is not a simple outcome of a one-way process. Indeed, state regulation of citizens' sexualities constitutes a terrain for intense political struggle. The gay rights lobby in particular plays a key role in activism around sexuality. There is some disagreement, however, on how these political struggles should proceed – a theme that is taken up in the next four papers of this collection.

Paul Skidmore's essay, 'Sexuality and the UK armed forces: judicial review of the ban on homosexuality', discusses the anti-homosexual policy in the UK armed forces. He examines the political strategies that gay pressure groups outside of the mainstream political parties adopt in their challenge to anti-homosexual policies. Although there is at present no legislation affirming the right to equal treatment of homosexuals with heterosexuals in the UK, a legal strategy is nevertheless being pursued to overturn discriminatory policies. Gay activists and, in particular, the pressure group Stonewall have complemented their lobbying work with litigation strategies.

It has been argued by some gay and lesbian rights lobbyists that campaigning strategies against sexual orientation should be directed towards the European Union, in the hope that transnational institutions will prove more sympathetic to action against sexual-orientation discrimination than some of the member states. Although the regulation of citizens' sexualities mostly takes place on the level of the nation-state, policies are also being developed on an international level. In Europe, the European Union especially plays an increasing role in the politics around sexual 'difference'. This role is examined in Mark Bell's essay, 'Sexual orientation and anti-discrimination policy: the European Community'. The European Parliament has prominently campaigned for EU action against sexual-orientation discrimination. However, Bell shows that its various resolutions become empty rhetoric in the face of opposition by the European Commission and the Council of Ministers. His analysis illustrates the limits to the powers of the European Parliament, and he shows that the Council of Ministers is particularly unsympathetic to policy opposing sexual discrimination. The anticipation of the Council's hostility leads the Commission to withhold its own support. Therefore, Bell argues, the gay and lesbian rights movement needs to lobby the Commission in order to ensure European Union backing for action against sexual-orientation discrimination.

Stevi Jackson and Momin Rahman disagree with the type of political strategies analysed by Skidmore and Bell. The quest for equal rights within gay politics is criticised by Jackson in her essay, 'Sexual politics: feminist politics, gay politics and the problem of heterosexuality', and by Rahman in his essay, 'Sexuality and rights: problematising lesbian and gay politics'. Both point out that the politics of sexuality is intimately connected with gender politics. The pursuit of equal rights with heterosexuals, they argue, endorses social institutions such as the heterosexual family, which feminists, lesbians and gays have long problematised. In their uncritical stance towards heterosexuality, many gay men in particular tend to foster the hope that they can gain equality as gays while retaining patriarchal privileges as men. The mobilisation of the discourse of rights in the realm of sexuality is problematic, so Jackson and Rahman argue, in that it constructs a political agenda that does not seriously question the way in which sexuality and sexual identities are constructed socially within a heterosexual context. Heterosexuals, so they argue, are not equal to each other as such, but unequal as men and women, so discourses of 'equal rights' and 'human rights', as deployed to argue for equality between sexualities, are contradictory and counterproductive.

Theorisations of sexuality: identity and political agency

The theorisation of sexuality and sexual identity as a site of political agency is the second theme of this anthology. While the preceding essays centre on the activities of the state, the contributions to this section expand the analysis to include the different social and political discourses and practices that produce sexuality. In 'Sexuality and nationality: gendered discourses of Ireland', Alan Finlayson scrutinises the connections between discourses of national identity and sexuality through a case study of Irish nationalism. Finlayson shows how Irish national identity is both the product of discursive processes and the object of political contestation and argumentation. He demonstrates how representations of sexuality infuse ideas on national identity that help to constitute both the state and its citizens. Irish nationalist discourse, he argues, relies heavily upon ideas about sexual and bodily behaviour that are articulated within a unified vision of the national and social body. This discourse of Irish nationhood is based on a vision of a past rurality evoking the gender roles that supposedly sustained it. Ireland's identity is defined in terms of womanhood and motherhood. This reductive conception of women's sexuality, Finlayson believes, conditions Irish political discourse to a considerable extent. In particular, it serves as a discursive legitimisation for sexual politics that limits female citizens to their sexual and reproductive functions.

The nationalist discourses that Finlayson analyses share a preoccupation with controlling sexuality and, in particular, with the control of female sexuality and homosexuality. Arguably the stress on constraining sexual activities implicitly suggests that sexuality is a potential threat to the current social and religious order. This disruptive potential of sexuality is also emphasised by Gail Hawkes's essay, 'Sexuality and civilisation: Weber and Freud'. In her discussion of the parallels between Weber's and Freud's ideas on the key dynamics of modernity, Hawkes points out that both authors were profoundly pessimistic regarding the 'advances' of civilisation. The impact of modernity on sexual expression received less detailed attention from Weber than from Freud. Nevertheless, there is a common emphasis in their work on the constraint of emotional and sexual expressions that the civilising process entails. According to Hawkes, Weber's and Freud's writings exemplify the more general preoccupation with sexuality signalled by, in particular, the rise of sexual science during the nineteenth century. The central preoccupation of the new sexual science was to name and exclude any forms of sexual desire that did not conform to the idea of 'normality'. This preoccupation with the routinisation of desire, Hawkes suggests, implies a recognition of the disruptive potential of sexual desire and pleasure for the modern social order.

Given the particular prestige of scientific discourse in modernity, the rise of sexual science is a key factor in the construction as well as the theorisation of sexuality, as emphasised both by Hawkes and by Véronique Mottier in her essay 'Sexuality and sexology: Michel Foucault'. Hawkes and Mottier adopt different positions, however, in their assessment of sexological discourse. Whereas Hawkes interprets the 'scientific' construction of sexual normality in repressive terms, Mottier believes that although sexology forms the basis for disciplinary discourses, it can also support counter-positions. Using a Foucauldian framework, she argues that sexual identities produced by 'scientific' discourses on sexuality can be articulated within conflicting political positions. It is not so much the type of discourse – essentialist or constructionist – that allows for political transformations of identities and meanings, Mottier contends, but rather the connection of these positions to specific value-orientations. Sexological discourse normalises, but it can also be a reflexive resource for fashioning the sexual self. Sexuality, Mottier argues, is therefore not just the locus of repressive power, as sexual liberation theories contend. It is also the site of active practices of self-fashioning.

The practices of self-fashioning that constitute sexual identities are further explored in Moya Lloyd's and David Boothroyd's essays. Lloyd's argument in 'Sexual politics, performativity, parody: Judith Butler' is developed through a discussion of Butler's theorisation of the construction of gendered identity, and in particular of the relation between two of Butler's core concepts, 'performance' and 'performativity'. Butler's perspective on gender identity as a performance is important for political theory in that it construes gender identity as both a mechanism of constraint and a locus for critical agency. However, the concept of performativity is largely limited to the construction of a particular subject as a gendered being. As a consequence, Lloyd believes that there is a risk of neglecting the space within which performance occurs, and in particular neglecting the others involved in the performance of gendered identity. Moreover, not all individual discontinuities in performance are necessarily transgressive of gender norms. The political effects of performativity, Lloyd argues, are context-dependent.

Similar to Lloyd's analysis of Butler's ideas, Boothroyd's discussion of Irigaray examines how sexual difference can be a basis for, rather than an obstacle to, political agency. In his essay, 'Sexuality and the politics of difference: Luce Irigaray', Boothroyd argues that conventional readings of Irigaray's work in essentialist terms miss the point of Irigaray's philosophical and political project. Irigaray argues for a discursive reappropriation of the female body, which involves a rethinking of sexual difference beyond biological naturalism. Irigaray's problematisation of traditional notions of politics and identity is useful, Boothroyd argues, in emphasising potential theoretical and practical problems that occur in the realm of feminist sexual politics.

Commodification of sexuality: economic activity and public policy

The final section of this volume focuses on national and international public policies around women's bodies and sexuality. Whereas, in the first section of the book, Gibbins uses postmodern ethics to argue for minimal intervention by the state in sexual politics, other authors prefer a more interventionist perspective. What if the 'freedom of sexual expression' of one person threatens that of another person, or that person directly? What happens when the persons threatened are always or generally women? The necessity may arise for the state to intervene actively rather than to withdraw from sexual politics. The essays in this third section examine some of the controversies surrounding such state interventions in women's reproductive options, sexual harassment and prostitution. In her essay 'Sexuality and the International Conference on Population and Development: the Catholic Church in international politics', Palena R. Neale examines how the Roman Catholic Church, the Holy See and the Pope operated within the international arena both prior to and during the International Conference on Population and Development, sponsored by the United Nations, in Cairo 1994, in order to influence policies around women's sexuality. Neale argues that the Catholic definition of women's reproductive options and sexuality, in combination with the doctrine of papal infallibility, serves as a legitimisation for political strategies to exercise power over women's roles and over their bodies as 'wom(b)an', who is defined and confined in religious and cultural politics as wife and mother.

While Neale's analysis is concerned with transnational politics concerning women's reproductive options, Delila Amir and Orly Benjamin examine such policies on a national level. Their essay, 'Sexuality and the female national subject: contraception and abortion policy in Israel', analyses the state's regulation of women's sexual and reproductive behaviour in the Israeli context. Amir and Benjamin's study of practices and discourses around abortion procedures, seen in the context of the integration process of immigrant women from the former Soviet Union, demonstrates that the state's control of women's sexual and reproductive behaviour is linked to the constitution of Israeli national identity. They argue that the encounter between pregnancy-regulation committees and women seeking abortion categorises women in relation to national identity. In particular, the sexual and reproductive behaviour of immigrant women, who routinely use abortion as a substitute for conventional Israeli contraceptive practices, is seen to conflict with the imperatives for affiliation to the national collective. This category of women is therefore constituted as 'other' with respect to Israeli female national identity, which, like male identity, is constituted through specific processes and representations.

Similar to Amir and Benjamin, Celia Valiente's essay, 'Sexual harassment in the workplace: equality policies in post-authoritarian Spain', illustrates how the politics of sexuality is intertwined with representations of national identity. In the Spanish case, appeals to cultural identity played an important role in the lack of implementation of state policy on sexual harassment. Her analysis shows that, although sexual harassment policy has existed in Spain since 1989, it suffers from an implementation deficit. Not only do trade unions and employers show little interest in acting against unsolicited sexual advances in the workplace, but also very few victims use the existing legal channels. Indeed, few complaints have been filed. According to Valiente, the hostility towards state intervention in this area of sexual politics is supported by a cultural argument. A policy of this type, Valiente claims, is seen as foreign to Latin cultures, and therefore lacks support. Spanish femocrats and feminist trade-union leaders are neither very active nor very efficient in promoting regulatory policies. Although sexual-harassment policy is therefore not well implemented in Spain, Valiente believes that it never-theless has an important symbolic value as a first step towards changing gender relations in the workplace.

Like Valiente, Katrina Gorjanicyn and Joyce Outshoorn discuss the influence of femocrats and feminist activists on the policy process. Focusing on the commodification of sexuality, they demonstrate that the categorisation of sexual activities as a moral issue, as a public health problem, or in terms of economic activities involving questions of remuneration, exploitation and work results in different forms of state regulation. To the extent that these categories are frequently contested by feminist as well as other political actors, the commodifi-cation of sexuality constitutes an arena for struggles over meanings as well as over policies. Both Gorjanicyn and Outshoorn thus emphasise the power of 'naming' in relation to policy decisions regarding commercial sex and, in partic-ular, prostitution.

In her essay, 'Sexuality and work: contrasting prostitution policies in Victoria and Queensland', Gorjanicyn examines the processes through which prostitution law was reformed in Australia under Labor governments. Her study reveals the ambivalence and divisions within Australian feminism towards prostitution. For some feminist activists, prostitution victimises those women who participate in it, and should therefore be abolished altogether. Other feminists argue that women are free to use their bodies in whatever ways they choose, agreeing with the defi-nition of prostitution as a form of work. The latter group, attuned to the dominant categorisation of commercial sex, was more involved in the policy process. In contrast, confronted with local governments' stance on the necessity to regulate prostitution as a form of work, the abolitionist feminists failed to affect the policy outcome results very significantly.

Joyce Outshoorn's essay, 'Sexuality and international commerce: the traffic in women and prostitution policy in the Netherlands', also looks at the involvement of feminists in the policy-making process on prostitution. Her analysis of policy on the trafficking of women in the Netherlands shows that Dutch feminists have been actively involved in the policy-making processes on prostitution and inter-national traffic in women. Contrary to the Australian case discussed by Gorjanicyn, Dutch feminists have mostly adopted a pragmatic rather than an abolitionist approach. Although femocrats and women's groups have managed to influence policy outcomes significantly in the arena of commercial sex, Outshoorn nevertheless thinks that the treatment of prostitution in terms of economic activities remains problematic from a feminist point of view. The construction of prostitution as work and gender-neutral definitions of 'traffic in persons', she argues, have led to the disappearance of themes such as (male) sexuality and sexual domination from official discourses. In the process, these issues are now no longer politicised.

Summary

The essays in this anthology raise central issues in the politics of sexuality. This collection, we believe, demonstrates the need for political science to expand both its subject matter and its methodological discourse. The neglect of sexual politics within the domain of political science is all the more problematic as these political issues become increasingly prominent inside and outside traditional political arenas. In providing theoretical discussions as well as empirical case studies, we hope that this volume will clarify some of the questions and problems faced by those interested in the connections between sexuality and politics, which are multifaceted and increasingly intertwined with issues that represent the usual concerns of political scientists. The one thing that the politics of sexuality is not, however, is 'private' or 'pre-political', something that can be treated as peripheral or of merely personal interest. Beyond that, there is substantial disagreement concerning the ways in which the politics of sexualities and of sexual identities are interpreted. As editors, our purpose has been to reflect this variety of viewpoints, and to provide a forum for ongoing debates.

Part I

Citizens' sexualities

'Difference' and unequal treatment

1 Sexual citizenship
Gendered and de-gendered narratives

Terrell Carver

In this chapter I propose to examine some of the ways in which citizenship is produced as a productive and disciplinary category, which is regularly deployed within formal and informal relations of power. To do that I shall argue that constitutional and other legalistic definitions and 'guarantees' are readily and characteristically linked to more popular forms of understanding, conceptualised here as 'narratives'. These narratives, so I claim, are characteristically deployed in both gendered and de-gendered forms, of which I cite examples. In order to explain this political phenomenon, I examine very closely the concept of gender in the light of recent theorisations and my observation of contemporary usage. I draw attention to the disjunction between gendered and de-gendered narratives of citizenship, and to the way that this discursive strategy operates within the current politics of sexuality. In conclusion I reformulate a number of political questions in ways that are subversive of traditional hierarchies of power.

Citizens/aliens

At first glance citizenship seems to be a simple on/off kind of concept. Either you have citizenship (and are 'a citizen'), or you do not have it (and are 'not a citizen'). If you have citizenship, then you have the rights and obligations as constitutionally and legally specified, and if you do not have citizenship but are 'in the country', you are an 'alien'. For example, citizenship may cover rights to work, reside, vote, obtain benefits such as education and welfare, etc., as well as corresponding obligations to pay taxes, perform national service or civil functions such as jury service, etc. These are, of course, subject to qualifications of age and residency, and also to nullification procedures that may require the suspension or loss of citizenship wholly or in part, such as imprisonment, renunciation, revocation and loss of voting rights or rights of movement.

Needless to say there are innumerable local variations on these themes within the constitutional and more or less democratic societies around the world. Non-constitutional, authoritarian regimes award fewer rights, if any, and sometimes follow very loose notions of legality, but some of the relevant categories survive, at least on paper, and even if only to satisfy some international agencies (e.g. UN conventions) and to put others off (e.g. Amnesty International).

Mirroring citizenship there are categorisations of 'alienness' and non-citizenship that exclude people altogether, allow entrance for specified periods and purposes, and sometimes give limited status within the polity (even voting, in some fairly rare cases, such as Irish nationals in the UK). Dual or multi-country citizenship creates areas of overlap and non-efficacy, as sometimes both states will contest for sole nationality (usually to the detriment of the person involved), and sometimes neither state will assume responsibility for a person, so as not to give offence to another state (see Dummett and Nichol 1991).

Yet if we dig further, the picture becomes even more complex, and the categories of citizen and alien do not merely fragment. Rather the fragments begin to form hierarchies. This view is clearly argued by David Evans:

> The full weight of civil, political and social rights machineries is employed to define *degrees of citizenship* or, to be more precise, the non-citizenship of those manifestly outwith [i.e. outside] the absolute reified standards of the moral community. Furthermore, these degrees of non-citizenship incite the further fragmentation of communities with sectionalised access and activity to and in specialised *markets*, they define degrees and forms of consumer status and lifestyle…citizenship *machineries* enhance state management of the 'life-world'.
>
> (Evans 1993: 6, 63; my emphasis)

Evans develops the argument with respect to sexuality/ies, but other descriptors that fall within 'the moral community' (e.g. 'race'/ethnicity, language use, religion, (dis)ability) could also be figured this way:

> The logic of the distinction between private and public behaviour [for instance] was that the legal penalties for *public* displays of sexuality could be strengthened as private behaviour was decriminalised, but given the strict definition of 'private', elaborate policing of civil society became *de rigueur*. By concentrating on public manifestations of sexual deviance in the buffer zone between moral and immoral communities, this policing has effectively penetrated all 'private' territories.
>
> (Evans 1993: 63–4)

This analysis, drawing equally on Foucault and Marx, presents citizenship as *gradations of esteem* – for example, with respect to the way the state conceives, represents, polices, educates, regulates, defines, criminalises and taxes what its various agencies take to be 'sexuality' or sexualities. The 'community' is then moulded, by state action and through political representation, to conform to what these disciplinary practices attempt to do.

Or is the community rather the source of the conceptions and representations according to which the state then moulds its activities? In an examination of the ways in which historical writing has been construed, Callinicos expounds the work of White, who draws attention to the links between popular culture and education, on the one hand, and the state and citizenship, on the other:

> White argues that by allowing their audience to imagine a reality that is whole and complete, they [historians] contribute to 'the production of the "law-abiding" citizen'...Historical narratives, by virtue of their tropological organisation, will always fail in their attempt to represent reality...[B]y depicting, through the device of narrative closure, a world that is whole, historical narrative helps to turn out good citizens.
>
> (Callinicos 1995: 50–2, quoting White 1987: 21, 87)

'Historical narrative', of course, can be broadened out to cover the whole realm of popular culture, such as commercial 'Hollywood' cinema. Babington and Evans (1993), for example, survey numerous narratives among various cinematic genres, some of which were (and perhaps are) central to conceptions of citizen-virtue in the United States:

> Among the...ancient/modern parallelisms two further sets predominate, idealistically linking [ancient] Israel with America as in King David's feder-alistic, melting-pot deathbed speech in *Solomon and Sheba*...The first equivalence sees two God-inspired democratic nations fighting to free the world from slavery. The second parallels two 'chosen' people formed out of the frontier, both looking nostalgically back to those origins from present urban corruptions...In De Mille's second *The Ten Commandments* both themes are foregrounded...the politics of freedom versus slavery...and the Israelites are shown in images underlined by the commentary as virtuous free-enterprisers.
>
> (Babington and Evans 1993: 55, 57)

Reimagining the community is thus an everyday form of cultural work conducted within and between realms that are rather irrelevantly designated political or non-political (see also Finlayson, Chapter 8 of this volume). It is this form of cultural work that I designate 'narratives' of citizenship. This is to say that collective experiences, or even individual experiences, in so far as they purport to tell us what 'actually' happened and/or what 'it means', are merely mobilisations of metaphors within discourses of certainty, authority and exclu-sion. Events or 'history' are not 'there' to be represented 'correctly' or 'incorrectly', but are rather realms of representation – whether near the time, much later or speculatively (and sometimes circularly) to do with the future.

Contemporary narratives of citizenship, in my view, are likely to incorporate factors such as the following:

*   nation-states as geographical conceptions;
*   formalities of official approval, such as documents of birth;

- hierarchies like federalism and transnational political communities;
- boundaries that are physically policed;
- entry and rejection, incarceration and deportation;
- renunciation, revocation, statelessness, 'asylum seekers';
- civil rights and obligations that are supposedly exclusive and defining.

However, no list could be completely inclusive. This is to say that citizenship is a movable metaphor of 'belonging' and 'inclusion' that is deployed at different times for various purposes. It has no universally or regularly agreed boundaries; rather there are contradictory and subversive accretions that are often used as counters in other political struggles. Citizenship is another exercise in the power/knowledge game, in that it is disciplinary and productive at the same time in terms of social relationships. Any structure distributes advantages and disadvantages, and a structureless world would have neither.

So far the analytical perspective here is individualist, because only individuals are citizens, and citizens can only be individuals. Who are the individuals? On the one hand they are human creatures with biological (though culturally conditioned) life cycles of birth, immaturity, (so-called) maturity, ageing and death. Family and community are metaphors frequently mobilised to cover some or all of these. On the other hand, citizens (as legally and morally categorised in terms that typically include age, sex, reproductive expectations and sexuality) are subjects in and of states. But before examining the ways in which these categories are manipulated in the sort of documents that are typically involved in reimagining the citizen-community, it is important to look more closely at 'ways in which sex and sexuality become political' – my working definition of 'gender' – in the light of recent theoretical work.

Gender(s?)

In the last hundred years or so, sex has become established as a 'biological' category, supposedly derived from observation of the body. Gender is often (though not exclusively) regarded as a 'sociological' category referring to the ways in which sexual behaviour is manifested by individuals in social circumstances. Once it was noticed that, for example, 'masculine' behaviour is not always manifested by males, and can indeed be manifested by females (and vice versa for 'feminine' behaviour), then two strategies emerged: one was to create categories of deviancy (such as effeminate and/or homosexual men – on various assumptions), and the other was to slide the unit of analysis away from sex as a binary aspect of the body towards sexuality as a manifold realm of 'behaviours', or at least 'orientations' (Connell 1987).

In about the last fifty years, feminist analysis and politics have raised the issue of 'gender' in the context of the ways in which women are oppressed or at the very least disadvantaged by men individually and collectively, and the ways in which overarching presumptions about men and women, masculinity and femininity, work to structure and reproduce this behaviour. Thus in many contexts today a reference to gender is a reference to women, as if men, males and masculinities were all unproblematic in that regard, or indeed perhaps simply nothing to do with gender at all, though there are of course circumstances where gender is used to indicate both sides of a binary (Carver 1996: 4–5). A usage of gender to designate women, while putting men to one side, can very readily become a way of making women problematic, once again, in a way that marginalises them as 'a problem'. This leaves men where they have always been, doing pretty much what they like, or more accurately, what some of them like. On the whole there have only been minimal concessions in power relations from men to women, and none at all in the basic construction of gendered – that is, power-ridden – identities derived rather incoherently from presumptions about sex and sexuality. These identities, or perhaps rather identity claims, are the real stuff of the asymmetrical social relationships that are culturally and politically transmitted across the generations. Few people, if any, really 'have' these identities with utter consistency and conviction. Rather they claim them as they are performed, and in doing this they establish the symbolic codes from which disciplinary and (re)productive practices emerge (Butler 1990; Lloyd 1998).

In the common parlance of recent times, 'gender' has also become a euphemism for sex: that is, male or female, M or F, man or woman, as biologically, socially and legally defined. These definitions, though, are hardly unambiguous. In doctrines of 'family', 'parenthood' and 'personal dignity' (cited in 'cases' of transsexuality) considerations of individual preference and social functionality begin to cross-cut the commonplace stereotyping on which our elaborations of the two supposedly 'opposite' yet 'co-requisite' sexes are based. This synonymy of 'gender' for 'sex' seems to me to be a step backwards, or at least it marks a kind of inertia. It constantly reinscribes the supposedly obvious and supposedly well-understood categories male and female, men and women, back into political ideas, just when these ideas are starting to be really problematic, politically interesting and interestingly complex. Why map gender onto sex as one-to-one, just when the term was helping to make visible the ambiguities of sexuality, orientation, choice and change that have been under cover for centuries? Indeed modern technologies of the body, and modern methods of political mobilisation, have rendered these questions not just visible but very pressing within the media, the institutional apparatus of courts and legislatures, and all the professions in society (see Waites, Skidmore and Bell, Chapters 2, 4 and 5 of this volume).

A one-to-one mapping of gender onto a commonplace categorisation of sex as male/female is over-simple, even with respect to biology and medicine, as there are chromosomal variations and syndromes, not to mention morphological and behavioural ones, that create genuinely ambiguous individuals. Even supposing that 'normality' with respect to the M/F distinction (as medically and socially enforced) is good enough for most analytical purposes, why then limit gender to a restatement of that? Indeed the term was coined to do more than restate the (supposedly) obvious, by decoupling (simplified) biology from (stereotyped) behaviour. Discourses and practices of toleration and liberation have to some extent replaced the more sinister approaches and institutions – utilising concepts of normality and deviance – which historical and sociological work on the history of the human sciences have exposed as disciplinary or worse. There is yet more room in political life for discourses of variation or 'difference'. Indeed it seems to me that we simply do not know how many genders there are, as the answer must vary according to what is assumed about sex and sexuality before any particular concept of gender is then constructed.

For instance, if there are normal or characteristic ways of *being of the male or female sex*, called masculine and feminine, and if these are socially learnt rather than biologically determined, then there are four genders, rather than two, as masculine men, masculine women, feminine women and feminine men become logically possible and empirically observable. If gender is the way in which *sexuality is expressed* between the sexes, then perhaps there are two genders, heterosexuality and homosexuality (or three, if celibacy is an option), on the assumption that these categories include both Ms and Fs, depending on whether sexuality is M to F and F to M (heterosexuality), or M to M and F to F (homosexuality). Alternatively perhaps there are four or six genders, as the line-up might then be heterosexual men, heterosexual women, homosexual women, homosexual men, celibate women and celibate men. Perhaps historically there were three genders (heterosexual men, heterosexual women, celibates) or four (heterosexual men, heterosexual women, celibate women, celibate men), before homosexuality as a sexual identity was developed, or at least as a sexual identity that we would recognise as homosexual, or that the social actors themselves would identify as such (Weeks 1985). Adding bisexuality as either one further gender or two 'sexually' differentiated genders then runs the total up further.

In terms of object of desire (a male or a female), then perhaps there are two genders, one encompassing heterosexual women and homosexual men (desiring men), and the other encompassing heterosexual men and homosexual women (desiring women). Arguments in some sex-discrimination cases are going this way, i.e. sexuality is mapped back onto object-choice: men and women should be equally free to choose a man as a sexual partner, and equally free from disadvantage for doing so (see Skidmore, Chapter 4 of this volume). The former (heterosexual women and homosexual men) is actually a well-known combination as 'best friends', whereas the latter (homosexual women and heterosexual men) does not seem to have attained much social reality or visibility that I know of. If bisexuals are added, then in terms of object of desire they are definitely one gender unto themselves, as the differentiation into 'women who desire women and men' and 'men who desire women and men' seems rather pointless, since genital identity seems transcended on both sides of the equation.

Once the mapping of gender has turned from bodily organs (which may or may not have anything much to do with reproduction, i.e. conception, pregnancy, parturition, lactation, etc.) to objects of desire (see also Jackson, Chapter 6 of this volume), whether human or otherwise, or to performance and 'dressing up' (see Lloyd, Chapter 11), then the variations and possibilities move swiftly towards infinity. How one defines the bounds of sexuality is by no means unambiguous. This is relevant, for example, even to an activity that is often *presented* as somehow asexual and only guiltily of the body, namely parenting. This then raises issues of power and politics. If gender is part of a political identity, a group basis for political coalitions, a field of individual interest where people find common cause in *similarity*, then perhaps 'parent' is itself a gender, transcending the bodily differences that are usually identified as not just sexual but 'opposite'.

Considerations of *difference* can also be relevant here, as women in feminist politics were not the first to discover. But this immediately raises the question of *similarity* against which 'difference' is supposed to be pertinent. Class and 'race'/ethnicity among women were points of reference from which quite different notions of gender politics were constructed in terms of substantial demands and coalition strategies. The notion of gender politics as necessarily a politics of sexual *polarisation* has been made highly problematic: could it be that the gender politics of working-class women should be oriented away from issues of 'male domination' and towards *solidarity* with working-class men in an anti-imperialist struggle? Perhaps the masculine as a threat to feminist politics was correctly located in rich, white, capitalist societies, and not in 'men of colour' in any significant way?

If gender is tied to gender politics, rather than to individualised conceptions of sex and sexuality, then perhaps privileged white men and poor exploited men are in different genders as political subjects, as well as political objects? Gender politics among men is not a topic that often surfaces in political theory. It works to divide them as men and, when divided, to draw them together in ways that may be hierarchical or egalitarian, 'homosocial' or homoerotic, within the divisions that are created around sex and sexuality (Hearn and Collinson 1994). Gender politics among men is thus by no means always in opposition to women or to conceptions of women's interests. On the one hand, naturalised or commonplace categories like sex, gender, class and 'race'/ethnicity are manipulated in politics to construct inclusions and exclusions with respect to groups, an inside and an outside with respect to a 'border' or boundary-line, and various maps of identity and difference such that allies and enemies, partners and opponents, powerful and powerless are produced as societies apparently 'function'. On the other hand, however, these constructions, despite all the disciplinary apparatuses employed, map poorly onto the varieties of experience that individuals can still manage to generate in living out their lives as human agents (see Edwards 1994).

My 'working definition' of gender as 'ways in which sex and sexuality become political' is not supposed to legislate what gender is (always and already, as the phrase goes), but is rather intended to alert readers to the ways in which the term is used. In my view, using gender to mean M/F is an attempt to erase or silence the complexities of sexuality into some essentialist or reductionist idea of what is supposed to be right, culturally validated, natural, desirable or whatever. This is not only a matter of the complexity that marginalised sexualities add to 'the heterosexual matrix'; as Butler (1990) says, heterosexuality denies its own variousness, as well. Heterosexuality is undertheorised and underinvestigated, and so are men generally, and 'straight' ones in particular (see Connell 1995).

Narratives

This brings us to the founding narratives of citizenship, which in popular terms are narratives about 'straight' men, patriarchal households, and then hierarchies of disadvantage, marginalisation and exclusion that are supposed to follow, explicitly and/or implicitly. Whether we take the documents and traditional narrations concerning the US constitution, or various national constitutions, 'basic laws' or public policies, we get much the same tale – though there are important differences. Among these there are stories of founding fathers, husbandly and fatherly authority over women and children, transitions to adulthood, manhood and wifehood/widowhood/motherhood. Transitions from girlhood to spinsterhood do not seem to occur, never mind to women as independent citizens. Assumptions and statements about language use and tests, how to 'raise the next generation' (that is, within the hetero-family), responsibility to elders who are 'blood relations', marriage laws (that is, creating a relationship between two people that is special in some sense in terms of rights and obligations), laws and presumptions about inheritance via degrees of consanguinity, which trace the heterosexual matrix out further into society than the nuclear family – all these have been documented, chiefly in feminist analysis and gay studies.

However, one of the things that interests me in this material is the narrative strategy of evasion. The US Constitution (1787), as originally drafted, does not mention women, family, reproduction, education, race or language or ancestry or slavery – directly. It refers to 'people', 'Electors', 'Indians not taxed', 'whole number of free persons', 'all other persons', and 'natural born citizen'. The right to vote was 'left to the States' as well as regulation of these matters, so there is a message-by-implication in the text, which is to endorse a political strategy of conserving social relations as they were already disciplined and policed. Only in later amendments and Supreme Court rulings are there references to concepts like 'race', 'color', 'previous condition of servitude', 'male citizens' and 'sex' (allowing women to vote!), and it is easily adduced that these issues were finally made explicit after strategies of evasion had failed (Shapiro 1973). Thus there is clearly a case for reading the silences of the text, and for setting the texts within the political flow, if we are to decode the messages.

Locke's *Second Treatise of Government*, first published in 1689, is often used to interpret such documents and sometimes serves as the raw material for judicial interpretations. In any case it is a reasonably concise reflection of power/knowledge, served up in a discourse of 'plain truths' that persist through cultural processes that do not reference the work explicitly. As a founding narrative (it was translated into French in 1691, and the ideas entered democratic discourse generally), it presents a wonderful mêlée of signifiers: 'the rational and the industrious', 'wild Indians'/'savages', 'the husband is the stronger and abler', etc.

However, there is another interesting and more subtle discursive strategy at work in this text that can be readily traced elsewhere in political practice.

When the narrative claims to be de-gendered, using terms such as 'man', 'subject', 'citizen', 'member', it has been convincingly shown – with reference to what Locke does say about women (and Indians), for instance – that he has white males of the propertied class in mind (Pateman 1988). But my claim here is that his narrative was not only gendered covertly – it had to be gendered overtly as well, precisely because an account of human society, community and citizenship requires a narrative of birth, education, transition to adulthood, etc. And to do that, sex and sexuality had to be confronted out in the open (which is not to say that there is much subtlety about it – rather the opposite). So Locke does discuss marriage, offspring (legitimate ones), the family, husbands and fathers, wives and mothers, the obligations of adult offspring to parents, etc. Why then did he construct a de-gendered narrative within the other one?

Current constitutions and 'basic laws' and bills of rights do much the same. Unlike the US Constitution, where these issues are strategically evaded, some constitutions explicitly protect marriage, 'the family', and the care of children (Basic Law of the Federal Republic of Germany, Article 6), and also in various other cases minorities both inside and outside the boundaries, cultural differences of certain sorts across zones or regions, etc. – gender-like realms of ascribed difference.

Yet constitutional and other documents of democratic politics also contain a discourse of presumed de-gendered sameness in terms of citizenship, couched in terms of 'equality'. Thus the founding ideas of democracy contain gendered narratives (overt as well as covert). Though covertly gendered, the de-gendered narratives still have a life of their own, and function today as the framework within which much sexual politics is conducted. Risking a generalisation, I would say that feminists agree that de-gendered narratives have been rightly exposed, in the founding texts, as covertly gendered. But they divide as to whether genuinely – rather than merely apparently – de-gendered narratives of equality can be sustained as a practical framework either for transcending difference or for negotiating difference in practical terms (Phillips 1991; Mouffe 1992). These debates concerning 'difference' could, of course, be generalised more widely beyond the female/male binary, and indeed they are.

My point here is that citizenship traditionally generates gendered narratives (overt and covert) of power hierarchy, and also a de-gendered narrative of citizenship among equal 'men'/persons. Gendered narrative establishes hierarchies of citizenship (as gradations of esteem) in ways to do with sex and sexuality. De-gendered narratives go over the same ground, but in a different and disjunctive way, when they treat 'man' or 'men' or 'persons' (or, for example, 'French nationals of either sex', as in the Constitution of 1958) as 'equal citizens'. Hierarchies of power *are noticed and then forgotten* within discourses that are consistently represented as quintessentially egalitarian – so we forget we forgot, as Nietzsche memorably remarked. The net effect is that gendered hierarchies of power are somehow disengaged by the egalitarian claims that constitutional and other foundational texts of democracy so boldly state, even though narrations of democracy make little sense without the 'broader' accounts of hierarchical social relationships that are explicitly or implicitly invoked.

More controversially I would argue that discourses of equality are self-contradictory, in that they represent sameness as difference: 'You're different, we're treating you differently, but the result is somehow "equal" – that is, supposedly the same in terms of some common factor.' Exactly what this common factor is – what it is in terms of sameness that transcends or underlies the differences under consideration – is never satisfactorily identified. Is it in virtue of some sameness as 'persons' that citizens are able to vote (leaving aside the effect of voting systems on a supposed equality of votes between different 'persons')? Or is it rather that voting is one of the few cases in which such an (approximate) equality can actually be worked out between people who are otherwise enmeshed in hierarchies of difference, particularly those to do with sex and sexuality? Equality narratives typically function to evade hierarchies of difference and to keep important inequalities intact *by overlaying yet not negating* traditional accounts of difference that maintain power hierarchies, notably the heterosexual matrix.

Rethinking

Given that citizenship narratives slyly construct these hierarchies, which masquerade as equality, how can this be subverted? As Butler (1990) says, gender is a strategy that constructs hierarchies around a presumed binary difference, and binary difference is actually constructed and policed at points within a continuum of talents, capacities, attributes, desires – whatever humans want, need, do. Thus people may be more or less good at, for example, parenting, managing, cleaning or doctoring, but enforced concepts of binary difference exclude, marginalise and degrade. Moreover each side of the binary of gender – as the heterosexual matrix – is usually conceived monotonically as mothers/fathers, wives/husbands, manly/womanly, etc. – again in defiance of how people manage to be and/or of the way they want to be, or might be if gender as the heterosexual matrix were not inculcated, inscribed, policed and defended.

Though society is itself an exercise in repressively and constructively rounding differences into uniformities, it is apparent politically that gender goes too far, as feminist politics and feminist analysis have amply demonstrated. Subverting it ought to involve more than just 'turning it round' or 'turning it over' – for example, 'women on top' or 'homosexual marriage'. Why not just put some questions clearly and allow different sorts of answers?

For example: what does it mean to have a legally recognised (for entry and exit) relationship with another person or persons – with respect to resources, obligations, inheritance, assignment of pensions? What is it to be 'next of kin'? How much kinship connection legally survives 'coming of age'? What are the proofs of relevant interests?

And further: what are the duties and obligations of biological, birth and/or

adoptive parents? What makes someone a 'carer'? Are there numerical boundaries to a 'family'? Does sex make a difference? Does sexuality? Much of the
philosophy and legal 'argument' employed to 'sort this out' is actually imbued
with the confusions of gendered (overtly and covertly) and de-gendered (apparently and genuinely) narratives of the person, men/women, adults entitled to
rights or subject to obligations, i.e. citizens (see also Rahman, Chapter 7 of this
volume). Given answers to these questions, and going beyond statutory privileges
and obligations of citizens, what representations of 'the citizen' or 'typical citizens' should the state construct, if any? This raises the question of
exemplification and demonisation – and consequent gradations of esteem – that
I began with.

Citizenship is at the heart of what 'we' think 'we' should be like – and,
perhaps more importantly, *not like*. The conceptual relationship between 'the
good man' and 'the good citizen' is a topic of debate as old as political theory
itself. What has shifted recently is the way in which these categories are now
construed as disciplinary and disadvantaging (in graded ways), as well as productive and enabling. An even bigger shift has been the recognition that sex and
sexuality play a very large narrative role in filling out these categorisations in
practice, and that re-theorisations of sex and sexuality are central to the re-
visioning of human(e) society.

References

Babington, B., and Evans, P.W. 1993. *Biblical Epics: Sacred Narrative in the Hollywood Cinema.*
    Manchester: Manchester University Press.
Butler, J. 1990. *Gender Trouble: Feminism and the Subversion of Identity.* London: Routledge.
Callinicos, A. 1995. *Theories and Narratives: Reflections on the Philosophy of History.* Cambridge:
    Polity Press.
Carver, T. 1996. *Gender is Not a Synonym for Women.* Boulder CO: Lynne Rienner.
Connell, R.W. 1987. *Gender and Power: Society, the Person and Sexual Politics.* Cambridge: Polity
    Press.
—— 1995. *Masculinities.* Cambridge: Polity Press.
Dummet, A., and Nichol, A. 1991. *Subjects, Citizens and Others.* London: Weidenfeld &
    Nicolson.
Edwards, T. 1994. *Erotics and Politics: Gay Male Sexuality, Masculinity and Feminism.* London:
    Routledge.
Evans, D.T. 1993. *Sexual Citizenship: The Material Construction of Sexualities.* London: Rout-
    ledge.
Hearn, J., and Collinson, D. 1994. 'Unities and differences between men and between
    masculinities'. In *Theorizing Masculinities*, ed. H. Brod and M. Kaufmann, 97–118.
    Newbury Park CA: Sage.
Locke, J. 1993. *Two Treatises of Government.* Ed. Mark Goldie. London: Everyman/Dent.
Mouffe, C. (ed.). 1992. *Dimensions of Radical Democracy: Pluralism, Citizenship, Community.*
    London: Verso.
Pateman, C. 1988. *The Sexual Contract.* Cambridge: Polity Press.
Phillips, A. 1991. *Engendering Democracy.* Cambridge: Polity Press.

Shapiro, M. (ed.). 1973. *The Constitution of the United States and Related Documents*. Arlington Heights IL: Harlan Davidson.

Weeks, J. 1985. *Sexuality and its Discontents: Meanings, Myths and Modern Sexualities*. London: Routledge & Kegan Paul.

White, H. 1987. *The Content of the Form: Narrative Discourse and Historical Representation*. Baltimore MD: Johns Hopkins University Press.

2 Sexual citizens

Legislating the age of consent in Britain

Matthew Waites

This chapter outlines the emergence of the concept of an 'age of consent to sexual intercourse' in Britain over the past century. It considers three moments of legal change at which the age of consent has been formulated, in 1885, 1967 and 1994, discussing the forms of power and resistance that have shaped age-of-consent law. The analysis shows that contemporary debates often ignore even the recent history of the concept. The meaning of an 'age of consent' has historically been linked to exclusionary assumptions about the gender and sexuality of sexual subjects conceived in law. This makes any history of steadily expanding consent problematic.

Sexual citizenship

To map the changing implications of the age of consent, this chapter employs the contested concept of 'citizenship'. Citizenship must be understood as a product of an individual's entire social existence, beginning with the civil, political and social rights identified by T.H. Marshall, but also including forms of cultural access, representation and belonging that go beyond rights (Marshall 1950). Recently, sexuality theorists have attempted to rework the term by coining 'sexual citizenship' and 'intimate citizenship' (Evans 1993; Plummer 1995: 144–80; see also Carver, Chapter 1 of this volume). David Evans does not regard 'the sexual' as a new sphere in Marshall's schema, but as an aspect of citizenship cutting across these spheres. Alternatively, Ken Plummer's conceptualisation of 'intimate citizenship' covers a wider range of issues, but is proposed as an additional sphere in Marshall's original schema. For the purposes of this chapter, the term 'sexual citizenship' is used, since the age of consent issue is clearly 'sexual'. But the phrase is used simply to summarise all the sexual aspects of citizenship, without any intended adherence to Evans's conceptual schema (Waites 1996).

Conceptualisations of legal boundaries between age groups in relation to sexuality have changed dramatically during the past century, so finding a language to theorise them is highly problematic. Each articulation of such a legal boundary involves corresponding and mutually constituting definitions of the groups both below and above that age. These definitions, linked to a range of assumptions about the gender and sexuality of these groups, amount to articulations of the forms of sexual citizenship granted by the state. Hence examination of debates over the age of consent can provide a lens through which to analyse the forms of sexual citizenship granted to persons both above and below the age of consent over time.

The UK has the lowest age of criminal responsibility in Europe: 10. In March 1997 the Labour Party's [then] shadow Home Secretary Jack Straw proposed ending the assumption in law that 13–16-year-olds are incapable of understanding the meaning of evil. British society holds under-16s responsible for crime, but does not grant them the right to consent to sexual acts, to govern their own bodies. There is confusion at the heart of conceptions of the shift from childhood innocence to adult responsibility and citizenship.

This is one set of important questions about the sexuality of children and young people that academic work on the age of consent has addressed. In doing so, however, researchers have sometimes set aside another interesting question. How has the sexual citizenship of those *above* the age of consent been articulated? Has a 'right to consent' emerged as constitutive of adult citizenship? This is the question, perhaps a more surprising one, that this chapter addresses.

'Consent' means 'voluntary agreement'. But being above the so-called 'age of consent' has not always meant a right to choose – indeed it still does not. To understand the contemporary meaning of the age of consent in relation to its history means reflecting upon the changing subjectivities to which that term has applied, the changing contexts of its application, and the social forces that have brought change about. As will become clear, a key issue is to decide whether the changing knowledges through which people both above and below the age of consent have been imagined reflect genuine changes in how society views the experiences of these people, or whether the emergence of a language of citizenship and consent merely obscures the absence of change.

1885: The age of consent for women

In 1885 the Criminal Law Amendment Act created the age of consent law for young women; it still stands on the statute book in Britain (Bland 1995; Walkowitz 1980, 1992; Weeks 1989). The Act was passed in the context of a public outcry over prostitution among young girls, magnified by a series of articles entitled *The Maiden Tribute of Modern Babylon* by the editor of the *Pall Mall Gazette* (see Walkowitz 1992). The change in the law occurred as the movement for social purity began to overcome previous *laissez-faire* Victorian attitudes to the role of the state in governing intimate relationships.

The Act prohibited sexual intercourse with a woman aged less than 16, raising the age from 13. Though the new law was discussed as an 'age of consent', recent feminist commentaries have demonstrated that this was a misnomer, since the rationale behind the law was prohibitive rather than empowering in its attitude to women. It was actually conceived in paternalistic terms as an 'age of protection', below which the state was responsible for protecting young women – a negative prohibition, placing limits upon the rights of men to sexual access. The Act did not create any right to consent to sexual intercourse above that age, as legal rape within marriage demonstrated until very recently. The law represented a limit upon male agency, a prohibition, rather than a recognition of women's equal agency or right to consent (Edwards 1996).

What we now think of as the 'heterosexual age of consent' was formulated in 1885, prior to the invention of the concept of heterosexuality (Katz 1995). The law was intended to protect only women, not men, a fact that belies the assumption of mutuality when a 'heterosexual age of consent' is discussed in contemporary debates. Furthermore, the existence of same-sex sexual behaviour was not contemplated in the debate over the age of consent. Although the Labouchere amendment creating the crime of gross indecency between males was passed as a last-minute adjunct to the Criminal Law Amendment Act, this did not influence debates over the age of consent. The Labouchere amendment in any case did not encode 'homosexuality' into law, and ignored female homosexuality (Weeks 1977; Moran 1996).

The age-of-consent legislation in the Criminal Law Amendment Act was founded on a polarised view of male and female sexuality whereby 'the beast' of male lust required legal containment to preserve the virtue of a passive female sexuality. Prevailing views of gender saw men as more rational, yet also more potentially lustful. Women were divided neatly between the virtuous virgins and mothers and the whores who became the most demonised figures in popular iconography. The morality of women was reconciled with their less rational status through the common understanding that women were governed by emotions linked to their essential womanly nature (Bland 1995: 48–9). The question of whether there should be an age of consent for men did not arise, due to the overwhelming assumption that women did not initiate sexual activity that might be against a man's wishes. The age-of-consent law was thus profoundly gendered in its conception and initial enforcement.

Since 'consent' is only meaningful when it is informed, one must question the meaning of an age of consent at a time when there was much confusion in popular beliefs about sexuality, no sex education in schools, and girls were given minimal information about sex to protect their 'innocence'. Even when the *British Medical Journal* responded to the *Maiden Tribute of Modern Babylon* by calling for commencement of sex education in schools, it remained ambivalent about such education being extended to girls, for fear of undermining their purity (Bland 1995: 59). Many girls would not have known what they were consenting *to* – including the risks of pregnancy and sexually transmitted diseases.

To understand the age of consent's formation in 1885 involves examining the reality behind representations of young women as passive victims. Judith Walkowitz and Jeffrey Weeks are agreed that the portrayal of young girl prostitutes as sexually innocent passive victims of individual evil men ignored the opportunities offered to young women by prostitution to combat poverty and dismal employment prospects (see also Gorjanicyn and Outshoorn, Chapters 16 and 17 of this volume), with the consequence that social purity's moral campaigns ignored the need for structural social reforms (Weeks 1989: 88;

Walkowitz 1992). Weeks argues that campaigns that continued until the 1930s to raise the age of consent, even to 21, were misguided in assuming a total lack of agency.

The problem in assessing the legacy of the rise in the age of consent to 16 is to weigh the benefits of increasing recognition by the state of its responsibility for children and young people against the new cultural formations that emerged at this time, constructing children as passive potential victims. It is important to consider the dangers of reading a contemporary agenda of sexual empowerment and autonomy into a previous century. Reliable contraception and treatments for diseases such as syphilis have surely changed the context in which the law operates.

1967: The age of consent for male homosexuals

In 1957 *The Report of the Departmental Committee on Homosexual Offences and Prostitution*, subsequently known as the Wolfenden report, was published (DCHOP 1957). The report, from a Home Office departmental committee investigating homosexuality and prostitution, advocated the partial decriminalisation of male homosexual acts in private between consenting adults (DCHOP 1957: 115). It provided the dominant rationale employed when this measure eventually came about in England and Wales, after a period of sustained lobbying, through the 1967 Sexual Offences Act, though not in Scotland until 1980, or in Northern Ireland until 1982. Decriminalisation created a male homosexual 'age of consent' at 21, the age of majority (voting age) when the report was written (Grey 1992; Hall 1980; Weeks 1989).

Decriminalisation, however, did not represent homosexuals beginning to be granted equal citizenship with regard to the age of consent. As the Wolfenden report said: 'It is important that the limited modification of the law which we propose should not be interpreted as an indication that the law can be indifferent to other forms of homosexual behaviour, or as a general licence to adult homosexuals to behave as they please' (DCHOP 1957: 44). The Wolfenden report stated, in accordance with the near unanimous view of its medical witnesses, that a young man's sexual orientation is fixed 'in the main outline' by the age of 16, although its call for more research and advocacy of hormone treatments suggests residual doubts about the fixity of sexual orientation. However, it argued after long deliberation that he could only take decisions that might set him apart from society after the age of 21 (DCHOP 1957: 25–8). Taken at face value, this suggests an interesting disjunction between physical maturity – the fixity of desires – and emotional, rational and ethical maturity, the attainment of moral responsibility. Given this mind–body split, only the attainment of certain mental capacities could legitimise the acquisition of the right to choose as a full citizen. This disjunction suggests that whereas young women in 1885 were defined largely by their biological maturity, male homosexuals in 1967 were accorded consent on the grounds of ability to exercise choice and agency, more in the manner we would expect of citizens. However, homosexuality implied a funda-

mental flaw that limited the scope of these consenting capacities to the management of deviant desires. Homosexuals could never join the dominant moral
community.

The sphere of consent was to be the sphere of privacy, a carefully delimited
realm, tightly patrolled at the boundaries where public order and decency were
threatened (DCHOP 1957: 9–10, 12, 20). Though the formal definitions of both
consent and privacy were intended by the Wolfenden committee to be the same
as for heterosexuals, their scope was delimited by a late parliamentary amendment (DCHOP 1957: 25). A universalistic, humanist language of an equal right
to consenting acts in private for all citizens was employed (DCHOP 1957: 20).
But this disguised contrary intentions with regard to real, meaningful citizenship:
of enhancement and promotion on the one hand, of containment and disappearance on the other (Hall 1980; Weeks 1989; Moran 1996). The Wolfenden
report stated that lesbian and male homosexual acts are 'reprehensible from the
point of view of the family' (DCHOP 1957: 22).

Much regulation of consensual activities between adults remained. Partial
decriminalisation did not remove the Labouchere amendment, which installed
'gross indecency' in law, but was a sole exception to legal prohibition. Buggery
and 'gross indecency' (sexual acts between men other than buggery, such as
fellatio and mutual masturbation) remained illegal except in strict privacy.
Medieval sodomy laws remained on the statute book, and new stricter sentences
for buggery with 'minors' below the age of consent were introduced. Soliciting
(cruising or propositioning men) and procuring (inviting, encouraging and facilitating homosexual acts) remained illegal. A legal judgment in 1972 by the House
of Lords decided that the 1967 Act exempted homosexuals over 21 from criminal penalties without making their actions 'lawful in the full sense' (Weeks 1989:
275). The merchant navy and armed forces were exempted from decriminalisation. Furthermore, the law imposed new regulations upon public behaviour. A
new definition of 'privacy', stricter than for heterosexuals, and subsequently
interpreted by police and courts to mean anywhere where a third person was not
likely to be present, was introduced in the House of Lords to widen the scope of
'public' acts. The law was tightened with regard to importuning.

Decriminalisation represented a pragmatic decision to recognise that the law
was not a deterrent, largely on the basis of the Wolfenden report's conclusion
that homosexual identity in adults was a *fait accompli*. It did not represent the
granting of a general right to consent above the age of 21. It signalled an ethic
of limited tolerance, and efficient regulation of public behaviour, rather than
equal rights and equal respect (Weeks 1989). The report's continuing interest in
research seeking a cure for homosexuality illustrates that it did not regard
consent as implying freedom to choose between equal options.

Lesbianism was largely absent from the debates over decriminalisation.
Female homosexuality continued to escape criminalisation by British law at any
age, despite a lack of clarity as to whether an age of consent existed for lesbian
acts. Implicit in this silence was the continuing invisibility of lesbians, and
assumptions of women's lack of sexual agency, especially the impossibility of

women abusing children. The lack of a lesbian age of consent was never a positive endorsement of women's right to consent. The Wolfenden committee did
consider whether the offence of 'indecent assault' could apply to lesbians
(DCHOP 1957: 36–8). But the committee was unable to find a single instance of
such an act having been directly committed against another female, and
continued to assume 'homosexual offences' were male (DCHOP 1957: 38;
Moran 1996: 97–101).

In some respects the (male) homosexual age of consent was conceptualised in
negative terms similar to those that had structured the age of consent for young
women in 1885. To a large extent the age of consent at 21 represented a prohibition upon activity below that age, rather than an endorsement of equal sexual
citizenship for those above. It was conceptualised by Wolfenden as an age above
which young men no longer needed protecting from themselves, or from
seducing older homosexuals. The taboo against paedophilia, historically stronger
in relation to male homosexual acts as opposed to heterosexual or female homosexual acts, played an important part. Homosexuals over 21 were not imagined
as fully rational beings, deserving of the equal citizenship status accorded to
those deemed to possess full moral and rational faculties. Decriminalisation on
the whole signalled a limit to state protection, rather than a right to consent.

However, in other respects the conceptualisation was significantly different
from that applied to the age of consent in 1885. The male homosexual age of
consent proposed by the Wolfenden report was 21, the general age of majority at
the time the report was written and when legislation was passed – though the age
of majority was subsequently reduced to 18 in 1969, leaving the homosexual age
of consent at 21 as a clear anomaly. This was intended to be high enough not to
encourage homosexuality.

This shows that the idea of an age of consent *had* begun to shift, or was being
used in a different way from in 1885. The fact that the (male) homosexual age of
consent was linked by Wolfenden to the age of majority indicated the existence
of a new liberal ideology that accepted adult citizens should be responsible for
their own decisions over homosexuality, rather than being ruled by church or
state. The homosexual age of consent did imply the granting of a limited degree
of citizenship, since it accepted the principle of self-determination within a
tightly defined sphere of acts, recognising limited moral and rational capacities
for responsible decision-making among homosexual men over 21. However, this
was an extremely partial, second-class sexual citizenship conceived as being
granted to a homosexual subject who could never be a full citizen, but would
remain necessarily compromised by deviant sexual desires requiring constraint.

1994: The gay age of consent

By 1994 sexual acts between male homosexuals were the only activities prohibited for young people until the age of 21 but permissible thereafter. Twenty-one
was also the highest age of consent in Europe, and there was an equal age of
consent in twenty-one out of twenty-eight Council of Europe states (Stonewall

1993). In 1994, following campaigns for lesbian and gay equality, the male homosexual age of consent was reduced from 21 to 18 (427 votes to 162 in favour), but not to the 'heterosexual' age of 16 (307 to 280 votes against). The vote in Parliament on 21 February 1994 followed the first full parliamentary debate on the subject since the partial decriminalisation of male homosexuality in 1967 (Waites 1995).

When considered in the light of the very partial decriminalisation of homosexuality in 1967, the debate in 1994 over what was commonly described as the 'gay age of consent' takes on a very different emphasis. The idea of a 'gay age of consent' was being invented, though often those engaged in the debate seemed unaware of the historical shift that had taken place, and drew simplistic parallels with previous 'age of consent' legislation. The Sexual Offences Act continued to make a wide range of consensual acts between men illegal, yet this was largely forgotten during the course of the 'gay age of consent' debate as reported in the press and on television.

There had been a shift from 'homosexual' to 'gay', and also a shift in the meaning of 'age of consent', shifts that signalled a complex set of changes in public understandings. Previously the 'homosexual age of consent' had been conceived as permitting a very limited set of actions for a medicalised sexually deviant group. Now claims were being articulated in 'gay' terms, with all the positive terms of equality that the word implied through the legacy of gay liberation. Where a 'homosexual age of consent' had applied to a medicalised category of deviants, as a pragmatic legal response to their affliction, the 'gay age of consent' recognised the agency of gay men and lesbians, their capacity to make claims to citizenship and define themselves. To some extent the gay age of consent implied recognition of claims for equality that were both lesbian and gay (see also Skidmore, Bell, Jackson and Rahman, Chapters 4, 5, 6 and 7 of this volume).

The language of an age of consent had been appropriated from 1885 and 1967, but given new meaning. Both the homosexual subject and his consenting sexual acts had been reinterpreted. Whereas previously the consenting homosexual subject of Wolfenden had been granted partial citizenship only as a means to govern deviant desires, now the gay sexual subject was articulated by supporters of equality as deserving equal rights precisely due to his fixed desires (see also Jackson, Rahman and Mottier, Chapters 6, 7 and 10 of this volume). Equality supporters still insisted upon the fixity of desires, indeed Stonewall and others cited the evidence for this produced by Wolfenden in 1957 (Waites 1995). But the language of perversion and deviancy was replaced by a neutral language of equality, thus reframing the meaning of medical claims for fixed sexual orientation. In the language of equality supporters, the right to perform consensual sexual acts became an indicator of citizenship, a mark of equality. The 1994 debate provides evidence for the emergence of a new set of assumptions about sexual citizenship.

In 1994, by contrast with 1885, the 'heterosexual age of consent' was often discussed as though it applied equally to men and women who were deemed equally capable of giving active consent, whereas before women were seen as essentially passive. The law remained the same, though there was some ambiguity over whether its interpretation had changed – could a young man be prosecuted for having sex below the age of 16 with an older woman? A shift in gender ideologies over the course of the past century, particularly due to the equalising effects of second-wave feminism, had transformed the assumption that women needed protection towards a belief that women and men had equal capacities to consent – though this has certainly not been fully achieved.

By 1994 the image of the seducing older homosexual continued to play a central part in public debates about the age of consent. But a significant disjunction between concepts of paedophilia and homosexuality had occurred, as homosexuality became included in what is normal and acceptable, while paedophilia remained illicit. 'Gay' and 'age of consent' were in fact in tension, since the aspiration to equal citizenship embodied in 'gay' was contradicted by the reality of the homosexual age of consent, which had been formulated as an age of protection to safeguard young men from becoming the victims of seducing older homosexuals.

The 1994 debate took place with lesbianism remaining largely off the agenda. There was some ambiguity over whether the Criminal Law Amendment Act needed reinterpretation to create an age of consent for same-sex acts between women, but no outcry that there existed no clear age of consent for sexual acts between women, or that this age should be lower than for gay sex. Lesbians remained sufficiently invisible for their legal status to remain ambiguous. This was partly the legacy of a view that young women did not require protection from lesbians.

The history of the law on homosexuality illustrates the inadequacy of widespread common-sense public assumptions about the meaning of an age of consent. The legacy of the Labouchere amendment in 1885, the partial decriminalisation of male homosexuality in 1967 and the lowering of the male homosexual age of consent in 1994 form a legal framework that is built upon prohibitive exclusions from citizenship, mitigated by liberal tolerance, utilitarian pragmatism and piecemeal reform. Consideration of homosexuality evidences the inadequacy of the widely held view that the age of consent in British law represents a positive endorsement of sexual citizenship.

Conclusion

In the light of the argument above, one is drawn to look afresh at familiar international comparisons of the age of consent, such as those employed by equality campaigners in 1994 (Stonewall 1993; Tatchell 1992). How must the individual national trajectories of law, and the different cultural formations informing them, compromise such easy comparisons between states? Is the age of consent the same thing, or does it operate in the same way, when the histories of the age of consent in each country reveal similarly distinctive formations?

In the UK the meaning of consenting sexual acts for both women and male homosexuals was predicated upon a model of an imagined sexual subject, compromised by their gender or perverse desires. Their consenting actions could only imply submission for women, or a pragmatic outlet for perversity for homosexual men, never actions that could raise them to a status of full sexual citizens. In the cases of both women and male homosexuals, the 1994 debate provided evidence that the age of consent had been reinterpreted in the aftermath of the sexual liberation movements, feminism and gay liberation. The granting of a right to consent had become an issue of respect between citizens, the granting of autonomy.

This occurred through two dimensions. After the sexual liberationist movements of the 1960s and 1970s, adult women and homosexuals claimed equal respect and thus became increasingly regarded as capable of decision-making. At the same time sexual relations themselves became issues of citizenship (see also Carver, Chapter 1 of this volume), and hence rights to consent were linked to general citizenship. However, the legal framework has remained unchanged, and continues to restrict sexual citizenship (see also Gibbins, Chapter 3 of this volume). Meanwhile in relation to those below the age of consent there have also been claims made for partial citizenship and an extension of consent on the basis of democratic principles applied to sexual relations. The language of democracy is now used to debate young people's empowerment in sexual relations.

It can be argued that present trends suggest that the scope of consent is progressively expanding for individuals above the age of consent. The unique law on gross indecency may soon be abolished, and in any case represents a legal anachronism, no longer reflecting public attitudes. The same can be said of the Criminal Law Amendment Act. The homosexual age of consent has been lowered, and is likely to be equalised, following a ruling in the European Court of Human Rights on 7 October 1997 that inequality constitutes illegal discrimination. The Labour government has promised a free vote in Parliament on the issue. The law on rape in marriage has also been reformed, mirroring greater respect for consent.

The emergence of an adult sexual subject who has rights to consent in public language, such as in the 1994 debate, may signal the demise of any shared sense of citizenship, rather than the construction of a new sexual dimension of citizenship. The language of citizenship employed by Stonewall and equality supporters in 1994 may be misleading, since it may be destroying the state's role in articulating shared citizenship ideals in the face of radical difference, rather than generating new forms of shared citizenship. In relation to 'negotiated', 'consensual' relations for those below the current age of consent, however, there is little evidence of any desire to expand sexual citizenship. There may be greater recognition that the desires and experiences of young people should be a part of the process of decision-making, but this is not interpreted widely to mean a lowering of the age of consent.

This chapter shows that a contemporary narrative searching for the gradual opening of a sphere of consent is highly problematic for several reasons: first, because the rationale behind legislation in 1885 and 1967 was largely prohibitive; second, because the meaning attributed to consent by women or by homosexuals was intertwined with prevailing knowledges of women and homosexual men as having compromised subjectivities, which rendered them outside the scope of full citizenship. Only when women and gay men had made claims for citizenship, articulating their biology and desires in new frameworks linked to social equality, did the age of consent become reimagined to include them, and it still remains unchanged in law even as the idea of a right to consent has entered the political imagination. Nevertheless, it may yet be possible to trace an emergent enlightenment vocabulary of equality, autonomy and consent applied to adult sexual relations back through voices of resistance raised in previous moments, even where dominant definitions imposed by the powerful denied these liberating possibilities.

References

Bland, L. 1995. *Banishing the Beast: English Feminism and the Sexual Morality 1885–1914*. Harmondsworth: Penguin.

DCHOP 1957. *Report of the Departmental Committee on Homosexual Offences and Prostitution* (Chair: Sir John Wolfenden). Cmnd. 247, 1957. London: HMSO.

Edwards, A. 1996. 'Gender and sexuality in the social construction of rape and consensual sex: a study of process and outcome in six recent rape trials'. In J. Holland and L. Adkins (eds), *Sex, Sensibility and the Gendered Body*, pp. 178–201. London: Macmillan.

Evans, D.T. 1993. *Sexual Citizenship: The Material Construction of Sexualities*. London: Routledge.

Grey, A. 1992. *Quest for Justice: Towards Homosexual Emancipation*. London: Sinclair-Stevenson.

Hall, S. (ed.) 1980. 'Reformism and the legislation of consent'. In National Deviancy Conference (ed.), *Permissiveness and Control: The Fate of the Sixties Legislation*, pp. 1–43. London: Macmillan.

Katz, J.N. 1995. *The Invention of Heterosexuality*. London: Penguin.

Marshall, T.H. 1950. 'Citizenship and social class'. In T.H. Marshall (ed.), *Sociology at the Crossroads*. London: Heinemann.

Moran, L.J. 1996. *The Homosexual(ity) of Law*. London: Routledge.

Plummer, K. 1995. *Telling Sexual Stories: Power, Change and Social Worlds*. London: Routledge.

Stonewall. 1993. *The Case for Change: Arguments for an Equal Age of Consent*. London: Stonewall.

Tatchell, P. 1992. *Europe in the Pink: Lesbian and Gay Equality in the New Europe*. London: Gay Men's Press.

Waites, M. 1995. *The Age of Consent Debate: A Critical Analysis*. Unpublished dissertation submitted for MA in Sociology of Culture and Society. Department of Sociology, University of Essex.

—— 1996. 'Lesbian and gay theory, sexuality and citizenship'. *Contemporary Politics* 2: 139–49.

Walkowitz, J. 1980. *Prostitution and Victorian Society*. Cambridge: Cambridge University Press.

—— 1992. *City of Dreadful Delight: Narratives of Sexual Danger in Late Victorian London*. London: Virago.

Weeks, J. 1977. *Coming Out: Homosexual Politics in Britain from the Nineteenth Century to the Present.* London: Quartet.
—— 1989. *Sex, Politics and Society: The Regulation of Sexuality since 1800,* 2nd edn. London: Longman.

3 Sexuality and the law

The body as politics

John R. Gibbins

The body, and in particular 'sexy bodies' (Grosz and Probyn 1995), have become the focus of several high-profile legal cases and political contests in recent years. The right of citizens to control their bodies, to change and exchange body images and to change their legal gender is at present being contested in the European Courts (see Skidmore, Chapter 4 of this volume). The legal right to obtain sex-change operations; the legality of marriages involving a transsexual and his/her occupational rights (see Bell, Chapter 5); the right to sex-altering drugs and the rights of a spouse to their partner's frozen sperm or eggs; sodomitic rights and the legality of sadomasochism are just a few of the issues that are being contested in Britain today. With a few notable exceptions, such as the work of Squires (1993a, 1993b), few of these contests have attracted research from political scientists, many of whom did enter into the debates over homosexual rights and feminism. Meanwhile in disciplines outside political science, the subjects of sexuality, the body and the politics of the body – sometimes inspired by contemporary continental philosophy – have become a focus of some of the most interesting and productive theories and debates. My aims are both to focus attention on some key issues in the politics of sexuality and the body and to apply insights from post-structuralism and postmodernism in theorising normatively about them.

Postmodernism and postmodernist writers deal with problems faced by citizens and the state alike in contemporary Western societies, problems that can be related to sexuality (Gibbins and Reimer 1995; Connolly 1991; Rosenau 1992; Yeatman 1994). How can a mushrooming plurality of distinct, diverse and apparently incommensurable selves and groups coexist in the same time and space? What roles, if any, should politics, government and the law play in regulating the behaviour of citizens? In this chapter I shall problematise the history of the state's involvement in regulating sexual behaviour by using the work of Foucault (see Mottier, Chapter 10 of this volume), and then I shall elaborate and deconstruct theories of the proper role of the state by suggesting new models and discourses of sexuality, the body and the law. To provide a focus for debate, I shall present a study of the state regulation of citizens' sexualities (see Carver, Chapter 1 of this volume), in this case sadomasochism, using the infamous 'Spanner case' (*R. v. Brown*, [1993] 2 WRL 556; [1992] 2 All ER 75). In that case a group of forty-four adult consenting males were prosecuted, and ultimately sixteen were convicted in the UK in 1989, for 'inflicting actual bodily harm'.

Participants in those activities, such as sadomasochism, that are troubling the state are sure that they have the bodies and minds of *adults* and not children. They are not forced into activities but rather *consent* to them in the pursuit of *pleasure* that transcends pain. There are no *victims* and very little real *harm*, only mutually satisfied or pleasured participants. In what follows, as illustrated by the Spanner case, I refer only to apparently consensual adult sex, and exclude all acts of violence and sexuality that do not involve apparent consent or that are forced upon unwilling participants, or those whose capacity to judge is not yet formed, or has been disrupted by illness, drugs or deprivation (Lee 1994: 125).

Problematising history

In the history of political thought there are many answers to the question of why and how the state ought to regulate the conduct of its citizens, including sexual conduct. Plato considered the legitimation for state involvement to be the realisation of justice, the strategy being to defend reason from the barbaric needs of the body. For Aristotle, the aim was to reconcile conflicts, the body being regulated to allow individual and social development. For Saint Augustine, bodily regulation was a means to salvation of the soul. For Marsilius of Padua, regulation was necessary to defend the body politic, limiting the natural desires of the individual body only to that extent. In the modern liberal tradition, regulation is to be minimal and determined only by concerns to protect individual rights to life, liberty and property from threats. Marxists theorised regulation as a rationalisation of class rule ensuring efficient and effective management of workers' bodies for the good of capitalism; socialism, by contrast, would regulate bodies on the basis of social welfare, either by scientific forms of birth control and eugenics or by the liberation of Eros from civilisation and capitalism, as in the works of Reich and Marcuse.

Since 1945 in the West we have seen a multiplication and diversification of arguments for and against regulation, with sexual liberation arguments put by sex therapists at one extreme and legal moralism at the other. For government this revolves round the need to find a 'rational' solution to problems posed by governments themselves about the management of mass populations enclosed in confined spaces. 'Government rationality' or 'governmentality' is aimed at maximising 'social defence' or 'security', and so to construct 'techniques of power' and power/knowledge complexes that allow the surveillance, disciplining and control of both individual and group behaviour (Foucault 1991; Burchell *et al.* 1991). Government sees the need to control growing populations, dangerous bodies and rogue reproduction, and it develops 'bio-power' to do this. Controlled populations respond by developing 'counter-conducts'. This conflicts with the very freedoms liberal governments are committed to protect, so they become trapped in the logic of governmentality and by problems of governability (Burchell *et al.* 1991: 46–8).

In modernity, an ideology of individual freedom, choice and rights to private expression between consenting adults is proffered, but problematised by warning discourses of health risks, sexual diseases, and dysfunctions. Legal discourses warn of rape and violence, sociological and feminist discourses warn of exploitation and poverty for deviants; psychological discourses warn of repression and dangerous drives for domination and release. Therapy, health promotion, and counselling provide discourses and practices that are aimed at helping the individual to handle anxieties resulting from knowledge and awareness of these risks. Under the ethical ideals of neutrality, non-prescriptiveness, mutual regard and empowering others, these new discourses and practices provide, however, the opposite of a liberating experience, imposing instead a new regulatory system governed by surveillance, discipline and power (Dreyfus and Rabinow 1982; Rabinow 1994).

This is the inheritance of the modern regime of 'bio-politics', where knowledge, power and regulatory apparatus are focused on the individual body and on the social body, a metaphor for the collective (Hewitt 1983: 71–3). Of importance to us here is the argument that this bio-power creates the very problems and crises that it then attempts to solve through its regulatory mechanisms.

Problematising language

To explain how and why sexuality is so regulated, we can look at the construction of the supposedly essential and foundational truths that create grids of meaning and structures of social reality. According to Levi-Strauss (1962; 1963), binaries such as male/female, straight/bent, heterosexual/homosexual, normal/abnormal, natural/unnatural, proper/perverse, human/bestial, civilised/barbarian and right/wrong are part of a social, psychological and political ordering system. They signify acceptability, provide moral scales, express emotional and cultural revulsion; they prescribe as well as describe and legitimate through the myths that contain them. Above all, they inform us as to what is a problem and what needs addressing as an issue. So myths about women, the 'fall' and Adam's rib set up the classificatory system that delegitimates women's rights and sexuality, and effectively shapes masculinity. The post-structuralist objection to Levi-Strauss is that he is wrong in considering that the need for these binaries is a deep structural necessity, even if the contents are contingent. Rather it could be, as Foucault claims, that this need is also contingent and political. Nor, according to post-structuralists, could it be presumed, with Durkheim, that each society has a functional necessity to regulate deviancy in order to preserve the social order, because the type of order is itself the subject of debate. Thus regulating 'deviants' follows from their construction in language as a 'discovery', and not from the dynamics of the social order, nor from a psychological, biological or anthropological necessity.

Three methods that are available to the analyst, and also to citizens engaged in the politics of sexuality, are deconstruction of binaries, inflation of metaphor, and self-labelling. In the first, the concepts and metaphysical presumptions that function to include and exclude possibilities are subject to a critique through which their status as 'laws' is made problematic. This is done by highlighting differences in usage and meaning. Derrida in particular has presented this approach by arguing that it opens up a space for creativity and invention. Accused variously of illogicality, relativism and making scholarship impossible, he has answered his severest critics by claiming that philosophy is both still possible and helpful in itself, and that it functions as a political tool by highlighting differences, challenging and transforming canonical 'truth' and preventing closures in debate, even if individual redemption and social emancipation are not possible (Derrida 1989: 209–28).

Lacanians and post-Lacanians, such as Irigaray, prefer the second approach, advocating new styles of discourse, new ways of speaking, new poetics and a shift in metaphors, teasing out space for possibility (see Boothroyd, Chapter 12 of this volume). By taking to task the language of sexuality, and of Freud in particular (see Hawkes, Chapter 9), Irigaray reveals the linguistic play that puts citizens, especially women, and their sexuality always at a deficit (Irigaray 1974, 1977). Of relevance here are the changing analogies and metaphors around politics, state and body. Historically, the most potent was the metaphor of the 'body politic' for 'the state' (Weldon 1953). This analogy, which reduces citizens to functional roles, has been subject to extended critique, but for its users it was obvious that the body was the 'something known about', and the state the unknown object (Mabbott 1958; Ortony 1975). Today the situation is less clear, as the body is now problematic, and the state seemingly better known. We have moved from the 'body politic' to the politics of 'the body' and 'the body' in politics.

Seeking removal of regulation, sexual citizens have utilised a third method. Self-labelling is a strategy of street-politics performative action supported by academics such as Weeks, Butler and Squires, who support, for example, female fetishists' preference for calling themselves and their behaviour 'pervy' or 'pervy practices', gays calling themselves 'queer' and lesbians defining themselves as 'dykes' (Harwood *et al.* 1993: 20). Not only is this an 'outing' challenge and a statement of affirmative pride, it also reflects an absolutism of difference, in which groups can assert their uniqueness (Butler 1997: 163).

Problematising sadomasochism

Sadomasochism (S/M) is a modern linguistic, political and legal invention. In British law, sadomasochistic behaviour was not officially a crime until the legal process involving the 'Spanner' defendants was completed (Spanner was the police officer in charge). They were arrested in 1987, and their final appeal to the Law Lords was rejected in 1993 (Thompson 1994: 197). Since then, a whole range of activities, from bondage and flagellation to owning or selling images of these, have been criminalised. In addition, people who practise S/M or own images of S/M are not only likely to be under surveillance by police, social workers and the media (and sociologists), but they are also likely to have their premises raided and property removed. In the eyes of journalists, social workers, the police, judges and politicians, sadomasochism is a perverted practice that justifies the surveillance, discipline and perhaps control of its participants. Far from an enlightened liberal and permissive regime, the state activities focused on S/M are conspicuously regulatory.

Prior to 1990 a series of high-profile cases brought under the Obscene Publications Act of 1964 had failed to lead to prosecution. The 'Moral Right', as Durham (1991) calls them, were united and vocal in attacking the 'permissive society' and in putting pressure on the Home Secretary, Members of Parliament, the police and local authorities to act against a wide range of practices and persons identified as unnatural and bestial, in order to cleanse the community and to restore 'family values'. One additional factor, as Thompson notes, was the widespread belief that a nauseous type of video was in current circulation, one that allegedly depicted actual torture and execution: the 'snuff movie' (Thompson 1994: 231–2, 255).

In London in the 1980s a group of male homosexuals met occasionally in twos or threes for sexual activities, which they sometimes filmed and then circulated to other group members. All were adults, none was mentally ill, driven by poverty into prostitution, or otherwise incapable of rational judgement, though evidence that some defendants had used alcohol and soft drugs was later adduced. A police raid produced videos that depicted bondage, cutting flesh, dripping hot candle wax, flagellation, passing wire through skin and, in one case, passing a small nail through a scrotum. The police believed they had discovered 'a dangerous international satanic-ritual, child-abusing, snuff-movie-making gang'. Suspecting murders, they dug up gardens and held various men under the Obscene Publications Act of 1964. Their suspicions proved increasingly unfounded, however, and, fearing a failure of the original charge, they decided to prosecute under the Offences against the Person Act of 1861. In the absence of legislation outlawing consensual S/M, the prosecution decided that they would seek to prove that there was 'infliction of actual bodily harm and wounds' (Thompson 1994: 2–3).

The prosecution's case was eventually proved, and sentences of between twelve months and three years were imposed. These were reduced to three and six months on appeal, but were eventually restored at the High Court. This remains the legal situation surrounding S/M activity in the UK today, as the recent ruling by the European Court of Human Rights on 19 February 1997 unanimously upheld this position. While recognising that all adults were entitled to privacy in their sexual lives, the three European judges held that health dangers and the possibility of damaging the moral welfare of others were relevant factors. In a later case brought against a husband who had branded his wife's buttocks, the Court of Appeal in the UK ruled in favour of the appellant, arguing both that it was a private matter and that it was no more dangerous to health than tattooing (*Guardian*, 1 May 1996: 5).

It seems then that among adults a right to privacy can sometimes be overruled on grounds of health and moral risks to the self or others. If privacy and informed consent are no defence against a charge of assault, this could leave rugby players, boxers and other contact-sports enthusiasts apparently exposed to criminal charge (Spanner 1996). Prosecution of enthusiasts for S/M activities is rare in the rest of Europe, though Califia reports a more variable situation in the United States (Califia 1988: 21–7).

Problematising the law

Here I shall present only an outline critique of the 'Spanner' judgment (for further detail, see Thompson 1994: 180–241; Stychin 1995: 117–39; Spanner 1996). At the appeal hearing Judge Templeman ruled that 'society is entitled to protect itself against a cult of violence. Pleasure derived from the infliction of pain is an evil thing. Cruelty is uncivilized' (Stychin 1995: 119). This reflects the paternalist view of law associated with Devlin (1965). Not only is this philosophically contestable, but the trajectory of most contemporary legal rulings on moral/legal issues has favoured the harm principle developed by Hart, namely that the action of consenting adults in private should be no concern of the law (Hart 1963; DCHOP 1957).

In his major ruling, Judge Templeman asserted that existing privacy legislation did not apply to assaults, though convention allowed this in cases of games, piercing and tattooing. Wounding or causing actual bodily harm to another 'for no good reason' was considered to be against the public interest, and the victim's desires and consent do not amount to a good reason. Pleasure/pain was a binary that attracted lengthy legal debate. The majority of the judges concerned with the case ruled that S/M was the infliction of pain, and that no gratification associated with it could change this fact. Most scholarship on S/M rejects this, and asserts that the primary motivation of both sadist (top) and masochist (bottom) is the giving and receiving of pleasure (Squires 1993a, 1993b; Harwood *et. al.* 1993; Valverde 1985: 170–6). The close proximity of partners during the experience, the fact that the same nerve endings transmit both pleasure and pain, and that one person's pain is another person's pleasure, reveal how hard this binary is to police. 'The mix of pleasure and painful pleasure which lies at the heart of sexual experience will always defy the phenomenological precision which the law apparently requires' (Polhemus and Randall 1994: 134; Thompson 1994: 134–42).

Violence is another contentious feature of the legal and other discourses around S/M. While hard to define, violence does involve the notion of being excessive, uncontrolled, unjustifiable and forceful – usually resulting in harm or injury. Throughout the academic literature the predominant argument is that in S/M the participants take part in 'Rituals of Love' (Polhemus and Randall 1994), which involve consent to control another or to be controlled oneself, a notion of agreed levels of discipline, agreement on a code to indicate cessation of control, and force only up to the point of agreed limits. Polhemus considered it to be common practice for participants to agree the limits of what will be done, how and to what degree something will be administered, code words to invoke cessation, safety procedures to prevent danger, and measures for hygiene and health promotion (Mitchell 1995: 25–7; Thompson 1994: 130–4; Polhemus and Randall 1994: 114–15). In fact the bulk of literature on S/M suggests it is almost completely about theatre, role play and fantasy, where the apparent violence is largely simulation, and a play of signifiers, ritual and fetish (Thompson 1994: 150–79; McClintock 1993; Gamman and Makinen 1994: 57–9). This line of argument also deals with cruelty, which is usually only apparent, and is desired and consented to, hence giving gratification, and not a gift that is 'without pity or merciless'. In the Spanner case, by contrast, there was a suggestion that all sadomasochists are members of devilish groups and on a slippery slope towards paganism, barbarianism and bestiality. One judge referred to 'blood lust' (Thompson 1994: 200), or 'addiction' (Stychin 1995: 127–32). A quick browse through the literature, web sites, and practices of S/M will at least dispel this as a mere first impression, as Thompson and others have argued (Thompson 1994: 150–79, 227–34, 250–4).

Other legal problems abound with the charge of assault, and the question of whether a consenting person can be assaulted. Consent is not a defence in cases of actual bodily harm and grievous bodily harm. The judges in the Spanner case, except for one appeal judge, agreed that consent was disallowed as a defence. An assault had to be intentional and reckless, in most cases, and the judges agreed, dubiously, that both factors were present (Thompson 1994: 185–6). More widely, any ethical or scholarly debate around S/M must involve definitions of sadism, masochism and sadomasochism, perversion and fetishism. Extended investigations by Thompson, Squires and Valverde reveal the absence of agreed definitions and understandings with respect to these matters (Valverde 1985: 170–6). Masochism means variously: (1) a desire to be conquered, (2) desire for roughness in sex, (3) sexual pleasure from the infliction of pain, (4) the non-sexual or sexual desire to be humiliated, (5) ritualistic versions of the above using symbolic props. Sadism has the same five correlate meanings but referring to giving rather than receiving. Several of these, especially (1) – (3), are seen by some as normal parts of most male and female sexual practices and identities, and of 'reciprocal erotic power'. In their submission to the Law Commission, the group Countdown to Spanner defined S/M as 'obtaining pleasure from an exchange of power and/or pain in consensual sex play or sexual fantasy'. A glance at many advertisements suggests that (5), female fetishism especially, is present in everyday media and fashion. Most authorities see S/M as about exchange not imposition, in which the biggest problem is finding a partner to share your narrative; it is about play and not violence, about equality and not inequality. Finally, the female authors of the *New Formations* issue on 'Perversity', the Squires book *Principled Positions*, the Harwood collection *Pleasure Principles*, Grosz and Probyn on feminist carnalities, as well as Valverde and the infamous Della Grace (see Grace 1993) all reject the 'disavowal of female fetishism' in so much feminist writing (Harwood *et. al.* 1993: 97–108). Women, so they all insist, are as likely and as entitled to enjoy 'pervy' sex as men.

It should now be apparent that traditional legal and jurisprudential categories and arguments are inadequate for dealing with S/M. The liberal harm principle founders on the deconstruction of the binaries harm/benefit, self-regarding/other-regarding and private/public. These binaries are hard to police, and terms such as 'harm' and 'private' are hard to define. One recent essay tries to apply the concept of psychological harm in this context, but I think it fails (Lee 1994: 131–5).

Legal moralism and paternalism founder on the claims that S/M involves violence, harm, assault, pain and degradation recklessly given to victims, when the practitioners themselves assert that it invokes caring, gratification, consent, pleasure and self-realisation given in the spirit and context of trust (Stychin 1995: 121–3). Feminist legal theory is over-focused on binary male/female sexuality, and on the association of violence, domination, fetishism and sadomasochism with males (Califia 1988: 19–22; Califia 1993). In short, political and legal theory, like the dominant discourse about S/M, is constructed and bounded in such a way that S/M appears so abnormal, abhorrent, beastly, vile, degrading, violent, patriarchal and unpredictable that no normal person or society could allow it. It follows that its practitioners should become 'a despised sexual caste' (Stychin 1995: 121; Vance 1984: 267, 269).

Conclusions

Civil law is essentially the law that governs relations between individuals, who are considered to have a private social status within the public world or *res publica*. The statute law or constitution is the public articles of association gleaned from past practice and modified in political activity. Politics in a civil society is not so much about policies designed to take a united consensual group with a shared identity to some new place or condition, but about the public negotiation of the changes necessary to allow divergent individuals and groups with no shared identity to live together without resort to violence and suppression. Politics is then the public activity of negotiating the constitution or rules for relating a plurality of groups with divergent aims, and not about agreeing the ends and means for state-managed public policy.

The proper role for the police and judiciary in the contemporary state should not be that of enforcing one form of life, imposing one identity or set of aims, but of keeping the peace between contending individuals, groups and lifestyles (Kleinig 1996: 27–9, 233). However, we can argue for something more. Defenders of the minimal state – mainly liberals and new-right conservatives – have misused the civil tradition and canon in order to construct an abstract ideology of natural rights for individuals, in which the state plays the role of protecting only life, liberty and private property (Hayek 1969; Nozick 1974). In fact, the civil tradition is so diverse and often infused with a republican spirit that it not only allows but also advocates a more interventionist role on the part of the state in enhancing citizenship and in providing citizens with the preconditions for participating in, and deriving benefits from, public life. In its modern form these ideas have surfaced in contemporary writings on citizenship by Plant (1990), Keane (1984, 1988a, 1988b), Walzer (1983), and the more affirmative postmodernist writings on citizenship and sexuality by Squires (1993a, 1993b),

Yeatman (1994), Weeks (1995), Evans (1993), Beck (1996), and Gibbins and Reimer (1995). In my view, while respect for the rights of individuals and of groups to be different should be embraced, the role of government is to be understood to imply both protection and enablement. Hence government should facilitate sexual citizenship by providing not only guarantees of protection and tolerance, but also education, healthcare and access to public spaces and public goods that make the right to difference efficacious (Evans 1993).

A civil society that referees the minimal rules necessary to uphold civil life and facilitates respect for and the right to diversity needs to be supplemented by a civil and sexual ethics. We need to go on and ask: why we should, as individuals, as groups, and as civil bodies, respect, tolerate or care for someone with a different sexual identity, even one that affronts and conceivably threatens our own. We need to advance a more detailed formulation of a second-order set of principles, a formal set of rules for a postmodern ethics along lines indicated by Bauman (1993) and Weeks (1995), in order to circumvent the currently arbitrary and oppressive prejudices that surface when the government and legal system discipline and punish the body and, in particular, 'sexy bodies'.

References

Bauman, Z. 1993. *Postmodern Ethics*. Oxford: Blackwell.

Beck, U. 1996. *The Reinvention of Politics*. Cambridge: Polity.

Burchell, G., Gordon C., and Miller P. (eds). 1991. *The Foucault Effect: Studies in Governability*. London: Harvester Wheatsheaf.

Butler, J. 1997. *Excitable Speech: The Politics of the Performative*. London: Routledge.

Califia, P. 1988. *Macho Sluts*. Boston MA: Alyson Publications.

—— 1993. *Sensuous Magic*. New York: Masquerade Books.

Connolly, W.E. 1991. *Identity/Difference: Democratic Negotiations of Political Paradox*. Ithaca NY and London: Cornell University Press.

DCHOP 1957. *Report of the Departmental Committee on Homosexual Offences and Prostitution* (Chair: Sir John Wolfenden). Cmnd. 247, 1957. London: HMSO.

Derrida, J. 1989. 'On colleges and philosophy'. In L. Appignanesi (ed.),*Postmodernism: ICA Documents*, 209–28. London: Free Association Books.

Devlin, P. 1965. *The Enforcement of Morals*. Oxford: OUP.

Dreyfus, H.L., and Rabinow, P. 1982. *Michel Foucault: Beyond Structuralism and Hermeneutics*. Brighton: Harvester Wheatsheaf.

Durham, M. 1991. *Sex and Politics*. London: Macmillan.

Evans, D. T. 1993. *Sexual Citizenship: The Material Construction of Sexualities*. London: Routledge.

Foucault, M. 1990. *The Care of the Self: The History of Sexuality*, vol. 3. Harmondsworth: Penguin.

—— 1991. 'Governability'. In G. Burchell, C. Gordon, and P. Miller (eds), *The Foucault Effect: Studies in Governability*, 87–104. London: Harvester Wheatsheaf.

Gamman, L., and Makinen, M. (eds). 1994. *Female Fetishism*. London: Lawrence & Wishart.

Gibbins, J. R., and Reimer, B. 1995. 'Postmodernism'. In J. van Deth, and E. Scarbrough (eds), *The Impact of Values*, 301–31. Oxford: Oxford University Press.

Grace, D. 1993. 'Dynamics of desire'. In V. Harwood, D. Oswell, K. Parkinson, A. Ward (eds), *Pleasure Principles: Politics, Sexuality and Ethics*, 90–6. London: Lawrence & Wishart.

Grosz, E., and Probyn, E. 1995. *Sexy Bodies: The Strange Carnalities of Feminism*. London: Routledge.

Guardian. 1996. 'Judges clear man who branded wife'. 1 May 1996: 5.

Hart, H. L. A. 1963. *Law, Liberty and Morality*. Oxford: Oxford University Press.

Harwood, V., Oswell, D., Parkinson, K., and Ward, A. (eds). 1993. *Pleasure Principles: Politics, Sexuality and Ethics*. London: Lawrence & Wishart.

Hayek, F. A. 1969. *The Constitution of Liberty*. London: Routledge & Kegan Paul.

Hewitt, M. 1983. 'Bio-politics and social policy: Foucault's account of welfare'. *Theory, Culture and Society* 2: 67–85.

Irigaray, L. 1974. *Speculum of the Other Woman*. Ithaca NY: Cornell University Press.

—— 1977. *This Sex Which is not One*. Ithaca NY: Cornell University Press.

Keane, J. 1984. *Public Life in Late Capitalism*. Cambridge: Cambridge University Press.

—— 1988a. *Democracy and Civil Society*. London: Verso.

—— (ed.). 1988b. *Civil Society and the State*. London: Verso.

Kleinig, J. 1996. *The Ethics of Policing*. Cambridge: Cambridge University Press.

Lee, J.R. 1994. 'Sadomasochism: an ethical analysis', in R.M. Stewart (ed.), *Philosophical Perspectives on Sex and Love*, 125–37. New York: Oxford University Press.

Levi-Strauss, C. 1962. *The Savage Mind*. London: Weidenfeld & Nicolson.

—— 1963. *Totemism and Taboo*. London: Beacon Press.

Mabbott, J.B. 1958. *The State and the Citizen*. London: Arrow Books.

McClintock, A. 1993. 'The return of female fetishism and the fiction of the phallus'. In J. Squires (ed.), *New Formations* 19: 1–22.

Mitchell, T. 1995. 'The art of safe bondage'. *Desire* 5: 25–7.

Nozick, R. 1974. *Anarchy, State and Utopia*. Oxford: Basil Blackwell.

Ortony, A. 1975. *Metaphor and Thought*. Cambridge: Cambridge University Press.

Plant, R. 1990. 'Citizenship and rights'. In R. Plant, and N. Barry, *Citizenship and Rights in Thatcher's Britain: Two Views*. London: IEA Health and Welfare Unit.

Polhemus, T., and Randall, H. 1994. *Rituals of Love: Sexual Experiments, Erotic Possibilities*. London: Picador.

Rabinow, P. 1994. *The Foucault Reader*. Oxford: Blackwell.

Rosenau, P. 1992. *Postmodernism and the Social Sciences*. Princeton: Princeton University Press.

Spanner. 1996. http://www.warwick.ac.uk/~esrhi/euroSP.html

Squires, J. 1993a. *Principled Positions: Postmodernism and the Rediscovery of Values*. London: Lawrence & Wishart,

—— (ed.) 1993b. *New Formations* 19 ('Perversity' issue).

Stychin, C. F. 1995. *Law's Desire: Sexuality and the Limits of Justice*. London: Routledge.

Thompson, B. 1994. *Sadomasochism: Painful Perversion or Pleasurable Play*. London: Cassell.

Valverde, M. 1985. *Sex, Power and Pleasure*. London: The Women's Press.

Vance, C. (ed.). 1984. *Pleasure and Danger: Exploring Female Sexuality*. London: Routledge & Kegan Paul.

Walzer, M. 1983. *Spheres of Justice: A Defence of Pluralism and Equality*. Oxford: Martin Robertson.

Weeks, J. 1995. *Invented Moralities: Sexual Values in an Age of Uncertainty*. Cambridge: Polity.

Weldon, T. D. 1953. *The Vocabulary of Politics*. Harmondsworth: Pelican.

Yeatman, A. 1994. *Postmodern Revisionings of the Political*. London: Routledge.

4 Sexuality and the UK armed forces

Judicial review of the ban on homosexuality

Paul Skidmore

'*No surrender*: forces ban on gays will stay says Portillo as poll backs him.'
(*Daily Mail*, 4 March 1996)

'Portillo panders to forces' homophobia'
(*Independent*, 5 March 1996)

Thus, reactions differed to the Ministry of Defence (MoD) decision in March 1996 to retain the absolute ban on homosexuality in the British armed forces. Between 1991 and 1994 alone, this ban, which outlaws all homosexuals, practising or celibate, led to the discharge of 260 servicemen and women (Hall 1995). This chapter examines the discourse of prejudice mobilised to justify the prohibition on homosexuals in the British military. It focuses on the court challenges to the ban and the process of change that flows from the use of litigation.

Rights struggles and pressure groups

Challenges to the military ban on gays and lesbians in both the UK and USA have raised profound questions for queer theory and politics, in terms of the legal categorisation of 'homosexual' (Stychin 1995: 91–101; Stychin 1996), media representation of gays and lesbians (Meyers 1994), and in general the direction of gay and lesbian politics. Sullivan, in his assimilationist essay *Virtually Normal*, argues that formal public equality is the goal: 'The military ban deals with the heart of what it means to be a citizen' (Sullivan 1995: 178). Tatchell (1995), in contrast, offers a radical critique of the military issue, adopting an agenda that seeks to question the role of the military in society and that addresses pacifist concerns. He points out the state's hypocrisy in accepting gay and lesbian personnel willingly in times of armed conflict – such as the Gulf War, Vietnam – but discharging them as soon as possible thereafter. The difficulties and shortcomings of engaging with the state in the process of gay and lesbian politics have been particularly identified by Cooper (1993), Herman (1994), and Rahman (Chapter 7 of this volume). These include the acceptance of (1) the hegemonic nature of the state as a given, thus working with(in) institutions such as the Church, family and military, (2) the categorisation 'homosexual' for legal discursive purposes, (3) the labelling of lesbians and gay men as 'other' and different, and (4) the tensions felt between lesbians and gay men whose interests and experiences are not congruent (see also Jackson, Chapter 6 of this volume). Nevertheless, the experience of struggles for gay and lesbian rights is not necessarily negative (Cicchino *et al.* 1995), with positive public images of lesbians and gay men having both educative and self-affirming functions.

The challenge to the military ban that has been mounted in the UK fits firmly into the formal public equality model, marginalising the views of Tatchell. There has been no serious debate as to the strategic costs and benefits of challenging the military ban. The organisational nature of the campaign may well explain this.

The first attempt in the UK to organise around the gays in the military issue was when the pressure group Rank Outsiders was formed in 1991 (Hall 1995: 166). This group is closely linked with the gay and lesbian lobbying organisation Stonewall, which campaigns for legal change on a range of issues affecting gays and lesbians (see also Waites, Chapter 2 of this volume). Stonewall's director, Angela Mason, summarising its claim for 'full civil rights', argues for action with regard to 'sexual offences reform, anti-discrimination laws, partnership recognition and parenting rights' (Mason 1995). The organisation's approach is to argue for equality for all, seeking to have the bars and disadvantages encountered by gays and lesbians systematically removed. It is essentially a campaign for the 'same' treatment.

Stonewall is a well-organised group, with paid staff, a regular newsletter, and over 6,000 individuals providing financial support. Its campaigns have three distinct strands. First, it seeks to lobby MPs and members of the House of Lords directly, persuading them to introduce and support bills to improve the position of gays and lesbians. Second, it encourages its members to become involved in these lobbying activities, particularly through letter-writing. Third, it has used test-case litigation to achieve change by judicial means.

The use of litigation by pressure groups has a well-documented history going back over 250 years (Harlow and Rawlings 1992). Once it is realised that the judiciary, as much as the legislature, makes law, then it is not surprising that litigation is such a favoured tactic. It is also important to note that the technical success of the case (win/lose) is not always significant in measuring the impact that the pressure group has on the political process. Harlow and Rawlings suggest that 'sharp issue focus' (O'Connor 1980: 22–3) is useful, but by no means determinative, in predicting success. Whether gays and lesbians should be allowed to serve in the armed forces undoubtedly provides a clear focus for a campaign, and is also an issue that is easily understood and readily attracts media attention. Given such factors predicting success, what reasons might underlie a challenge to the military ban?

First, the armed forces symbolise 'the Establishment', and thus a challenge to them, if successful, provides access to the very core of society. Second, the armed forces are a locus of production of male (hetero)sexuality, with its aggressive 'macho' culture and misogyny, assuming women either to be sexually

available or lesbian. To valorise gay and lesbian military experience and achievements through the litigation process might help change public attitudes. Third, a
successful campaign on the military issue might have important spill-over effects
with regard to employment discrimination more generally. If the armed forces
were made to change their policy, so that homosexuality *per se* could not provide
grounds for dismissal, it would then be anomalous if employees in civilian life
did not also gain that protection.

When in December 1994 legal advice indicated that a case could be
mounted, it is not clear that Rank Outsiders or Stonewall had a litigation test-
case 'strategy' in mind, in the sense of a clear plan of campaign to run several
cases if necessary. Four servicemen and women who had recently been
discharged on grounds of their homosexuality brought actions for judicial review
(*R. v. Secretary of State for Defence* ex parte *Smith and others*). The Divisional Court
(Lord Justice Simon Brown and Mr Justice Curtis) rejected their case in June
1995. Their appeal was also rejected by the Court of Appeal (Sir Thomas
Bingham, Master of the Rolls, Lord Justices Thorpe and Henry) in November
1995, and leave to appeal to the House of Lords was refused in March 1996
([1996] QB 517; Skidmore 1995, 1996). Thus in technical legal terms, the case
was a failure, but in campaigning terms, it helped considerably in exposing the
prejudice of the armed forces. The applicants' grounds of challenge and the
judicial response will be examined below.

Prejudice unmasked

The affidavit produced by Sir John Willis (Vice-Chief of the Defence Staff) in
the Divisional Court proceedings gave four reasons for the ban: (1) national security, (2) communal living, (3) *in loco parentis*, and (4) morale and discipline.

The national-security argument was dropped in court, given the government's
removal of the blanket ban on homosexuals serving at the highest levels in the
civil and diplomatic service (Hansard HC 23.7.91 col. 474). It had been argued
that gay service personnel constitute a security risk, because they are likely to be
blackmailed on account of their sexuality. Moran (1991) argues that the link
made in the UK between male homosexuality and the threat to the interests of
the state is culturally and temporally specific. Lesbianism has not been
demonised as a threat to national security in the same way, despite the fact that
only in the armed forces has lesbianism ever been unlawful in the UK.

The national security argument is particularly circular, as blackmail depends
on the risk of dismissal for homosexuality. If this risk were removed, then a
homosexual serviceman or woman would be no more and no less likely than any
heterosexual to be blackmailed. However, it is argued that they would not want
their family and friends to know that they were gay. This suggests that generalised homophobia and the 'presumed heterosexual' construction of societal
relations was used to justify the MoD's policy of prejudice, relying on the prejudice of others to validate their own.

With respect to communal living, the MoD suggested that heterosexuals would find it intolerable to have to share living quarters with gays, because of lack of privacy. The particular fears of heterosexuals were not articulated – perhaps unwanted sexual advances? The practice of 'hot-bunking' – sailors working different shifts using the same beds for sleeping at different times of the day – does not explain why another's *sexuality* should make it more unpleasant to use the same bed. The MoD again based its argument on the perceived prejudice of others, on this occasion other personnel.

The armed forces are *in loco parentis*, i.e. responsible for the welfare of recruits under the age of 18. It was argued that young people needed to be 'looked after and protected appropriately', hinting that the presence of homosexuals posed a risk. No evidence was offered to suggest that young people were liable to be 'converted' by the presence of older gays and lesbians. Nor does such a policy take into account the needs of 16- and 17-year-old lesbians and gay men. The notion of 'protection' shows the MoD relying on the perceived prejudice of others – parents and recruits – to justify their policy. The prejudice behind the unequal age of consent in the criminal law (certain male homosexual acts are criminalised when one or both of the participants are under 18) was used by the MoD to argue a particular need to protect male recruits under 18.

With regard to morale and discipline, the MoD feared that personnel would not be able to work together in combat situations if their team were known to include non-heterosexuals. The MoD also argued that homosexual officers might not be able to command the necessary respect. Again, prejudice, assumed to exist in the minds of servicemen and women, was used to justify the MoD policy.

Two further factors clearly expose the MoD prejudice. First, the MoD discharges anyone who admits to a homosexual orientation, so it is sufficient to self-identify as gay or lesbian to be discharged. Second, it is highly likely that there will be serving gay and lesbian members of the armed forces who are engaged in military duties, but whose sexuality is unknown or hidden, against whom the MoD has no complaint. This lends credence to the view that sexuality is of itself irrelevant to the performance of military duties, strengthening the argument that it is the views and attitudes of others that cause the MoD's complaint and not homosexuality *per se*. If knowing the sexuality of another changes that person's attitude, it would seem to locate the problem in the mind of the knower.

The judicial response

The applicants' first argument was irrationality, an argument of national administrative law. An administrative decision can be declared 'irrational' if it is 'so outrageous in its defiance of logic or of accepted moral standards that no sensible person who had applied his mind to the question to be decided could have arrived at it' (Lord Diplock in *CCSU* v. *Minister for the Civil Service* [1985] 1 AC 374). This test has been developed by the judiciary, who have asserted their right to control executive action (Craig 1994; Wade and Forsyth 1994). The executive has not willingly accepted this; nevertheless, Lord Justice Simon Brown insisted on the courts' right to supervise the executive, even in relation to the disposition of the armed forces. The scope of judicial review is limited to testing the legality of the government action and not its merits; the court must not substitute its own view for that of the Minister.

The weakness of the irrationality test is the absence of an externally defined norm against which the Minister's action can be measured. Thus the test leads to unpredictable results, dependent on judicial prejudice, blurring the distinction between the review of legality and that of merits (*Wheeler* v. *Leicester City Council* [1985] AC 1054). The test is only likely to find unlawful those decisions where the Minister acts in bad faith or deliberately ignores a vast body of evidence when making her or his decision. Where the Minister simply gives greater weight to one argument than to another, applying a different set of values from those contended for by the applicant, the irrationality plea is likely to fail.

The applicants showed that the MoD was isolated in its approach and that other NATO and Western defence forces permitted homosexuals to serve, with their counsel exposing the MoD arguments as prejudice. They also referred to changing attitudes to homosexuals in civilian and public life. These arguments found sympathy with many of the judges:

> I have to say that the balance of the argument...appears to me to lie clearly with the applicants. The tide of history is against the Ministry. Prejudices are breaking down; old barriers are being removed. It seems to me improbable, whatever this court may say, that the existing policy can survive for much longer.
>
> (Simon Brown LJ)

> The consideration that impresses me the most on the merits is the complete absence of illustration and substantiation by specific examples...in the respondent's [MoD's] evidence filed in the court below.
>
> (Thorpe LJ)

The judges hinted that if they could determine MoD policy they would permit homosexuals to serve, subject to some disciplinary code regulating sexual conduct. Nevertheless, they allowed the prejudice of *others* to provide a valid basis for the Minister's decision, despite the complete absence of supporting evidence.

> The existing policy cannot in my judgement be stigmatised as irrational at the time when these appellants were discharged. It was supported by both Houses of Parliament and by those to whom the Ministry properly looked for professional advice.
>
> (Bingham MR)

> It would be quite impossible to say in my judgement that the Court is enti-
> tled to interfere with the Secretary of State's application of a policy which
> clearly commands a wide measure of general support.
>
> (Thorpe LJ)

These comments make it clear that the more widely held a belief is, however
erroneous and unsubstantiated it may be, the more the Minister is entitled to
take it into account in the decision-making process. The position of the majority
of the judges is confusing. On the one hand, they asserted their personal belief
that the policy should not be founded on prejudice. On the other hand, they
permitted the prejudice of others to justify the ministerial decision. If rational
judges are unpersuaded by prejudice, why should rational ministers be permitted
to take it into account? The judiciary are (re)producing prejudice, despite
appearing to denounce it. Beneath the rhetoric of human rights and sound bites,
the message is that it continues to be acceptable for *other people* to be prejudiced
against gays and lesbians. Thus the latent prejudice of the judges prevails.

The second argument contended that MoD policy breached Article 8 of the
European Convention on Human Rights – the right to private and family life
(including right to a sexual life as a homosexual) (*Norris* [1988] 13 EHRR 186).
As the Convention is not incorporated within UK law, and does not give individ-
uals enforceable rights in the national courts, the argument was bound to fail.
The national court was powerless on these grounds alone to overturn the MoD
policy, even if they decided that it breached the Convention. To pursue the
Convention argument, the applicants had to work their way through the lengthy
mechanisms of the European Commission and Court on Human Rights in
Strasbourg (Feldman 1993: 47–50).

Judges may nevertheless take note of the Convention in deciding a case on
other grounds (*Brind* [1991] 1 AC 696). Here, the judges considered that the
right under Article 8 did not add anything to the irrationality test. This could
have been the end of the story (as Justice Curtis suggested), however the other
judges indicated their belief that the applicants did have a good case under the
Convention.

> I for my part strongly suspect that so far as this country's international obli-
> gations are concerned, the days of this policy are numbered.
>
> (Simon Brown LJ)

Despite rhetoric sympathetic to the human rights arguments, the judges' rejection of the European Convention point nevertheless permitted the discourse of
prejudice to continue.

The third argument for the applicants was that the policy breached the EC
Equal Treatment Directive (76/207), which requires equal treatment for men
and women in employment (see Bell, Chapter 5 of this volume). This Directive is
part of English law, and the courts are required to give effect to it and to provide
remedies should it be breached. The jurisprudence of the European Court of

Justice (ECJ) has interpreted the Directive as preventing sex-based treatment, i.e. where the sex of the employee determines the employer's attitude or policy towards him/her.

The applicants argued that sexual-orientation discrimination was included within sex discrimination, not through linguistics or the ontology of sex and sexuality, but because discrimination on grounds of sexual orientation arises out of sex-stereotyping. This argument is circulating around the world, including Canada (Wintemute 1994) and the UK (Pannick 1983; Bamforth 1994; Wintemute 1997; Skidmore 1997a), as prejudice against homosexuals is challenged. An employer who dismisses a woman for having a relationship with a woman, but who does not also dismiss a man for having a relationship with a woman, is discriminating on grounds of sex. The employer is using a sex-based criterion in the decision-making process, which is unlawful according to ECJ jurisprudence.

The judges in the Divisional Court appeared confused by the argument, and could not get beyond a basic reading of the legislative text, looking for discrimination between women and men. They held that the applicants' argument was an ill-founded extension of the principle contained in the Directive, which could not be justified when looking at the document as a whole or in the context of the EC Treaty. The argument was dismissed:

> [D]iscrimination is very often based on stereotypical assumptions as to gender characteristics. Orientation is however quite another thing. If, of course, an employer were willing to employ lesbians but not male homosexuals, that would be discrimination on grounds of sex. Where…an employer refuses to accept homosexuals of either sex, that is discrimination on grounds of orientation.
>
> (Simon Brown LJ)

The Divisional Court denied that there was sex discrimination where gay men and lesbians are treated equally badly. In the Court of Appeal there was little greater attempt to grapple with the applicants' argument, as the judges instead discussed the purpose of the legislation when drafted in the mid-1970s. They saw that purpose as being a narrow one of sex discrimination and did not respond to the arguments with regard to sex-stereotyping. They rejected a creative approach to interpretation, nor were they willing to consult the ECJ for a ruling on the meaning of the Directive.

Reactions and repercussions

The decision of the Divisional Court in June 1995, despite being a legal victory for the MoD, nevertheless provoked an internal inquiry – Homosexuality Policy Assessment Team (HPAT) – to reassess the issue. One of the main issues it sought to address was the criticism levelled by the judges that there was no evidence to support MoD arguments. The HPAT report was published in

February 1996, presenting the views of the many service personnel who wished to see the ban maintained. Its data were regarded as controversial (HMSO 1996: 99–102), with queries raised as to anonymity and methodology in general, as respondents were asked to agree/disagree with statements such as: 'All homosexual acts are perverted.' Nevertheless, its publication – timed to coincide with the Select Committee hearings on the Armed Forces Bill – was highly influential in persuading the Committee to recommend no change in policy:

> We are persuaded by the surveys summarised in the MoD report...of the strength of opposition throughout the armed services to any relaxation of the current bar. We accept that the presence of openly homosexual servicemen and women would have a significant adverse impact on morale and ultimately on operational effectiveness.
>
> (HMSO 1996: xiv)

Respondents were invited to speculate on the consequences of permitting gays and lesbians openly to serve. Those surveyed feared that violence, harassment and ostracism of homosexuals would result, making it more difficult to maintain discipline. The survey evidence bears out the strength of these feelings:

> Homosexuals would get beaten up...I like many others would quite happily smash their faces in if I found any in my unit...Regimental pride would be dented if there were any homosexuals within the ranks.
>
> (MoD 1996: 72)

These bigoted views were not exposed as such, but treated respectfully as evidence justifying the existing policy, despite the initial premise underlying the inquiry that 'homosexual men and women are no less physically capable, brave, dependable and skilled' (MoD 1996: 26).

The (male) heterosexuality of the armed forces was emphasised by many respondents:

> Soldiers talk about their sexual exploits all the time and homosexuals could not fit in...Everyone would question people's behaviour if homosexuals were allowed. Why did that officer not invite a woman to that event?...The very fact that a heterosexual has shared a room or tent with a homosexual leaves them open for accusation or suspicion.
>
> (MoD 1996: 115, 136, 68)

Yet the very fragility of this heterosexuality is evident from the *in loco parentis* arguments, which suggest that heterosexuality could be easily undermined if gays and lesbians were allowed to serve.

The Court of Appeal had noted particularly the international comparisons regarding the experience of other NATO and Commonwealth forces, which had changed their policies to allow homosexuals to serve, wondering why the UK should differ. The HPAT report countered this by arguing the uniqueness of UK forces, stating that the majority of respondents were 'particularly scornful and resistant to the idea that British forces should move to conform to any European average' (MoD 1996: 33). In conclusion, they recommended no change.

This recommendation was then debated in Parliament, when Edwina Currie MP introduced an amendment to the Armed Forces Bill at Stonewall's request, seeking to lift the blanket ban and to introduce a new discipline code that would apply to all personnel (Hansard HC 9.5.96 col. 481). The Commons debate is significant for two reasons: first, in its exploration of the notion of prejudice; and second, in showing the interaction of the legal challenge with the policy process.

Tony Banks MP summed up the issue of prejudice:

> It is no good saying that we will allow prejudice to determine policy. That is precisely what this is all about – not wanting homosexuals in the Army. I am sure that if the same people were asked, they would say that they did not want blacks or even women in the Army. Shall we allow racists and sexists to determine policy in Britain?
>
> (Hansard HC 9.5.96 col. 496)

Menzies Campbell MP identified the self-referential nature of services' opinion: 'The views of people in the services are conditioned by the ban' (col. 486). Despite the views of the many MPs who identified prejudice as the key to the whole issue and the need for Parliament to take a stand in resisting it, the government Minister was blind to this:

> If collective professional judgements about operational effectiveness are simply to be defined away in advance as irrelevant prejudice unless they fit abstract principles of equal treatment, servicemen and women will be disenfranchised…[It] would put at risk the cohesion and fighting power of our armed services.
>
> (Hansard HC 9.5.96 col. 509)

The amendment was defeated by 188 to 120 votes. In the course of the debate, several MPs had warned that if Parliament failed to take action at that stage, change would be forced on it by the European Court of Human Rights in Strasbourg or by the ECJ in its interpretation of the Equal Treatment Directive. Even those MPs opposed to change seemed to accept that it would ultimately be imposed by the courts, although there were suggestions that the UK should defy those courts in the event of an unfavourable ruling.

As predicted by MPs, the legal process continued to shape the policy agenda when the Divisional Court in March 1997 agreed to refer to the ECJ questions regarding the interpretation of the Equal Treatment Directive, asking whether it precluded dismissal on grounds of sexual orientation, and if so, the extent of any derogation for the armed forces (*R. v. Secretary of State for Defence* ex parte *Perkins* [1997] IRLR 297).

The Divisional Court's change of position on the relevance of the Equal Treatment Directive flows from the ECJ's decision in a case decided in April 1996 *P.* v. *Cornwall County Council* (case C-13/94 [1996] ECR I-2143; Skidmore 1997b), which held that the Directive did preclude the dismissal of a transsexual on the grounds of her gender reassignment. This decision of the ECJ could not have been predicted when the first judicial review of the military ban was launched in 1994. The timing of this development was fortuitous in providing an opportunity to keep the military ban on the policy agenda, thus allowing a litigation 'strategy' to develop (Barnard 1995: 263). Campaigners in 1997 were hopeful of success. First, it was unlikely that the ECJ would want to make difficult distinctions between homosexuals and transsexuals. If the ECJ were to hold that homosexuals were not protected by the Directive, this could lead to the absurd situation of a gay man or lesbian having to threaten to undergo gender reassignment in order to obtain legal protection from dismissal. In any event, as Justice Lightman observed in Perkins, transsexuals in English law are treated for marriage purposes as homosexuals: a female transsexual (born a man) is regarded always as a man and cannot in English law marry a man. Second, the Conservative government indicated that it would argue that personnel policy in military matters fell outside the scope of EC law. Even if the ECJ accepted that some aspects of military service lie outside the scope of the Directive, it was unlikely to hold a blanket ban compatible.

If Perkins is successful, change will be forced on the UK in a manner that circumvents the arguments of prejudice, ignoring the evolving justifications put forward by the MoD. Media reports following the Divisional Court decision in Perkins suggested that both the Army (*Financial Times*, 25 March 1997) and the incoming Labour government (*Pink Paper*, 23 May 1997) considered reviewing the ban. It was subsequently reported (*Sunday Times*, 5 April 1998), that the Army (but not the other services) intended to relax its absolute ban on gays and lesbians, but without according them equal status with heterosexual soldiers. However, in the absence of a clear government position on the issue, it may nevertheless take judicial action to force wholesale change.

Conclusions

Over the period 1994–6, a discourse of prejudice was effective in maintaining the ban on homosexuality in the armed forces. This discourse was perpetuated by the judiciary and Parliament accepting the prejudice fed to it by the MoD. But for a few members of the armed forces who articulated their own prejudice and hatred of gays and lesbians, the prejudice publicly relied upon was that of others. The actors involved distanced themselves from the prejudice, putting it into the third person, citing the reaction of the general public, parents and other serving members of the armed forces as evidence to uphold the ban. To attach any relevance to prejudice held by a third party must nevertheless suggest a latent unexpressed sympathy with that prejudice, or it would be dismissed as irrelevant. Deference to public opinion in this policy process has perpetuated the status quo. If the ban is lifted, this will flow from policy-makers (judges or politicians) recognising the civil rights of gays and lesbians, and acting in defiance of prejudice.

References

Bamforth, N. 1994. 'Sexual orientation and dismissal'. *New Law Journal* 144: 1402–3, 1419.

Barnard, C. 1995. 'A European litigation strategy: the case of the Equal Opportunities Commission'. In J. Shaw, and G. More (eds), *New Legal Dynamics of European Union*, pp. 253–72. Oxford: Clarendon Press.

Cicchino, P., Deming, B., and Nicholson, K. 1995. 'Sex, lies, and civil rights: a critical history of the Massachusetts Gay Civil Rights Bill'. In D. Herman and C. Stychin (eds), *Legal Inversions: Lesbians, Gay Men and the Politics of Law*, pp. 141–61. Philadelphia: Temple University Press.

Cooper, D. 1993. 'An engaged state: sexuality, governance and the potential for change'. *Journal of Law and Society* 20: 257–75.

Craig, P. 1994. *Administrative Law*. London: Sweet & Maxwell.

Feldman, D. 1993. *Civil Liberties and Human Rights in England and Wales*. Oxford: Clarendon Press.

Hall, E. 1995. *We Can't Even March Straight*. London: Vintage.

Harlow, C., and Rawlings, R. 1992. *Pressure through Law*. London: Routledge.

Herman, D. 1994. *Rights of Passage: Struggles for Lesbian and Gay Legal Equality*. Toronto: University of Toronto Press.

HMSO. 1996. Special Report from the Select Committee on the Armed Forces Bill HC (1995/6) 143.

Mason, A. 1995. 'From the Director's desk'. *Stonewall Newsletter* 3: 2.

Meyers, M. 1994. 'Defining homosexuality: news coverage of the "Repeal the Ban" controversy'. *Discourse and Society* 5: 321–44.

MoD. 1996. *Report of the Homosexuality Policy Assessment Team*. London: Ministry of Defence.

Moran, L. 1991. 'The uses of homosexuality: homosexuality for national security'. *International Journal of the Sociology of Law* 19: 149–70.

O'Connor, K. 1980. *Women's Organisations' Use of the Courts*. Lexington KY: Lexington Books.

Pannick, D. 1983. 'Homosexuals, transsexuals and the Sex Discrimination Act'. *Public Law* 279–302.

Skidmore, P. 1995. 'No gays in the military: Lawrence of Arabia need not apply'. *Industrial Law Journal* 24: 363–68.

——— 1996. 'Homosexuals have human rights too'. *Industrial Law Journal* 25: 63–5.

——— 1997a. 'Sex, gender and comparators in employment discrimination'. *Industrial Law Journal* 26: 51–61.

——— 1997b. 'Can transsexuals suffer sex discrimination?' *Journal of Social Welfare and Family Law* 19: 105–10.

Stychin, C.F. 1995. *Law's Desire: Sexuality and the Limits of Justice*. London: Routledge.

——— 1996. 'To take him "at his word": theorizing law, sexuality, and the US military exclusion policy'. *Social and Legal Studies* 5: 179–200.

Sullivan, A. 1995. *Virtually Normal: An Argument about Homosexuality*. London: Picador.

Tatchell, P. 1995. *We Don't Want to March Straight: Masculinity, Queers and the Military.* London: Cassell.

Wade, W., and Forsyth, C. 1994. *Administrative Law.* Oxford: Clarendon Press.

Wintemute, R. 1994. 'Sexual orientation discrimination as sex discrimination: same-sex couples and the charter in Mossop, Egan and Layland'. *McGill Law Journal* 39: 429–78.

—— 1997. 'Recognising new kinds of sex discrimination: transsexualism, sexual orientation and dress codes'. *Modern Law Review* 60: 334–59.

5 Sexual orientation and anti-discrimination policy

The European Community

Mark Bell

The European Community has a well-established competency to combat sexual discrimination. (Since the 1993 Treaty on European Union, it has become more common to refer to the former European Community as the European Union. However, social policy still operates under the aegis of the European Community Treaty, and for this reason the term European Community has been used throughout this chapter.) The commitment of the Community to advancing sexual equality is enshrined in the EC Treaty, by virtue of Article 119, which provides for equal pay between men and women. This is complemented by the Equal Treatment Directive (76/207/EEC, OJ 1976 L 39/40), which forbids sexual discrimination in employment. However, the role of the European Community *vis-à-vis* other types of discrimination is much less certain. This chapter will examine the case of sexual-orientation discrimination. It aims to provide a critical overview of the European Community's response to sexual-orientation discrimination and will outline the key stages in the evolution of the policy. It will then turn to consider the potential for future progress.

Slow progress: 1980–9

In 1983 the European Parliament Committee on Social Affairs and Employment produced the Squarcialupi report on sexual-orientation discrimination in the workplace (European Parliament 1984). The initiative for the report can be traced back to the decision of the European Court of Human Rights in *Dudgeon* v. *UK* (22.10.81; Series A: no. 45, p. 5), which states that the criminalisation of consenting adult male sexual relations was contrary to Article 8 of the European Convention on Human Rights ('everyone has the right to respect for his private and family life'). Indeed the Squarcialupi report concluded that, whereas the Court of Human Rights had concerned itself with discrimination in criminal law (see also Gibbins, Chapter 3 of this volume), the European Community should concentrate on combating sexual-orientation discrimination in the field of employment. The report was debated in the European Parliament on 13 March 1984, where it received the broad support of the parties of the Left and the Centre-Right. There was, however, opposition from a significant minority of Christian Democrats and the UK Conservatives. For example, the Irish

Christian Democrats abstained from voting on the Resolution on the basis that it exceeded the competency of the European Community; 'the Irish people are entitled to observe their own moral code and this Parliament has no right to dictate otherwise...The EEC has no competence to decide the moral attitudes of society or the pattern of the criminal laws in the Member States' (MEP Mr Ryan; Debates of the European Parliament No. 1–311/71, 13.3.84). Despite the objections, the report was adopted, with 114 votes for, and 45 against (OJ 1984 C 104/46). It called on the European Commission to submit proposals to ensure that 'no cases arise in the Member States of discrimination against homosexuals with regard to access to employment and dismissals' (para. 5b).

The report met with a favourable response from the Social Affairs Commissioner, Iver Richard, who agreed it was 'unacceptable that homosexuals should be refused employment or suffer victimisation and harassment at work'. However, he noted there were 'significant practical, legal and political problems' to consider. Action was made difficult by the absence of a specific Treaty provision authorising legislation on equal treatment for homosexuals. The Commissioner acknowledged, however, that action could be justified by recourse to Article 235 of the EC Treaty. This had already been employed as the legal basis for the 1976 Equal Treatment Directive, and the Commissioner accepted that there was no reason why this could not also be used to legislate against sexual-orientation discrimination. Nevertheless 'as a matter of practical politics', the Commissioner could not foresee such a measure being acceptable to the Council of Ministers 'at least in the immediate future' (Debates of the European Parliament No. 1–311/17, 13.3.84). Certainly at a time when even progress on equal opportunities between women and men was proving difficult, there was little prospect of the Member States agreeing to new EC legislation on sexual-orientation discrimination. Spencer comments, 'the Commission evidently decided that the issue was one on which it was fruitless to draw up proposals for legislation that would be rejected outright by the Council' (Spencer 1995: 142).

After 1989, the Commission's attitude to gay and lesbian issues changed considerably. In 1989 a new Social Affairs Commissioner assumed office, Ms Vasso Papandreou. The arrival of Papandreou coincided with the symbolic renewal of European social policy via the Community Charter of the Fundamental Social Rights of Workers (hereafter referred to as the Social Charter). The Charter was a non-binding declaration, designed 'to set out formally the broad principles underlying our model of workers' rights' (Jacques Delors, Debates of the European Parliament No. 2–380/94, 13.9.89). Around this time, lesbian and gay groups began to lobby the Commission with greater determination, organising together through the International Lesbian and Gay Association (ILGA). In particular, they capitalised on the 1992 single European market programme and argued that this required a common standard of protection against sexual-orientation discrimination throughout the Community. This was based on the logic that where differences in the legal rights of gays and lesbians existed between Member States, this could present obstacles to the free movement of persons (Tatchell 1992: 19). Furthermore, they lobbied for inclusion in the new Social Charter, and, to this end, the Parliament amended the Commission's proposed text to include a statement that priority should be given to 'the right of all workers to equal protection regardless of their nationality, race, religion, age, sex, sexual preference or legal status' (OJ 1989 C 323/44).

Nonetheless, the Commission rejected this amendment and replaced it with a more ambiguous text. The preamble of the Social Charter states, 'in order to ensure equal treatment, it is important to combat every form of discrimination, including discrimination on grounds of sex, colour, race, opinion and beliefs' (Commission 1990). The Charter's ambiguity is both its strength and its weakness. While it failed to include sexual orientation explicitly, by referring to the need to combat 'every form of discrimination', it left the door open for potential future progress.

Policy innovation from the European Commission

The absence of an explicit reference to sexual-orientation discrimination in the Treaty has clearly hampered the development of EC policy. However, many alternative options to binding legislation exist that allow EC policy to evolve, in spite of the aforesaid competency problem. Cram argues that the European Commission has become expert in competency expansion. She suggests that this is conducted via small-scale initiatives and non-binding 'soft law' instruments (Cram 1994: 209). Since 1990 a range of such initiatives on sexual-orientation discrimination have been instituted. At first sight, these seem rather fragmented and lacking in any common direction. Yet when viewed as part of a steady process of competency expansion, there begins to be a greater coherence between the various measures taken. Commission initiatives fall into a number of categories:

• Small-scale direct-expenditure programmes
• Soft law instruments
• Minor legislative innovations

Small-scale direct-expenditure programmes

On several occasions since 1990, the Commission has provided much-needed funding to lesbian and gay community groups. Much of the financial support provided by the Commission has been to fund policy research. For example, the Danish Gay and Lesbian Union (LBL) received a grant of ECU 40,000 for research into the visibility of lesbians, with specific reference to lesbians in the labour market (Sanders 1996: 87). This was followed in 1993 with the publication of the Commission-funded report *Homosexuality: A European Community Issue – Essays on Lesbian and Gay Rights in European Law and Policy* (Clapham and Waaldijk 1993). The Commission has also promoted various gay and lesbian community-development programmes. For example, in Ireland, the Commission funded a Lesbian Education and Awareness programme. The financial support for this scheme was provided under the aegis of the New Opportunities for Women programme, representing a tacit acknowledgement that one dimension of combating sexual discrimination is combating discrimination against marginalised groups of women, who may not conform to sexual stereotypes. Through such initiatives, one can see how the Commission builds up a working relationship with gay and lesbian groups and establishes the credentials of the European Community as an institution sympathetic to their objectives.

Soft law

One of the most important instruments for competency expansion is 'soft law' (non-binding legislation). Sceptics criticise non-binding measures as weak and ineffectual, but this tends to overlook the important role that these can play in forging common policies and principles within the EC legal order. McMahon and Murphy submit that soft-law measures have a 'political and psychological significance...Sometimes they can, for example, be a prelude to legal acts, and other times they may create "legitimate expectations" in interested parties' (1989: 159). Soft law has proven a productive alternative to binding legislation *vis-à-vis* sexual-orientation discrimination. In the wake of research that high-lighted the need for action to combat sexual harassment in the workplace (Rubenstein 1988), the Council of Ministers adopted a Resolution on 27 May 1990 (OJ 1990 C 157/3) calling on the Commission to draw up a Code of Practice on Sexual Harassment. During the drafting of the Code, the ILGA successfully lobbied for the inclusion of harassment based on sexual orientation (Collins 1996: 31). The Commission Recommendation on the dignity of women and men at work was adopted on 27 November 1991 (OJ 1992 L 49/1). The Code of Practice on measures to combat sexual harassment is annexed to the Recommendation and states that 'harassment on grounds of sexual orientation undermines the dignity of those affected and it is impossible to regard such harassment as appropriate workplace behaviour' (Introduction, para. 5).

While it is unlikely that this has produced a significant improvement in the working environment for gay and lesbian employees in the Community, the importance of this statement should not be underestimated. It was the first reference ever to sexual-orientation discrimination in an EC legislative instrument and thus assisted in establishing the principle that harassment based on sexual orientation is contrary to EC law. Furthermore, the Commission has signalled its intention to propose binding legislation governing sexual harassment in the workplace (Commission 1995b: 27). The Code of Practice currently greatly strengthens the arguments in favour of including sexual-orientation harassment within any future EC sexual-harassment directive, demonstrating how soft law may anticipate future legal developments.

Minor legislative innovations

In a logical progression from the adoption of soft-law measures, the Commission has also begun to integrate the principle of non-discrimination on grounds of sexual orientation into EC legislation. This has been an evolving concept, only coming to fruition in the mid-1990s. In 1994, Commissioner Bruce Millan informed the Parliament that henceforth the Commission would follow a systematic policy of non-discrimination on grounds of sexual orientation (Debates of the European Parliament No. 3–442/44, 7.2.94).

The Commission maintains its well-established position that the Community does not possess the necessary competency to adopt a general non-discrimination directive, which would apply throughout the Member States. However, it now accepts that it does possess sufficient powers to at least ensure that EC legislation is not implemented in a discriminatory fashion. This policy was put into effect with the draft parental-leave directive (Commission 1996). Following many years of wrangling over the 1983 proposal for a parental-leave directive, the Commission finally managed to make some headway with the proposal via consultation with the Social Partners (European employers and trade unions). However, when the text agreed by the Social Partners was presented to the Council of Ministers for approval, the Commission also proposed including an anti-discrimination clause stating 'when Member States adopt the provisions to implement this Directive, they shall prohibit any discrimination based on race or colour, sex, sexual orientation, religion or nationality' (Article 2(3)).

The Member States, though, regarded this provision as unacceptable and substituted for it an anti-discrimination clause in the preamble of the directive that did not refer to sexual orientation (Recital 17; OJ 1996 L 145/4). The rejection by the Member States of the Commission's first explicit proposal for an anti-discrimination clause does not augur well for future anti-discrimination initiatives. That the Member States could not even reach agreement on this relatively minor provision demonstrates the true extent of the obstacles to the adoption of an Equal Treatment Directive for gays and lesbians.

At the beginning of this section, a model of how the European Commission can expand EC competency was put forward. Yet does the evidence presented suggest that the Commission is strategically acting to expand EC competency for sexual-orientation discrimination? Certainly there is some evidence that the Commission has deliberately sought to enhance its role in this field. A significant number of policy initiatives have been taken through soft law, small-scale expenditure, etc. Nevertheless, it is not clear that these amount to a demonstrable policy on the part of the Commission to prepare the way for a more significant undertaking, such as an Equal Treatment Directive for homosexuals. What these initiatives appear to lack is a clear vision as to their underlying objective.

The opportunity for the Commission to demonstrate its intentions *vis-à-vis* sexual-orientation discrimination presented itself in 1994, with the publication by the Commission of the White Paper 'European Social Policy – A Way Forward for the Union'. The White Paper sets forth the future direction of

European social policy. However, no reference is made to sexual-orientation discrimination. The same is true of the Commission's 1995 Medium-Term Social Action Plan 1995–97. The absence of sexual orientation from these 'agenda-setting' documents suggests that the Commission has quite limited ambitions in this area. The Commission's current policy is aimed at ensuring non-discrimination on grounds of sexual orientation within EC law. Thus, where appropriate, the Commission will explicitly address gay and lesbian concerns, for example, in the Code of Practice on sexual harassment. Consistent with this policy, the Commission has also demonstrated itself to be willing to approve suitable applications for EC financial support from gay and lesbian organisations. Ultimately, the Commission's room for manoeuvre is constrained by the Council of Ministers, as demonstrated over the Parental Leave Directive. When the Council will reject even minor legislative innovations, the Commission has little scope to move beyond the handful of low-level initiatives that currently exist.

The 1994 Roth Report

In complete contrast to the low-key nature of the Commission policy, the Parliament continues to push for radical change. In the 1994 report on *Equal Rights for Homosexuals and Lesbians in The European Community* (European Parliament 1994), the Parliament proposed sweeping legal reforms to be initiated by the Community. The report went much further than any previous work by the Parliament, and proposed that MEPs should call upon the Commission to submit a draft Council Directive 'on combating discrimination on the basis of sexual orientation' (Article 13). It states that the Directive should 'at least' provide for an end to 'all forms of discrimination in labour and public service law', the creation of a European 'equivalent legal framework' to marriage for same-sex couples, and the extension of adoption rights to same-sex couples (Article 14). Unsurprisingly, the Resolution proved divisive within the Parliament. Support for the proposal was strongest amongst MEPs from the Green and the Socialist groups in Parliament and, correspondingly, support was weakest among the Christian Democrats and other right-wing parliamentary factions. Alongside the normal party-political divisions were discernible differences based on MEPs' national background. For example, Dutch Christian Democratic MEPs proved largely supportive of the Resolution, despite the formal opposition of the Christian Democratic group as a whole. This contrasts with the position in the 1984 debate on the Squarcialupi report, when the Christian Democrats backed the proposed Resolution, but faced dissent from Irish Christian Democrats opposed to gay and lesbian rights. This indicates that this is an issue that transcends mere party-political allegiance, and that attitudes to issues of sexuality are also informed by the different cultural traditions that prevail in the Member States.

Predictably, the issue of EC competency dominated the debate. It quickly emerged that few MEPs shared the opinion of the Rapporteur, Green MEP Claudia Roth, that the Community possessed the necessary powers to enact a

Directive on issues such as same-sex partnership and adoption rights. Pragmatically, the Socialist group proposed amending the Resolution to replace the call for the adoption of a Directive with a call for the Commission to propose a (non-binding) Recommendation to the Council of Ministers, and, as a result, the motion was passed (159 votes for; 96 against), with the support of the Greens, Socialists and a few MEPs dissenting from the Christian Democrats' official line of opposition.

However, the wisdom of adopting a Resolution that stands no chance of adoption by the Commission or the Council is surely open to question. This is especially true when it is clear that a less far-reaching proposal would have received much wider support from within the Parliament, and could have won tacit approval from the Commission. For example, a Resolution that had called for a Directive to prohibit discrimination in employment would have been a more realistic proposition than proposals for the EC to regulate marriage and adoption rights.

European Community policy on sexual-orientation discrimination

EC policy on sexual-orientation discrimination is still more defined by its absence than its substance. The Parliament has been at the forefront of efforts to push EC sexual-orientation discrimination policy forward but, in the face of overt hostility from the Council of Ministers, it has failed to convince the Commission that it would be productive to prepare legislative proposals. The weakness of the policy may be particularly attributed to two factors: disunity among the Member States as to the *appropriateness* of EC intervention; and the *fundamental disparities* that exist between Member States' national laws on sexual-orientation discrimination.

Again and again, the issue of the Community's competency for sexual-orientation discrimination has been raised. The Community does not possess an unlimited legislative competency, and it is necessary to discover what the EC Treaty does and does not permit. However, determining the correct interpretation of the Treaty provisions is a hazardous and often value-laden process. One's interpretation of the Treaty may be no more than a reflection of one's own political preferences. It is no coincidence that those from the Right who are sceptical about the merits of legislation against sexual-orientation discrimination have argued that the Treaty does not provide any basis for EC intervention. Conversely, those on the Left who wish to see such legislation enacted have interpreted the Treaty as presenting no obstacles to the adoption of such proposals.

While accepting that it may be difficult to make a truly 'objective' evaluation of the terms of the Treaty, two points may be made. Given the precedent of the Equal Treatment Directive on sexual discrimination, there is clearly a strong case to be made that the Community does possess competency to combat discrimination in employment. Alternatively, there is no precedent for the Community intervening on issues such as marriage and adoption. Consequently, it is considerably harder to sustain the proposition that the EC may legislate in these fields.

Even if the Member States were agreed that the Community had the power to act, and that it was an appropriate subject for EC legislation, the Member States would then have to agree the contents of any such legislation. Yet, when one considers the diverse national laws that currently exist, it is difficult to identify how any agreement could be reached on a harmonised approach to sexual-orientation discrimination. Some Member States, such as the Netherlands, prohibit discrimination on grounds of sexual orientation in all aspects of the employment relationship. Other Member States have legislation that offers more limited protection against employment discrimination. For example, in Ireland, it is unlawful to dismiss someone on the basis of their sexual orientation, but it is not unlawful to refuse to employ or promote an individual on the same grounds. Finally, there are other Member States, such as the UK, where there is no specific protection against sexual-orientation discrimination. Indeed, in the case of the UK, the government itself is an agent of discrimination, routinely dismissing members of the armed forces on the grounds of their sexuality (see Skidmore, Chapter 4 in this volume). Given such legal diversity, the obstacles to the adoption of common EC legislation on this matter seem immense. Yet, despite these twin obstacles to progress at the EC level, there is now a genuine opportunity for a dramatic turnaround in this history of haphazard and inconsistent policy development.

Potential avenues of progress

The legal barriers concerning the EC's competency to legislate on sexual-orientation discrimination have suddenly, and unexpectedly, been largely demolished, with the agreement of the 1997 Treaty of Amsterdam. This amends the original Treaties and, in particular, significantly expands the EC's competence in the sphere of anti-discrimination law. Throughout the intergovernmental conference (IGC), which negotiated the Treaty revision, the Member States had expressed support for the need to expand the powers of the Community to allow it to legislate against non-sex-based discrimination, most notably racial discrimination (Council-EU 1995: 22). Capitalising on this momentum, ILGA lobbied for the inclusion of sexual orientation in any such amendment. While this was included in a number of draft versions of the new Treaty, on two separate occasions, sexual orientation was deleted from the draft Treaty, first by the Italian government, in the spring of 1996 (Bell and Waddington 1996: 336), and then, surprisingly, by the Dutch government, in March 1997 (ILGA 1997). However, on both occasions, lobbying from the ILGA, MEPs and other Member States, such as Ireland and Austria, secured its re-insertion, and ultimately its inclusion in the final draft. Thus the Amsterdam Treaty inserts a new Article 6a into the EC Treaty, stating 'without prejudice to the other provisions of this Treaty and within the limits of the powers conferred by it upon the Community, the Council, acting unanimously on a proposal from the Commission and after consulting the European Parliament, may take appropriate action to combat discrimination based on sex, racial or ethnic origin, religion or belief, disability, age or sexual orientation' (EU 1997).

The importance of this amendment should not be underestimated. Symbolically, it is an unprecedented recognition by the governments of the fifteen Member States of the need to combat sexual-orientation discrimination. Substantively, the familiar argument from the Commission and the Council that they lacked the necessary legal powers to enact anti-discrimination legislation is clearly no longer valid. Assuming the Treaty is ratified in all the Member States, the main legal barrier to an anti-discrimination directive has now been successfully removed.

Notwithstanding this progress, Article 6a requires unanimity for the adoption of legislation, presenting formidable political obstacles on an issue as divisive as sexual-orientation discrimination. However, the political barriers to protection against discrimination may shortly be circumvented through the European Court of Justice (ECJ). In July 1996, a British industrial tribunal asked the ECJ to decide whether sexual-orientation discrimination is prohibited by EC law under the 1976 Equal Treatment Directive and Article 119 of the Treaty. In the case in question, C-249/96 *Grant* v. *South West Trains*, a lesbian employee challenged the refusal of a rail company to extend a free travel pass to her same-sex partner, a benefit that is generally available to the opposite-sex partners of employees (*Equal Opportunities Review* 1996: 2). The chances of a decision in favour of Ms Grant and her partner have been greatly increased following the decision of the Court in *P.* v. *S and Cornwall County Council* (C-13/94 [1996] IRLR 347). In that case, the Court held that the Equal Treatment Directive prohibited discrimination against transsexuals. The logic of the Court's reasoning would appear to support the proposition that the Equal Treatment Directive also covers discrimination based on sexual orientation (see Skidmore, Chapter 4 of this volume).

Moreover, a second case on the question is now also under way. In March 1997, in C-168/97 *R* v. *Secretary of State for Defence* ex parte *Perkins*, the English High Court referred to the ECJ a case concerning the legality of the ban on lesbians and gays serving in the armed forces. Again, the referral asks the Court to determine whether sexual-orientation discrimination may be regarded as sexual discrimination contrary to the Equal Treatment Directive. Importantly, the judge stated his conviction that 'after the decision in the Cornwall case, it can scarcely be possible to limit the application of the Directive to gender discrimination…and there must be a real prospect that the European Court will take the further courageous step to extend protection to those of homosexual orientation' (*Equal Opportunities Review* 1997: 45).

A favourable decision at the ECJ, combined with the ratification of the Treaty of Amsterdam, holds the potential to transform EC law and policy on sexual-orientation discrimination from a picture of intransigence to one of dynamism and creativity, placing the Community at the forefront of providing equal opportunities irrespective of sexuality. In referring *Perkins* to the ECJ, Mr Justice Lightman outlined the challenge now facing the EC institutions: 'Homosexual orientation is a reality today which the law must recognise and adjust to, and it may well be thought appropriate that the fundamental principle of equality and the irrelevance of a person's sex and sexual identity demand that the Court be alert to afford protection to them and to ensure that those of homosexual orientation are no longer disadvantaged...' (*Equal Opportunities Review* 1997: 45).

References

Bell, M., and Waddington, L. 1996. 'The 1996 Intergovernmental Conference and the prospects of a non-discrimination Treaty Article'. *Industrial Law Journal* 25: 320–36.

Clapham, A., and Waaldijk, K. (eds). 1993. *Homosexuality: A European Community Issue – Essays on Lesbian and Gay Rights in European Law and Policy*. Dordrecht: Martinus Nijhoff.

Collins, E. 1996. 'EU sexual harassment policy'. In R. Elman (ed.), *Sexual Politics and the European Union: The New Feminist Challenge*, pp. 23–33. Oxford: Berghahn Books.

Commission of the European Communities. 1983. 'Proposal for a Council Directive on Parental Leave and Leave for Family Reasons'. COM (83) 686.

—— 1990. 'Community Charter on the Fundamental Social Rights of Workers'. *Social Europe* 1/90: 46–50.

—— 1994. 'European Social Policy – A Way forward for the Union: A White Paper'. COM (94) 333.

—— 1995a. 'Medium-Term Social Action Plan 1995–97'. COM (95) 134.

—— 1995b. 'Fourth Medium-Term Community Action Plan on Equal Opportunities for Men and Women 1996–2000'. COM (95) 381, 19 July 1995.

—— 1996. 'Proposal for a Council Directive on the Framework Agreement on Parental Leave concluded by UNICE, CEEP and the ETUC'. COM (96) 26.

Council of the European Union. 1995. 'Reflection Group Report and other References for Documentary Purposes'. Brussels: General Secretariat of the Council of the European Union.

Cram, L. 1994. 'The European Commission as a multi-organisation: social policy and IT policy in the European Union'. *Journal of European Public Policy* 1: 195.

Equal Opportunities Review. 1996. 'ECJ to rule on homosexual rights'. 69: 2.

—— 1997. 'Sexual orientation discrimination to ECJ'. 73: 44–6.

European Parliament. 1984. *Report for the Committee on Social Affairs and Employment on Sexual Discrimination at the Workplace*. EP Doc. 1–1358/83, 13.2.84.

—— 1994. *Report for the Committee on Internal Affairs and Citizens Rights on Equal Rights for Homosexuals and Lesbians in the European Community*. EP Doc. A3 – 0028/94.

International Lesbian and Gay Association (ILGA). 1995. *ILGA*. Brussels: ILGA Administrative Office.

McMahon, B., and Murphy, F. 1989. *European Community Law in Ireland*. Dublin: Butterworth.

Rubenstein, M. 1988. 'Report on the Problem of Sexual Harassment in the Member States of the European Community'. Luxembourg: OOPEC.

Sanders, D. 1996. 'Getting lesbian and gay issues on the international human rights agenda'. *Human Rights Quarterly* 18: 67–106.

Spencer, M. 1995. *States of Injustice – A Guide to Human Rights and Civil Liberties in the European Union*. London: Pluto Press.

Tatchell, P. 1992. *Europe in the Pink: Lesbian and Gay Equality in the New Europe*. London: GMP.

6 Sexual politics
Feminist politics, gay politics and the problem of heterosexuality

Stevi Jackson

The politics of sexuality is inextricably interconnected with the politics of gender. Both were at one time frequently subsumed under the umbrella of 'sexual politics', a term used to encompass both feminist and gay politics, to denote opposition to both male domination and heterosexual hegemony. This usage dates from the early 1970s, when the gay and women's movements shared much common ground, and it was widely assumed that gay liberation, like women's liberation, required the dismantling of patriarchal structures and institutions. The alliances built in that period, however, proved unstable and short lived. As many lesbians withdrew from gay politics, putting their energies instead into feminism, the two movements parted company. It is not my purpose here to retell this story, since this has been amply recounted by others from both sides of the divide (Stanley 1982; Jeffreys 1990; Edwards 1994; Evans 1993). What does concern me is one legacy of this history: a form of gay activism within which the politics of sexuality has been divorced from the politics of gender.

Gender and sexuality in sexual politics

Of course this rift has never been total: there have always been feminists and gay men who have kept the relationship between gender and sexuality in view, and there has always been some collaboration between individual feminist and gay activists and theorists. In recent years some have sought to rebuild lapsed alliances in response to the resurgent homophobia of the moral Right and the global crisis of AIDS. Even the latter, however, has not been enough to bring all feminists and gay men together around a common cause. There are those gay men, such as Simon Watney (1987), who see feminist anti-pornography campaigners as part of the sex-negative culture that promotes homophobia and inhibits adequate political responses to AIDS. On the other side are those radical lesbian feminists, such as Sheila Jeffreys (1994), who see a range of gay male practices – from cruising to sadomasochism – as antithetical to the feminist goal of equality in sexual and social relations, and for whom lesbian realignment with gay men threatens to undermine feminism. There are feminists working around AIDS who are prepared to ally to varying degrees with gay men, but who continue to insist that there are gendered dimensions to the epidemic that need to be explored and campaigned around (see, for example, Doyal *et. al.* 1994), while some gay men are suspicious of feminist intervention into debates around AIDS.

These differences intersect with the acrimonious debates around sexuality that have divided feminism over the last two decades (see Jackson and Scott 1996). Yet despite the divergent perspectives that feminists have adopted on the politics of sexuality, most continue to relate it to the politics of gender. Whether heterosexuality is viewed as the root of gender divisions (MacKinnon 1982) or gender is understood as central to the maintenance of normative heterosexuality (Butler 1990; Jackson 1996), a link between the two is assumed. This is a common thread linking perspectives as diverse as Sheila Jeffreys's radical lesbianism and Judith Butler's Queer theory (see Lloyd, Chapter 11 of this volume). From the early 1970s onwards, feminist writings on sexuality have, at least implicitly, entailed a critique of institutionalised heterosexuality. This critique has become increasingly explicit, and, while its terms are hotly contested, continues to undergo further theoretical elaboration (see, for example, Wilkinson and Kitzinger 1993; Richardson 1996). In other words, feminist theory and activism have retained some sense of the old meaning of 'sexual politics' in which gender and sexuality are understood to be interrelated.

There is, however, a minority of feminists who, like Gayle Rubin (1984), argue that a radical politics of sexuality must be distinct from the politics of gender. Rubin's position has more in common with certain tendencies in gay theory and activism than with the central concerns of feminism. I wish to argue that the separation she calls for is already occurring, and that the consequential widening of the divide between feminist and gay politics has the effect of undermining, rather than enhancing, the radicalism of the latter. This is true not only of reformist gay politics – the main object of my critique here – but also of some self-defined radical tendencies within gay activism. I shall focus here on a recent report published in the UK by Liberty (1994), which argues for human rights for lesbians and gays. Although produced by a civil rights organisation rather than from within the gay movement, it was written in consultation with gay groups and draws heavily on the gay press. It can therefore be taken as representative of a range of gay opinion – although not of lesbian opinion, since it excludes the opinions of lesbian feminist campaigners.

Heterosexuality and human rights

I am acutely aware that speaking on these issues as a heterosexual feminist lays me open to charges of claiming to speak on behalf of gay men or preaching to them, that I lack the authority I might have were I a lesbian. I am not, however, speaking on behalf of either gay men or lesbians but as a feminist who remains committed to the view that women's oppression and the oppression of lesbian and gay men are interconnected, that both are sustained by the hierarchy of gender, in which male dominance is sustained in part through the heterosexual contract (Wittig 1992).

In the Liberty report, decades of feminist activism and scholarship on sexuality, as well as the work of radical gay theorists, have been ignored. As a result, the report reads as if no one had ever developed critical perspectives on the social construction of sexuality. Of course, a document such as this, which aims to further pragmatic political aims, is not the place for complex theorising. Nonetheless, some of its more glaring conceptual flaws could have been avoided had it been informed by the insights of academic feminist and gay research and theory. It lacks any rigorous or consistent conceptualisation of sexuality and gender, still less of their interrelationship. There is no consideration of homosexualities as oppositional to heterosexuality, nor of the place of institutionalised heterosexuality in maintaining patriarchal domination. Rather than seeking to question the structures and discourses that maintain the distinction between heterosexuality and homosexuality, and that confirm the former as the norm, heterosexuality's normative status is confirmed. It is taken as the standard on which human rights are founded, and hence the issue of rights is posed in terms of equality *with* heterosexuals.

Liberty frames gay rights as a human rights issue within the parameters of the United Nations (UN) International Covenant on Civil and Political Rights (ICCPR), which was produced as an addition to the Declaration of Human Rights of 1948. It is argued that discrimination on the grounds of sexual orientation can be considered an abuse of human rights on three grounds, the first of which is that 'sexual orientation is an immutable part of every person like their race or gender' (Liberty 1994: 11). In the very next paragraph, however, we read that: 'A debate continues about whether sexual orientation is a biologically innate characteristic or a conscious political choice.'

If sexual orientation is immutable, it cannot be a matter of choice. Liberty wants to have it both ways, because each of these options offers apparent grounds for arguing for protection against discrimination: 'either similar protection to that which is afforded women and ethnic minorities, or protection from discrimination because of political or other opinions' (1994: 11). The opposition between biology and choice is not confined to this document. It has been a feature of other recent debates and campaigns, such as those in Britain around Section 28 of the Local Government Act 1988 (which prohibited local authorities from 'promoting homosexuality') and the homosexual age of consent (Franklin 1993; Stacey 1991; Birke 1994; Evans 1994). It relies, as Lynda Birke (1994) argues, on a reductionist view of biology as a monocausal explanation for complex human behaviour. More importantly, it leaves no room at all for social structures and processes. In ruling out this third option, that sexuality is socially or culturally constructed, it ignores the social contexts that shape both biological research and the political (or other) choices we make. Not only is this view of sexuality as either biologically ordained or freely chosen conceptually flawed, but I am not convinced that either alternative provides a sound basis for advocating equality.

It is not clear whether the idea of sexuality as a political choice is a misunderstanding of social constructionist theories of sexuality or of political lesbianism or both. If the idea of choice derives from political lesbianism, it is a somewhat simplistic interpretation of it; the slogan may have been that 'any woman can be a lesbian' but, in fact, not every woman could. Lesbian feminist theorists such as Rich (1986) had a great deal to say about the material and ideological constraints that kept women heterosexual. Those who became lesbian for polit-ical reasons did so as a result of a particular analysis of sexuality, one that derived from the feminist movement: that sexuality was socially constructed within heterosexually ordered patriarchal relations. It was in this context that the possibility of challenging and transforming sexuality opened up, making new choices available. What was involved was never simply a matter of a voluntaristic effort of will. Moreover, although a discourse of choice has been important to feminist thinking on sexuality, feminists have also long been aware of the complexity of sexuality and the dangers of a liberal individualistic model of desire and identity (see Stacey 1991).

Locating oneself as lesbian or gay *is* potentially political, because it entails embracing an identity oppositional to the prevailing norm; it is precisely the *social* significance of homosexualities that creates this political potential. Following the logic of homosexuality as a choice, Liberty argues for gay rights as analogous to the rights of political belief and dissent. What Liberty does not consider is what gays and lesbians are dissenting from, if not compulsory hetero-sexuality. Those who have chosen to be lesbian (or, much less frequently, gay) for political reasons have done so as a result of a critical opposition to patriarchal heterosexuality – hence the last thing they want is to be just like heterosexuals. Yet the aim of the report is precisely that lesbians and gays *should* be treated just like heterosexuals. They should, it is argued, have the right to form heterosexual-style marriages, including entitlements to the pensions and tax allowances that derive from the economic inequality underpinning heterosexual marriage (see Bell, Chapter 5 of this volume). The goal is to be included into heterosexual privilege, rather than to challenge it. Political lesbianism, on the other hand, has always been seen as a challenge to institutionalised heterosexuality, a refusal to live within its boundaries (see, for example, Wittig 1992).

The defence of homosexuality in terms of freedom of belief and association is difficult to sustain. There is not, nor can there be, absolute freedom of action for any of us – if there were, there would be no criminal law. Liberty's impre-cisely stated notion that the ICCPR 'protects the right of people to enter into relationships' (Liberty 1994: 11) is similarly too general to hold up – none of us is free to enter into any relationship we choose, still less are we free to act as we please within those relationships that are permitted. Many feminists would dissent from the extreme libertarianism that such an argument could lead to. They would not countenance, for example, the right of an adult man to enter into a sexual relationship with a six-year-old child, nor the right of a man to abuse his wife. (Some libertarian and gay activists do support the right to enter into what they call 'cross-generational relationships' (see Rubin 1984).)

The alternative strategy offered by Liberty is the claim to rights premised on sexuality as an immutable characteristic. In the absence of a political understanding of sexuality as socially constructed, the idea of being 'born that way' becomes attractive to many gays and lesbians. The ease with which biological explanations can be woven into individuals' accounts of their sexual desires and identities itself depends on the cultural legitimacy of scientific narratives. These 'ring true', not because they are based on incontrovertible fact, but because they provide culturally approved ways of constructing a sense of self (see Plummer 1995; Whisman 1996; see also Hawkes and Mottier, Chapters 9 and 10 of this volume). A further reason for the popularity of biological determinism among gay activists is that versions of constructionism have been mobilised from the political Right, centring on the possibility of conversion to or the promotion of homosexuality (Stacey 1991; Evans 1994). This, however, is no reason to abandon social and cultural perspectives. If both choice and determinism can be used to defend gay and lesbian rights, they can equally be deployed against those rights – to damn lesbians and gays as genetic freaks on the one hand or moral degenerates on the other (see Sinfield 1994).

Liberty's assumption that immutable sexual nature is the only alternative to political choice is not, then, an isolated instance, but part of a more general turn to biological explanations among gay activists. Epstein has characterised this as the adoption of an 'ethnic' identity in current gay politics, contrary to the proto-constructionist thought of early gay liberationists (1992). This trend has been noted with alarm by many feminists, since it runs counter to some of their fundamental political convictions (Birke 1994; Franklin 1993; Stacey 1991). The notion of an innate sexual orientation offers no challenge to hierarchies of gender and sexuality. Moreover, pleas for rights based upon this – we deserve tolerance and protection because we can't help it – hardly seem a promising start for claims to equality.

Political intersections between gender and sexuality

It is somewhat ironic that the Liberty report takes the immutability of sexual orientations as analogous to gender (Liberty 1994: 11), given that gender is a concept developed by feminists precisely to refute essentialist, biological ideas about sex differences. It also leads the author of the report into further contradictions. Gender, we are told, is immutable, but because Liberty wants to defend transgendered individuals, it complains that 'the law does not recognise the right of people to have changes to their gender acknowledged' (Liberty 1994: 58). It does not recognise that it is the construction of gender divisions itself that is the problem, and that this is linked to the binary divide between hetero- and homo-sexualities.

Hegemonic heterosexuality entails a conflation of anatomical sex, gender and sexuality: to have female genitals is to be a woman; to be a woman is to desire men (and vice versa). At the core of heterosexuality is the gendering of object-choice (see Carver, Chapter 1 of this volume). Because homosexuality involves the 'wrong' object-choice, biological and psychological theories of homosexuality have often conceptualised it as a gender disorder. Some recent forms of biological determinism promoted by gay scientists and activists accept this. For example, LeVay (1993) relies on the idea that the brains of gay men are characteristically feminised, and thus assumes that if men desire other men they must be 'like' women (see Fausto-Sterling 1992). This concedes ground to the patriarchal and heterosexist ideology, which identifies gay men as failed men – and lesbians as failed women.

While the divide between homosexuality and heterosexuality depends on the prior existence of gender divisions (see Jackson 1996), there are also links the other way round. As Anne Fausto-Sterling points out, fear of homosexuality helps to enforce the boundaries of gender. Thus the political struggle about gay civil rights and gay acceptance inevitably becomes part of the power struggle about gender (Fausto-Sterling 1992: 256). The author of the Liberty report, like many gay male activists, fails to appreciate the political implications of the complex interrelationship between gender and sexual hierarchies. Feminists, on the other hand, have long been aware of the potential challenge that homosexuality – and more specifically lesbianism – represents. It threatens the hierarchy of gender on which heterosexuality as a system is founded (Wittig 1992).

The existence of such a threat, the potential for political change, depends on recognising that the current ordering of gender and sexuality is social rather than natural (Stacey 1991). This is perhaps another reason for the appeal of biological theories to the less radical wing of the gay rights movement. Indeed, such explanations appear to have been embraced precisely because they render homosexuality unthreatening. If gays are 'born that way', then there is no risk of their ranks being swelled by converted heterosexuals, no challenge to the hegemony of the heterosexual social order. This is the political stance taken by Simon LeVay (1993). For the same reason, the recent British survey on sexual behaviour (Wellings *et al.* 1994), for all its attempts to avoid categorising individuals as gay and straight, has been welcomed by some gay activists, because it can be used to suggest that homosexuals are an even smaller minority than had hitherto been assumed – and hence even less of a threat to the heterosexual norm. More radical lesbian and gay theorists contest this point of view, arguing that gay and lesbian communities are not reproduced biologically, but through social, cultural and political struggle (see Franklin 1993).

Those who endorse biological and genetic theories assume that lesbians and gays constitute a permanent, more or less stable, natural minority. To campaign for equal rights on this basis is misguided. Homosexuality is not a natural difference that has become stigmatised through some irrational prejudice, but a category that only exists in relation to normative heterosexuality. It cannot be equal to heterosexuality: it is necessarily in opposition to it.

Positing sexuality as immutable obscures the hierarchical ordering of heterosexuality and homosexuality within which the latter is constructed as the deviant category in relation to the former. This deviance is not accidental, but serves to define the boundaries of compulsory heterosexuality (Rich 1986; Stacey 1991): 'The trick is to have us here *but* disgraceful' (Sinfield 1994: 189). Homosexualities have been constructed as immoral since legal regulation began. Moreover, 'permissive' legislation does not necessarily revoke their deviant status. David Evans (1993) notes that the Wolfenden report, which recommended and facilitated the decriminalisation of 'adult' gay male sex, nonetheless condemned it as immoral. The limited rights already won since that time have produced ghettos for gays that are policed and contained; homosexuality may be legal within these imposed limits, but it remains beyond the pale of the dominant moral order (Evans 1993). Morality does not exist in a social vacuum, but is rooted in specific institutions and practices. To quote Sinfield again: 'It suits the system if we are ultimately intolerable; it holds us at the point where we may seem to underwrite the normative ideology of manly men and feminine women' (Sinfield 1994: 191). I would add that this moral frontier also serves to maintain the hierarchy of men over women.

The Liberty report, like some gay activists, appears to have only a limited understanding of what is involved in maintaining this moral divide. In detailing legislation on sexual offences they make it quite clear that public morality is an important justification for regulating gay and lesbian conduct (Liberty 1994: 31–2). At this stage the report does begin to question the narrow concept of public morality, but does not extend this into a critique of heterosexuality. While there is scope for using formal rights as a basis for legalising gay relationships and conduct (see Waites and Bell, Chapters 2 and 5 of this volume), this does not necessarily translate into an acceptance of homosexuality as of morally equivalent status to heterosexuality. The focus on rights misses the point that homosexualities will inevitably be regulated, oppressed and stigmatised while heterosexuality retains its privileged position as the unquestioned, institutionalised cultural norm. Nowhere in the report is this privilege challenged.

Given the lack of awareness of the intersections between gender and sexuality evinced by the report, it is perhaps not surprising that the author fails to recognise that heterosexuality is a fundamentally gendered institution. Heterosexuals are not an undifferentiated category, but fundamentally divided by gender (aside from all the other social divisions, such as class and 'race', which alter the meaning of heterosexual relations). Men and women do not share equally in heterosexual privilege, since heterosexual marriage has historically institutionalised women's subordination to their husbands (Pateman 1988; Wittig 1992; Guillaumin 1995). It is nonsense to claim equality with 'the heterosexual', when the condition of being heterosexual, virtually by definition, differs for women and men.

The gender division underpinning heterosexuality means that gays and lesbians are not simply commonly oppressed through their homosexuality but are located differently in relation to compulsory heterosexuality. Rights pursued by gay men may not, therefore, be rights for lesbians. There is some recognition of gender difference in the report insofar as it details the specific problems faced by lesbian mothers, but even here this is soon collapsed back into a gender-neutral notion of lesbian and gay parenthood (see Rahman, Chapter 7 of this volume). This completely obscures the gendered principles and practices applied in decisions about child custody and access to assisted conception that apply specifically to lesbians (see, for example, Harne 1984; Radford 1991; Rights of Women 1984; see also Rahman, Chapter 7 of this volume). The report almost totally disregards the experience of feminist campaigns around these issues and the insights they have yielded.

Another obviously gender-specific issue is the campaign for an age of consent that applies equally to heterosexuals and homosexual men. What is not widely recognised, and is not mentioned in Liberty's coverage of the issue, is that the age of consent is a gendered concept – it applies only to heterosexual women (see Waites, Chapter 2 of this volume). There is no age of consent for hetero-sexual men, but rather an age of assumed sexual capability – and therefore of criminal culpability – for such acts as rape. In other words, the law encodes a model of heterosexual acts as something men do and women merely consent to (or not). Feminists have long been aware that this derives from a history in which male sexual access to a women's body was an act of appropriation whereby a man gained rights over a woman's person, property and labour (Guillaumin 1995; Pateman 1988). This is evident in the necessity of consummation for a marriage (and all the rights men gain from it), and is expressed in the notion of men's conjugal rights. This history should not be ignored, for we do not yet live beyond its influence.

This omission is perhaps surprising since the National Council for Civil Liberties (now Liberty) argued in the early 1980s for the removal of the age of consent on the grounds of sex discrimination – an argument controversial at the time, since many feminists felt (and still feel) that it was necessary to protect young women from sexual violence and exploitation. The history of hetero-sexual age-of-consent legislation has also been much debated among feminists, particularly in terms of whether its protective intent was progressive for women or repressive of their sexuality (for differing views, see Walkowitz 1980; DuBois and Gordon 1984; Jeffreys 1985). It is surprising that this has been ignored, given that it was the same piece of legislation – the Criminal Law Amendment Act 1885 – that both raised the heterosexual age of consent to 16 and outlawed 'acts of gross indecency between men'.

The extension of the concept of the age of consent to gay men has been a result of the partial decriminalisation of homosexuality. It effectively positions (*sic*) gay men in an analogous situation to straight women: consenting to have 'it' done to them. This model of sexual relations certainly shapes the thinking of some of those who oppose parity, who see it as a license for men to bugger young boys. I am not suggesting that the campaign to lower the age of consent is misguided, merely that it should be recognised that it does not render gay men formally equal to heterosexual men but to heterosexual women. This holds true whether one regards the age of consent for women as repressive discriminatory legislation or as necessary protection against male sexual exploitation. It serves to underline the point, yet again, that the pursuit of rights 'equal' to those of heterosexuals is far from unproblematic, and that the way in which heterosexu-ality has been constructed and institutionalised should be questioned.

Throughout Liberty's report, the social construction of heterosexuality remains unexamined. This entails not only essentialist assumptions about gender and sexuality but also assumptions about the subjects who embody these gendered, sexual identities. The underlying premise is that sexuality is intrinsic to the essential private self, that it is an attribute of an individual, and that it has little to do with the social. Rights for individual gays and lesbians are projected onto this conceptually private individual. Essentialist conceptions of the self fit well with the discourse of rights and compound the difficulty of confronting the normative constraints of compulsory heterosexuality. In a democratic system based on majority consent, and one in which the heterosexuality of that majority remains unchallenged, any freedoms gained for homosexuals will inevitably be limited. We cannot even begin to challenge heterosexual hegemony while limiting our concept of equality to formal, individual rights. The fact that women have gained many such rights without attaining social equality should demonstrate the limitations of a discourse of rights in which the social is rendered invisible and outside the field of discussion.

Conclusions

This chapter has concentrated on the reformist quest for gay rights, but the refusal to critique heterosexuality is also evident in some apparently more radical tendencies with gay politics and practice. It is within the gay rights lobby, however, that this uncritical stance is most evident, particularly in its demand for equality with heterosexuals.

To whom, precisely, do these lesbians and gays want to be equal: heterosexual women or heterosexual men? I suspect that within the gay rights lobby, gay men are seeking equality with heterosexual men, and are quite happy to leave lesbians the less enviable goal of equality with heterosexual women. Lesbian feminists, of course, have continued to fight for equality for all women and an end to gender hierarchy. This does not mean equality with men, or being like men for, as Christine Delphy puts it, 'if women were the equals of men, men would no longer equal themselves' (Delphy 1993: 8). That is to say, since men and women are categories rooted in a hierarchical division of gender, without that hierarchy the categories would cease to be socially significant; or, at the very least, women and men would not be the same as the creatures we know today. The same logic can and should be extended to the division between homo- and heterosexualities. If real equality existed, heterosexuality would no longer be what it is today. To seek equality with heterosexuals is a logical absurdity, since it cannot happen without displacing heterosexuality from its status as privileged, institutionalised norm. Rather the goal should be to make the anatomical sex of one's chosen sexual partners socially irrelevant, of no more significance than whether they have blue or brown eyes. This itself requires that gender ceases to be a significant factor in the way we organise not only our sexual but also our social relationships and institutions.

This may seem a utopian and distant goal, but if we think that political struggle can effect change, it is one worth working towards. The subversive and liberatory potential of homosexuality, as is recognised by many lesbian feminists, lies in its challenge to the inevitability of heterosexuality as a majority sexual practice. An effective critique of heterosexuality thus implies abandoning essentialist frameworks that position gays and lesbians as permanent minorities (Epstein 1992; Weeks 1985). It also entails an appreciation of heterosexuality as an institution, not merely a sexual preference (see Jackson 1996). Most fundamentally, all of this requires sustained opposition to the array of social practices and institutions through which inequality between women and men is perpetuated. Ultimately the gay movement needs to reorder its priorities, to see the struggle for equality between men and women as critical for its own cause – instead of ignoring feminism, marginalising lesbians and endorsing patriarchal, heterosexual institutions.

References

Birke, L. 1994. 'Interventions in hostile territory'. In G. Griffin, M. Hester, S. Rai, and S. Roseneil (eds), *Stirring It: Challenges for Feminism*, pp. 185–94. London: Taylor & Francis.

Butler, J. 1990. *Gender Trouble*. New York: Routledge.

Delphy, C. 1993. 'Rethinking sex and gender'. *Women's Studies International Forum* 16: 1–9.

Doyal, L., Naidoo, J., and Wilton, T. (eds). 1994. *AIDS: Setting a Feminist Agenda*. London: Taylor & Francis.

DuBois, E., and Gordon, L. 1984. 'Seeking ecstasy on the battle field: danger and pleasure in nineteenth century feminist thought'. In C.S. Vance (ed.), *Pleasure and Danger: Exploring Female Sexuality*, pp. 31–49. London: Routledge & Kegan Paul.

Edwards, T. 1994. *Erotics and Politics: Gay Male Sexuality, Masculinity and Feminism*. London: Routledge.

Epstein, S. 1992. 'Gay politics, ethnic identity: the limits of social constructionism'. In E. Stein (ed.), *Forms of Desire*, pp. 239–94. New York: Routledge.

Evans, D.T. 1993. *Sexual Citizenship: The Material Construction of Sexualities*. London: Routledge.

—— 1994. 'Sexual citizenship'. Unpublished paper.

Fausto-Sterling, A. 1992. *Myths of Gender*. 2nd edn. New York: Basic Books.

Franklin, S. 1993. 'Essentialism, which essentialism? Some implications of reproductive and genetic techno-science'. In J.P. DeCecco, and J.P. Elia (eds), *If You Seduce a Straight Person, Can You Make Them Gay? Issues in Biological Essentialism versus Social Constructionism in Gay and Lesbian Identities*, pp. 27–40. New York: Harrington Park Press.

Guillaumin, C. 1995. *Racism, Sexism, Power and Ideology*. London: Routledge.

Harne, L. 1984. 'Lesbian custody and the new myth of the father'. *Trouble and Strife* 3: 12–14.

Jackson, S. 1996. 'Heterosexuality and feminist theory'. In D. Richardson (ed.), *Theorizing Heterosexuality: Telling it Straight*, pp. 21–38. Buckingham: Open University Press.

Jackson, S., and Scott, S. 1996. 'Sexual skirmishes and feminist factions: twenty-five years of debate on women and sexuality'. In S. Jackson and S. Scott (eds), *Feminism and Sexuality*, pp. 1–31. Edinburgh: Edinburgh University Press; New York: Columbia University Press.

Jeffreys, S. 1985. *The Spinster and her Enemies*. London: Pandora.

—— 1990. *Anticlimax: A Feminist Perspective on the Sexual Revolution*. London, The Women's Press.

—— 1994. *The Lesbian Heresy*. London: The Women's Press.

LeVay, S. 1993. *The Gay Brain*. Cambridge MA: MIT Press.

Liberty. 1994. *Sexuality and the State: Human Rights Violations against Lesbians, Gays, Bisexuals and Transgendered People*. London: National Council for Civil Liberties.

MacKinnon, C.A. 1982. 'Feminism, Marxism, method and the state: an agenda for theory'. *Signs*, 7: 515–44.

Pateman, C. 1988. *The Sexual Contract*. Cambridge: Polity.

Plummer, K. 1995. *Telling Sexual Stories: Power, Change and Social Worlds*. London: Routledge.

Radford, J. 1991. 'Immaculate conceptions'. *Trouble and Strife* 21: 8–12.

Rich, A. 1986. 'Compulsory heterosexuality and lesbian existence'. In *Blood, Bread and Poetry*. New York: Virago.

Richardson, D. (ed.) 1996. *Theorizing Heterosexuality: Telling it Straight*. Buckingham: Open University Press.

Rights of Women. 1984. *Lesbian Mothers on Trial*. London: Community Press.

Rubin, G. 1984. 'Thinking sex: notes for a radical theory of the politics of sexuality'. In C.S. Vance (ed.), *Pleasure and Danger: Exploring Female Sexuality*, pp. 267–319. London, Routledge & Kegan Paul.

Sinfield, A. 1994. *The Wilde Century*. London: Cassell.

Stacey, J. 1991. 'Promoting normality: Section 28 and the regulation of sexuality'. In S. Franklin, C. Lury, and J. Stacey (eds), *Off Centre: Feminism and Cultural Studies*, 284–304. London: HarperCollins.

Stanley, L. 1982. '"Male needs": the problems and problems of working with gay men'. In S. Friedman, and E. Sarah (eds), *On the Problem of Men: Two Feminist Conferences*, pp. 190–213. London: The Women's Press.

Walkowitz, J. 1980. 'The politics of prostitution'. In C.R. Stimpson, and E.S. Person (eds), *Women, Sex and Sexuality*, pp. 145–57. Chicago IL: University of Chicago Press.

Watney, S. 1987. *Policing Desire*. London: Routledge.

Weeks, J. 1985. *Sexuality and its Discontents: Meanings, Myths and Modern Sexualities*. London: Routledge & Kegan Paul.

Wellings, K., Field, J., Johnson, A.M., and Wadsworth, J. 1994. *Sexual Behaviour in Britain: The National Sex Survey*. Harmondsworth: Penguin.

Whisman, V. 1996. *Queer by Choice: Lesbians, Gays and the Politics of Identity*. New York: Routledge.

Wilkinson, S., and Kitzinger, C. (eds). 1993. *Heterosexuality: A Feminism and Psychology Reader*. London: Sage.

Wittig, M. 1992. *The Straight Mind and Other Essays*. Hemel Hempstead: Harvester/Wheatsheaf.

7 Sexuality and rights

Problematising lesbian and gay politics

Momin Rahman

In this chapter I question the pursuit of equal rights within gay politics. My worry is that, implicitly or explicitly, the equal rights agenda takes the normality of heterosexuality as given, as the natural condition of the majority, and hence fails to question the legitimacy of its institutionalisation (see Jackson, Chapter 6 of this volume). While my discussion ranges across various campaigns that have used the discourse of equal rights, I shall focus on a recent report by the civil liberties pressure group 'Liberty', which brings together many of the issues under contention: *Sexuality and the State: Human Rights Violations against Lesbians, Gays, Bisexuals and Transgendered People* (Liberty 1994).

The first theme in my criticism is whether rights are necessary or useful in trying to achieve social equality. Drawing on feminist political theories, I suggest that formal legal equality will have little impact on the current social construction of sexuality, which stigmatises non-heterosexuals. I argue that legal equality with heterosexuals will not produce social equality with heterosexuals, since their freedoms are founded on homosexual oppression; their rights are heterosexual rights, and gaining those will not transform non-heterosexuals into their equals. My second criticism is focused on the discourse of rights itself. I analyse the essentialism that underpins the individualistic conception of rights and argue that this may reinforce the essentialist understanding of sexuality, thus compounding the very problem we seek to overcome. In conclusion, I discuss the potential for common ground with feminist and normative theorists who have suggested alternatives to individualism, such as group-based rights (Young 1989) or rights that recognise differences in opportunity and ability (Kingdom 1991).

Rights trouble

Liberty's aim is to make rights 'a key theme for the 90s' (Liberty 1994: 5). Its emphasis is on civil and political rights, those 'guaranteed in law', the premise being that such rights are crucial to equality, and that sexual orientation is ignored by most conventions on rights. I do not dispute that rights are important to those whose activities are oppressively regulated and unjustly obstructed. As the report points out, rights in areas such as housing, immigration and employment would go some way to protecting lesbians and gays from discrimination.

However, it must be recognised that rights in themselves do not guarantee equality. There are a number of problems with rights in liberal democracies in general and also with claims to rights for gays and lesbians within a patriarchal and heterosexually ordered society (see Jackson, Chapter 6 of this volume).

Rights are generally conceptualised as individualistic, founded on the assumption 'that the individual is conceptually and ontologically prior to society and can in principle be conceptualised and defined independently of society' (Parekh 1994: 157). Moreover, the individual is seen as the fundamental unit of political life (Phillips 1994). We are attached to our rights because they are most definitely attached to us *as individuals*. As Parekh argues, the liberal tradition limits individuation to the organic body and therefore ignores the social relations that define who we are, or how we are treated. Thus within the discourse of rights it is difficult to deal with infringements of liberty that arise from structured social inequalities. When rights are mobilised to challenge social inequality there is, I would argue, a confusion of the cause and effect of that inequality. This confusion shifts attention onto individual attributes as the problem, rather than social hierarchies and cultural constructions of otherness.

This construction of the political individual renders invisible the social hierarchies and structures within which individuals are located and through which their identities are constructed. In this sense, rights are not essential but *essentialist*, in that the focus of politics becomes the organic individual rather than social relations. Rights are often ascribed on the basis of an essentialist construction of individuality, which casts certain differences as 'natural', and thus the antagonisms arising from these differences are similarly regarded as natural and inevitable. The political establishment in Britain justifies racist immigration-control policies through such a discourse whereby 'natural' racial differences are seen to give rise to inevitable (that is, natural) prejudice, rather than to the social conditions and naturalist ideologies that produce and sustain racism (Guillaumin 1995).

Does this matter? One could argue that, as long as rights guarantee legal and political equality for social minorities, the origin of their minority status is irrelevant. This is the classic liberal position whereby the state only guarantees freedom from coercion and constraint – 'negative freedom' (Berlin 1984). However, I would argue instead that this position on rights is particularly problematic when applied to differences that are regarded as essential (natural, biological, spiritual), as they are in sexuality.

When rights are used as a mechanism to deliver equality, there is an implicit attempt to reach the 'ideal' of individual subjects equal before the law. As Anne Phillips has put it, the abstract individualist tradition in liberal democracy 'may note the differences between us but says these differences should not count' (Phillips 1993: 104). Thus it should not matter that one's social freedom is limited by being a woman, gay, black or a lesbian – one is a citizen, and as a citizen one has rights in law: this is, of course, the basic rationale behind equal rights. As many feminists have argued previously, the liberal discourse of rights is limited in its scope to legal and political equality, whereas it is actually social relationships and hierarchies that produce and sustain inequality for most groups (Pateman 1988, Phillips 1994). What I want to suggest is that not only do formal rights fail to address the social construction of differences because of their limited scope, but also that the discourse of rights may serve to *compound* social inequality, since it is too often underpinned by essentialist constructions of differences. The legitimacy of rights as mechanisms to promote social equality is undermined when the basis of inequality is regarded as natural and thus inevitable. What seems important to me is that we press for rights that focus on the social causes of inequality rather than on the social categories that these inequalities produce, or the essentialist conceptualisation of individuals located within those categories. In this vein, Liberty's call for workplace anti-discrimination legislation focuses on 'other people's' attitudes and actions when they are faced with the 'difference' of homosexuality, rather than on individual sexuality as the cause of the problem.

However, even these minimal negative rights are contentious when demanded by lesbians and gays. They are often characterised as asking for particular, group-specific rights, which can then be interpreted as 'special rights', as has happened in the United States, both with affirmative-action policies and with gay rights ordinances (*The Economist*, 25 June 1996). 'Special rights' are politically unpopular with democratic majorities that are attached to the current discourse of universally applicable equal rights. A case in point is the recent rash of state-level actions in the USA aimed at overturning anti-discrimination measures that specifically included lesbians and gays. The anti-homosexual campaigners argued that anti-discrimination measures were 'special rights' for homosexuals that the majority did not have. Indeed, this was the main thrust of the successful campaign to pass Amendment 2 in Colorado, which altered the State's constitution to exclude lesbians and gays from anti-discrimination legislation and prevent any such legislation in the future. This amendment was challenged in the courts and in May 1996 the US Supreme Court declared it unconstitutional. The opinion of the Justices was that anti-discrimination measures were not special rights but rather mechanisms to deliver equality that others either did not need or already had (*The Economist*, 25 June 1996).

The Supreme Court demonstrated that the notion of special versus equal rights is a false opposition that, as Elizabeth Kingdom suggests, needs to be exposed as mere camouflage for the problem of social inequality (Kingdom 1991). The debate should not be about the equal allocation of rights but about which equivalent rights (therefore potentially both different and differentially applied) are needed to deliver or underwrite social equality. An emphasis on rights that accepts and promotes differences within a framework of equal treatment and opportunity is more productive than rights that merely guarantee formal equality. Feminists have shown that such abstract formal equality has little effect in a society where inequality is perpetuated, both materially and ideologically, at a social level (Phillips 1993, 1994; Young 1989; Pateman 1988).

Not only do we need to push for a reconceptualisation of rights that is non-essentialist, but we also need to broaden the legitimate scope and construction of rights as mechanisms for legal and political equality to considering them as part of the framework of social equality. This is necessary because the conditions under which formal rights are exercised are not the same for all social groups. Take, for example, the right to privacy, as set down under Article 17 of the ICCPR (International Covenant on Civil and Political Rights added to the 1948 UN Declaration of Human Rights). Liberty would like to see this incorporated into a bill of rights, since it is not, at present, constitutionally guaranteed in the UK.

This might indeed offer lesbians and gays some respite from the degree of surveillance to which they are now subject, but even if such a provision were technically applicable to all, this would not ensure that it would be equitably observed. The boundaries between public and private are already differentially demarcated in interpretations of what counts as consensual sex 'in private' (Liberty 1994: 46–7). Because the boundary between public and private is not absolute, it is always subject to contextually specific social definition. Precisely where it is drawn depends on the actors involved, their location within social hierarchies and the moral and political judgements applied to their conduct. The privilege of heterosexuality within essentialism makes it unlikely that the relatively large heterosexual 'private' sphere will *ever* be the standard for gays and lesbians while the essentialist hegemony remains intact.

Many of the freedoms enjoyed by heterosexuals are not, in any case, encoded as formal rights. For example, heterosexuals can flaunt their sexuality in public: they can hold hands or kiss in the street without censure or legal intervention. It is difficult to see how any formal rights could deliver the same freedoms for lesbians and gays. Such rights might be able to offer some protection from harassment and violence (not least by the police), but could not grant them the freedom to express their sexuality in public. In the case of sexuality, freedoms are determined by the social construction of sexuality that privileges heterosexuality. It is a mistake to think that rights currently enjoyed by heterosexuals, whether they be legal or social, are the result of the limited distribution of 'natural' rights, which, with the right political will, can be extended to all persons. These are not general human rights but, in many cases, profoundly heterosexual rights.

Heterosexual liberty

The focus on rights may imply that gays and lesbians are merely marginalised; that in some way a wider application of rights will bring them from the margins to the centre. In some areas this may be true, but in others this cannot be the case, since the rights sought are the rights that enshrine the privilege of heterosexuality. Sexuality is the basis of social categorisation as a result of relations of domination and subordination (Rich 1986; Delphy 1993; Guillaumin 1995): gays and lesbians are oppressed outsiders because of the institutionalisation of heterosexuality and the pivotal place it occupies in the normative order. Rights are but one arena of this institutionalisation.

The examples of women and racialised minorities must be borne in mind.

Rights have seldom acknowledged that their difference is based on the social construction of race or gender rather than innate characteristics. Equalising rights has in many ways meant an attempt to level racialised groups or women up to the ideal level of the abstract citizen. The abstract citizen, however, does not exist. Actual political citizenship was developed to accommodate propertied men and then extended to all adult men before the franchise was given to women (see Carver, Chapter 1 of this volume). For many ethnic minorities in Britain, political citizenship, deriving from nationality, is still an insecure and conditional status. We need to recognise that citizenship itself is gendered and racialised (Walby 1994; Phillips 1993; Young 1989; Parekh 1994). Giving a black woman the same formal rights as a white man does not endow her with his social and economic advantages.

I recognise that abstract citizenship rights may be more feasible objectives in some contexts than in others. Liberty's call for legislation to outlaw discrimination in employment is an example of where rights might serve to offer gays and lesbians equal protection against unfair dismissal (see also Bell, Chapter 5 of this volume). Here the intention is to redirect attention away from sexuality, to make it irrelevant to employment. Although this right, if enacted, would address only individual experiences of being gay or lesbian and does not therefore threaten heterosexual privilege as such, it could also be argued that this is a right that, in a limited and negative sense, recognises the 'difference' of homosexuality, since it would shift attention onto others' attitudes to lesbians and gays as part of the social conditions that sustain inequality.

However, in some sectors of employment sexuality does become an issue, and here there is greater resistance to formal equality: for example, in the armed forces, the one form of employment where the British government policy openly bans lesbians and gays (Liberty 1994: 24; see also Skidmore and Bell, Chapters 4 and 5 of this volume). The military position rests firmly on the essentialist construction of homosexuals as morally and psychologically unbalanced and as subsumed by their sexuality. Gays and lesbians are thus said to be innately unable to perform their duties or keep their mind on their job and their potentially disruptive effect on (presumably homophobic) colleagues overrides any individual rights they may have. In this example, the essentialist construction of homosexuals as deviant is very definitely the problem, rather than people's attitudes or institutionalised discrimination. I would suggest that this view of homosexuality is particularly strong in the military because it is an intensely homosocial institution that is rigidly divided by gender. These are near perfect conditions for homosexual encounters, but the military is part of the traditional patriarchal network of state institutions and so must project a rigorously heterosexual image.

Major problems arise in demands for rights in areas that are central to the institutionalisation of heterosexuality, notably 'the right to form a family' (Liberty 1994: 18; 37–44). The well-worn example of Section 28 of the Local Government Act (1988) demonstrates that the family, by definition, is heterosexual: gays and lesbians can only have 'pretended family relationships'.

However, diverse family forms are becoming widespread and visible, whereas a variety of state social policies reinforce the institutionalised heterosexuality and male dominance on which families are still founded. Liberty mobilises the idea of family diversity to argue that the ICCPR's provision on family rights could be extended to lesbians and gays, but the rights they argue for do not rely at all on ideas about diversity, but rather on the closest possible mimicry of conventional heterosexual domesticity. What is known about living arrangements and self-defined kin and family ties within lesbian and gay communities is suggestive of far more varied and fluid possibilities (see, for example, Weston 1991; Weeks 1996). Rather than looking for ways of enhancing such diversity, Liberty simply wants to give lesbians and gays rights modelled precisely on the heterosexual family. It would seem that Liberty is indeed advocating rights enabling lesbians and gays to establish 'pretended (heterosexual) family relationships'.

There has been a marked increase in campaigns to formalise same-sex marriage for lesbians and gays. What worries me is that although the meaning invested in marriage by lesbians and gays may not be wholly determined by its current heterosexual construction, the actual institution and the laws supporting it are still very much a reflection of a patriarchal and heterosexual contract. Surely our imaginations can stretch beyond this meagre union? Indeed, as the *Gay Times* issue on marriage points out (July 1996), it is already possible to secure legal agreements that ensure many of the rights encoded within heterosexual marriage – the difference, and in my view benefit, being that these rights must be specifically thought out, discussed and sought after by both partners. Perhaps this might even serve as a better model for heterosexuals? The point is that the condition of being part of a registered partnership, or even 'properly' married in religious or civil ceremony, will not, despite its symbolic impact, serve as a panacea for social acceptance or equality. Once couples are out of the registry office, it will not be more acceptable for them to hold hands, have children or do anything else that heterosexuals take for granted.

The granting of immigration rights to those 'who can demonstrate the exis-tence of a committed relationship' is another 'marital right' promoted by Liberty (1994: 62). What standards will be used to judge this (see also Carver, Chapter 1 of this volume)? Heterosexual monogamy? In the realm of immigration, even heterosexual marriage is not a sufficient condition for fair treatment. Western constructions of marriage and the family are the blueprint for immigration poli-cies. Country of origin and type of marriage, kinship structures and cultures are all taken into account in order to determine 'genuine' marriages. In effect, these policies are racist, since they are applied selectively to non-whites from non-Western cultures. To be a couple in a committed relationship, however that commitment and relationship is defined, is simply not enough to guarantee equal treatment, even if the couples are heterosexual and have copiously procreated.

Similarly, Liberty's defence of the rights of lesbians and gays to parent, and especially to foster and adopt, is couched in terms of the difficulties faced by lesbian and gay couples (Liberty 1994: 43). Once more Liberty ignores the diver-sity existing within gay communities, the variety of situations in which children might be reared (see Weston 1991). The problem lies in taking for granted the rights that accrue to heterosexual couples as a basic model for human rights. This presupposes the normality and desirability of monogamous coupledom. This might be merely strategic, an attempt to make gay rights appear respectable and reasonable (interesting, however, that Outrage!, an organisation not usually so concerned with respectability, has put its name to this enterprise). But if this move is more than strategic, then it is endorsing institutionalised heterosexuality as a model for human relationships.

Perverting liberty

Imbued with the dominance of heterosexuality, the discourse of rights is problematic in a number of ways. First, balancing positive and negative rights – freedoms to and freedoms from – is always difficult in democratic states, as are problems to do with competing negative rights. In classical liberal arguments, negative freedoms are seen as fundamental, which should produce an unassailable case for lesbians and gays to be free from discrimination and harassment. This is not what happens in practice. The reluctance to pass anti-incitement to hatred laws is justified on the grounds that it would erode freedom of speech (Liberty 1994: 53). Hence the right of racists and homophobes to say what they like is given priority over the right of black people, lesbians and gays to be free from abuse and harassment. For 'deviant' sexual identities, this can be attributed to the essentialist construction of sexuality which has a moral dimension at its core, in which those beyond the pale of decency as 'unnatural' are cast as unworthy of protection.

Traditional liberal theory accords liberty priority over morality, since liberty is seen as fundamental to being human – an absolute – whereas morality is seen as relative, a product of historically specific behavioural norms. However, in the case of sexuality, liberalism founders on the rock of compulsory heterosexuality. Hence morality in practice constrains liberty. The essentialism of the discourse of rights dovetails with the essentialist understanding of sexuality, which underpins the moral and social privilege of heterosexuality as the 'natural' ordering of gender and desire. This seals the reversal of the liberty–morality relationship. That this can happen suggests that morality is rather more than the product of behavioural norms, or that we should at least ask where these norms come from. They are not simply the result of traditional attitudes, but part of an ideology that legitimates a heterosexual and patriarchal social order. Liberal theory, as I have indicated, does not address such structural inequalities.

What lesbians and gays need to do is to pervert liberty; to stop it being the sole preserve of heterosexuality. Rights *are* essential mechanisms in the fight for social equality, given that rights discourse occupies a privileged moral position in democratic states (Kingdom 1991; Glaser 1995). However, lesbians and gays cannot remedy their lack of equality through rights unless they contest the defining influence of the essentialist construction of sexuality and morality on the liberty of sexual identities. This means displacing heterosexuality from its

institutionalised place in the normative order and replacing it with a conceptualisation of rights that recognises different values, practices and communities, and
also that these differences generate their own moralities. As Jeffrey Weeks has
argued, lesbians and gays need to contest patriarchal and heterosexist morality in
order to show that all such moralities are 'invented' and thus are neither eternal
nor transcultural truths (Weeks 1996). Furthermore, lesbians and gays need to
construct and project their social identities with a moral dimension – their own
moral framework – so that they can lay claim to specific rights, and to the more
general settlement of equal opportunity and treatment. This is not easy ground
to tread on; it involves discussions of morality, libertarianism, responsibility and
social equality. Each is fiercely contested territory, not least within lesbian and
gay communities of thought. At the core of each debate, in this context, must be
a consideration of social justice and liberty.

Perverting justice

As socially oppressed groups, lesbians and gays have an important contribution
to make to the formulation of an alternative conceptualisation of rights that is
based on the recognition of social differences, rather than on an abstract,
universal and essentialist construction of the individual. For example, the discussions of group representation in feminist theory have direct relevance for the
progress of lesbian and gay rights and representation (Young 1989). As yet, this
remains an uncharted area for lesbian and gay politics. Elizabeth Kingdom's
discussion of the problems with rights for feminist politics concludes that, while
the discourse of rights brings moral weight to political campaigns, its essentialist
baggage may be reduced by framing rights in terms of capabilities, competences
and capacities (Kingdom 1991). This is a conceptualisation of rights that takes
into account the differential abilities and conditions needed for different social
groups to exercise rights, given their locations within intersecting social hierarchies and their differences from a cultural norm. Like traditional communitarian
theory, this places the emphasis on rights related to a person's social location and
social duties (Glaser 1995).

There is already a tentative engagement with these issues at the level of
recognising sexual difference. Both Jeffrey Weeks's *Invented Moralities* (1996) and
Ken Plummer's *Telling Sexual Stories* (1995) centre on the importance of diversity
and on the need to accept and promote different social and cultural values as
equivalent to any dominant norm. Moreover, they suggest the need for political
identities that do not rely upon essentialism, or which, at the very least, recognise
that such identities are tactically or strategically 'necessary fictions' (Weeks 1996).

It should be acknowledged that rights for gays and lesbians will be different
from each other because of the defining way that gender constructs heterosexuality as the norm (see Jackson, Chapter 6 of this volume). An inevitable
consequence of contesting the discourse of rights is the implied challenge to
democracy as merely a process whereby a majority makes decisions and the state
guarantees only negative liberties. A central aim must be to reconceptualise the

discourse of rights so that rights are not only underwritten by an acceptance of social differences but they are also more broadly conceived as mechanisms to deliver social equality. This is necessary because formally equal rights do not, on the whole, address the inequalities that create and sustain experiential differences. Equal rights seem to work only in those situations where negative liberties are at stake.

In the realm of sexuality, I would argue that this cannot be done without an explicit engagement with normative political theory, including questions of morality and social justice. It may seem wilfully perverse to suggest that the argument should be moved to the emotionally charged territory of morality rather than focusing on apparently rational liberty, but it is clear that liberty is not rationally produced in the arena of sexuality. Indeed, it is completely bound up with the social construction of sexuality, rather than being an expression of a 'natural' or morally self-evident form of justice. We need to pervert justice away from its heterosexual bent.

There is already an engagement with these issues by some gay and lesbian theorists, and I would suggest that they have much to contribute to this debate. Normative theory has two major preoccupations: the role of the state and the related question of the methods it may use in the pursuit of social equality (Glaser 1995). As I have indicated, lesbian and gay inequality would seem to suggest a need for a non-essentialist conceptualisation of rights and, in complement to this, a more interventionist state when it came to matters of social justice. This would perhaps place us on the communitarian wing of normative theory, although this position would have to be balanced with the need for the individual ascription of protective rights in the current hierarchical organisation of sexual identities and freedoms. However, the involvement of lesbians and gays should bring something to the debate about what the state is for, and how it should go about achieving its aims.

Objections may be raised in that this kind of normative discussion is utopian in its aims of changing political culture and practice. Specifically, the oppositional nature of homosexuality to heterosexuality is so entrenched that it may be possible to achieve little beyond negative liberties. Against this I would argue that lesbians and gays must not forget that a range of social movements and radical academic theorists share their concerns with regards to freedom from oppression. Lesbians and gays should learn from them and realise that they may have something distinctive to contribute as well. The debate about the direction of gay politics is not new; many others have raised the dangers of sexual politics being de-radicalised and confined to traditional democratic forms based on an 'ethnic' identity (Epstein 1992; Altman 1980; Edwards 1994; Evans 1993). These problems and proposals may seem 'queer' to some folk, but properly thought out and considered, they are in fact central to issues of democracy, social justice, and liberty.

References

Altman, D. 1980. 'What changed in the 70s?'. In *Homosexuality, Power and Politics*, ed. Gay Left Collective, ch. 4. London: Allison & Busby.

Berlin, I. 1984. *Four Essays on Liberty*. Oxford: Oxford University Press.

Delphy, C. 1993. 'Rethinking sex and gender'. *Women's Studies International Forum* 16: 1–9.

Edwards, T. 1994. *Erotics and Politics: Gay Male Sexuality, Masculinity and Feminism*. London: Routledge.

Epstein, S. 1992. 'Gay politics, ethnic identity: the limits of social constructionism'. In E. Stein (ed.), *Forms of Desire*, pp. 239–94. New York: Routledge.

Evans, D.T. 1993. *Sexual Citizenship: The Material Construction of Sexualities*. London: Routledge.

Glaser, D. 1995. 'Normative theory'. In D. Marsh, and G. Stoker (eds), *Theory and Methods in Political Science*, ch. 1. London: Macmillan.

Guillaumin, C. 1995. *Racism, Sexism, Power and Ideology*. London: Routledge.

Kingdom, E. 1991. *What's Wrong with Rights?: Problems for Feminist Politics of Law*. Edinburgh: Edinburgh University Press.

Liberty. 1994. *Sexuality and the State: Human Rights Violations against Lesbians, Gays, Bisexuals and Transgendered People*. London: National Council for Civil Liberties.

Parekh, B. 1994. 'The cultural particularity of liberal democracy'. In D. Held (ed.), *Prospects for Democracy*, ch. 7. Cambridge: Polity Press.

Pateman, C. 1988. *The Sexual Contract*. Cambridge: Polity Press.

Phillips, A. 1993. *Democracy and Difference*. Cambridge: Polity Press.

—— 1994. 'Must feminists give up on liberal democracy?' In D. Held (ed.), *Prospects for Democracy*, ch. 4. Cambridge: Polity Press.

Plummer, K. 1995. *Telling Sexual Stories: Power, Change and Social Worlds*. London: Routledge.

Rich, A. 1986. 'Compulsory heterosexuality and lesbian existence'. In *Blood, Bread and Poetry*. New York: Virago.

Walby, S. 1994. 'Is citizenship gendered?' *Sociology* 28: 379–96.

Weeks, J. 1996. *Invented Moralities: Sexual Values in an Age of Uncertainty*. Cambridge: Polity Press.

Weston, K. 1991. *Families We Choose: Lesbians, Gays, Kinship*. New York: Columbia University Press.

Young, I.M. 1989. 'Polity and group difference: a critique of the ideal of universal citizenship'. *Ethics* 99: 250–74.

Part II

Theorisations of sexuality

Identities and political agency

8 Sexuality and nationality

Gendered discourses of Ireland

Alan Finlayson

This chapter analyses the interrelation between the two discursive 'regimes' of nation and sexuality. Discourse is understood to organise social relationships into conceptual frameworks, 'discursive formations', that produce a 'set of rules' by which objects, subject positions, and strategies are formed. Discourse analysis is concerned with this social practice of discursive articulation and with exploring discursive formations as the relationship between 'institutions, economic and social processes, behavioural patterns, systems of norms, techniques, types of classification, modes of characterisation' (Foucault 1989: 45).

This chapter further investigates the articulation of discourses of nation and sexuality into a unified ideological discourse (Laclau 1979: 81–142). Under the conditions of such a unity, interpellations on the basis of nationality can also be interpellations of specific sexual or gender roles, while interpellations on the basis of such roles can also invoke the category of nationality. Thus discourses of nation structure and blend with discourses and interpellations concerned with sexuality and gender (see also Mosse 1985; Parker *et al.* 1992; Amir and Benjamin, Chapter 14 of this volume).

Such discourse may be understood as 'identitarian', fixing itself by a claim to an inviolable and natural identity (in this case, a national identity). The category of national identity operates as if it were simply 'out there' producing the way we ought to be and acting as a kind of external 'guarantor' of a set of desired social/political arrangements. This, of course, obscures the ways in which a 'national identity' is itself the product of social/political discursive processes, themselves the object of political contestation and argumentation.

Where analysis of nations and nationalism may argue about what nations are, and the mechanisms of their formation, I am concerned not with the 'what' of nations but with the 'how'; the ways in which the concept of nation operates and is produced within ideological discourse. Benedict Anderson has suggested that nations be distinguished not in terms of their truth or falsity, but by the 'style of their imagining' (Anderson 1992: 6; see also Carver, Chapter 1 of this volume). My concern is precisely with the 'style' of national imagining and the way in which that 'style' produces specific categories of identification and behavioural norms pertaining to sexuality.

While the thought behind this chapter is general, the main focus is on a specific instance – Ireland. However, this does not represent a comprehensive study of Irish nationalist discourse. Rather I am pointing to some of the ways in which aspects of Irish nationalist discourse have produced not only visions of the nation but ideas about sexual and bodily behaviour. In the ideological discourse of Irish nationalism these two 'regimes' of thought come to be part of a unified vision of the national and social body.

Ireland as a woman

When Renan analysed Celtic culture he chose to portray the Celts as 'an essentially feminine race' (Renan 1897; Cairns and Richards 1988: 42–57). This notion is one of the most enduring elements of the 'style' of imagining Ireland. Imagining Ireland as woman has been a widespread practice in Irish culture, be it Yeats's Kathleen Ni Houlihan or Seamus Heaney's images of the bog queen. As one commentator has put it: '...in Ireland sexual identity and national identity are mutually inter-dependent. The images of suffering Mother Ireland and the self-sacrificing Irish mother are difficult to separate' (Meaney 1991: 3). Images of the vulnerable virgin and the mourning mother link the Irish woman-nation to religious iconography. Suffering Ireland can be seen as tormented by the bullying rapist of Britain, a portrayal that offers nationalism a 'mythic pedigree and exonerates it from aggressive and oppressive intent...virgin Ireland gets raped and pitied while mother Ireland translates pity into a call to arms and vengeance' (Longley 1990: 18).

The significance of this trope in pre-independence nationalist discourse can be illustrated by the *Catholic Bulletin*, a popular periodical published in Ireland from 1911 to 1939. The *Bulletin* mixed topical comment, short stories, poetry, book reviews and miscellanea with the aim of promoting 'good reading' among the Catholic Irish as well as a Gaelicised nationalist political vision. It is not my intention to suggest that the *Bulletin* represents a cross-section of nationalist opinion but rather to use this aspect of such opinion to illustrate some of the contours of Irish nationalist discourse as it intersects with questions of sexuality.

An edition from 1915 contains a very purple piece of prose entitled 'The Spirit of Erin', which follows the spirit of Ireland down through the centuries encountering various mythic events. Ireland is described as 'Ever Fair, ever Beautiful and ever Young....' She has 'inspired her sons and daughters with the highest hopes and ideals, and has ever wielded a sweet, strange influence over them'. Ireland is 'our own dear Caitlin', an ever watchful spirit guarding 'her four provinces with a warrior's courage and a mother's care', inspiring her children to fight new battles, 'keeping her honour untarnished, and holding a lofty contempt for all that is mean and ignoble' (*Catholic Bulletin* 1915: 922–5).

The piece concludes:

> Ah yes! Eire dear! your morn is breaking and the clouds are rolling by. Your long thraldom will sink into oblivion when the bright glory of a new Era shines upon your hopes and brings them fruition. No more will you gaze

upon your dark night of wrong. The brightness of day will dispel all the gloom and you will see your sons and daughters within your four seas with hands clasped once more in unity. Your heart will beat high with joy when your crown of victories is placed upon your stately brow, and rocks and glens and valleys will resound to the loud, glad shout of your children as they hail you, 'A Nation Once Again'.

(*Catholic Bulletin* 1915: 925)

Clearly this passage is heavily informed by religious imagery. The sufferings of Erin, after a time in the wilderness, are to be ended with the coming of a new age when a unified natural universe will resonate in harmony. The dawning of an Irish nation becomes the fulfilment of centuries of waiting, the foundation of a heaven on earth. Erin emerges as a complicated female figure, both beautiful magnificence to be adorned by her children and the mother that weeps for the loss of her saintly sons; mistress and servant to fallen heroes. The heroes themselves are religious-nationalist martyrs dying to defend the purity and chastity of their nation-as-religion. The entwining of Celtic with Catholic mythology produces the land as both a pagan living spirit and a Christian Madonna figure. The image of Mother (Mary) Ireland is a Sorelian myth, embodiment of, and itself, that to be maintained and achieved. This figure of the nation, and with it of woman, occupies an ambivalent position – in some moments divine in itself, in others the route through which divinity is achieved by martyrs, and in still others the figure of divinity yet to be achieved – one who must suffer in order to confirm the true nature of the nation-spirit.

Within this kind of discourse distinctive roles are offered to men and women. The man is the brave hero boldly defending Her, his motherland, the source of his being. But She is only this in as much as it is he that protects Her, worships Her, and defends Her honour. She is sometimes warrior, most times mother, passive yet an activating image, often weeping and always suffering. Her position is entirely dependent on the actions of the male heroes at the same time as they appear to be acting only in response to Her.

Irishmen – defenders of the woman-nation

Where women are positioned in the family or made into stoic, weeping heroines, the young man is portrayed as the spirit of the ancient Gael and seed of the future greatness of Ireland. Emphasis is placed on the full development of that male youth in his spiritual, moral, cultural and especially physical dimensions. These fuse with cultural nationalism in sport. The *Bulletin* is preoccupied with using sport, and the training associated with it, to assert a physical ideal, which in turn develops a spiritual and moral one. The advice offered on the correct training procedures forms part of discourses not only of the body but specifically of the Irish male body and the characteristics of Irish manhood. Emphasis is placed on the way in which national games can 'develop the qualities of determination and endurance'. It is 'one of the primary duties of our time to produce a generation eminently capable of fearless effort in the struggles that life always brings and in the national undertakings of the race'. The qualities embodied in Gaelic sports are conducive not only to good physique but also good character:

> The ideal physical man should display activity and possess endurance, and these qualities are best developed by the practice of field games…Out-door games supplemented by a rational culture of the body…will give a strong and shapely formation to the growing youth…the out-door game, under sympathetic guidance, encourages and develops the moral qualities and virtues of courage, promptness, presence of mind, resolution, comradeship and humanity.
>
> (*Catholic Bulletin* 1920: 171)

Where women were spoken of in direct connection to religious imagery and mythic archetypes, men are discussed in drier, 'scientific' and 'rational' terms, where physical control is utmost. The historicity and legendary status of Gaelic games is asserted, and their relation to national defence stressed: Hurling, 'the most ancient national game…had its origin with the infancy of the race, is inter-woven with the national legends and stories, with their prowess on a hundred battle fields, with their long and enduring struggle for national existence' (*Catholic Bulletin* 1920: 173). It is laid down as a principle that 'to give a healthy training to all is the object to be aimed at in the physical exercise of boys' (1920: 173; see also Mottier, Chapter 10 of this volume). The boy who refuses to play, from 'delicacy, awkwardness, or timidity due to previous conditions of life', must be taken firmly in hand and subjected to a strict regimen:

> [F]or the weak boy something akin to medical treatment will be needed – the luke-warm bath followed by a good rubbing, gradually leading in the warmer months of the year to a sponging of warm water succeeded by a cold shower-bath and a vigorous rubbing with a rough towel; sea bathing, suitable diet and walking. After a course of treatment of this kind many a weak boy will become normally vigorous and will take his part in almost any game. It is neglect during the early years of college life which often leads to chronic delicacy in boys of this type.
>
> (*Catholic Bulletin* 1919: 665).

Detail and 'scientificity' are of clear importance in this distinctly medicalised approach. This is instantly reminiscent of Foucault's remarks on training proce-dure in *Discipline and Punish* (1977). The bodies under analysis are subject to a power that 'regards individuals both as objects and as instruments of its exercise' (Foucault 1977: 170). As Foucault points out: 'The success of disciplinary power derives no doubt from the use of simple instruments: hierarchical observation, normalising judgement [both of which are in evidence here] and their combina-tion in a procedure that is specific to it – the examination' (1977: 170). Sure enough this has a place in the training of Young Ireland: 'to place the physical training of boys on a scientific basis, medical examination of the individual is a necessity' (*Catholic Bulletin* 1920: 45). A detailed record of each boy is to be kept recording his strengths and weaknesses: 'drill and gymnastic exercises may then easily be chosen for the rational development of the boys as a whole' (1920: 45). The production of such rationally developed bodies, as the ideal masculine national subject, is the outcome to which this practice is oriented.

Where women are immobile, in the home, a line of defence in their lack of movement and resolution, the male is definitively mobile – not to be confined in colleges with little space but to be outside engaging in full physical activity (*Catholic Bulletin* 1920: 171–2). However, this access to open space and engagement in physical activity is itself constrained by the precision with which these movements are defined by the discourse of Irish manhood. The potential contradictions of such a discourse are held in place by the oppositions around which it turns. The discipline and rigour of the rational training of manhood is opposite to the non-rational, mythic and pre-modern image of the women of Ireland. Within this context the demand for independence and modern statehood emerges from manhood, yet cannot threaten the traditional, 'pre-modern' mythology of ancient Ireland that is contained within the sphere of womanhood. In order to understand the importance of these oppositions we turn now to a central metaphor of this discourse – the body.

Bodies of Ireland

With the body, many signifiers converge, forming a point of confluence for a number of discourses. The body can represent the social body of the nation, which in turn can be represented by the female body imagined, like the nation, as under attack, pierced by the invasions of foreigners yet resolute. It is an immobile body that is a necessary grounding of social actions and political resistance, yet itself derives power and significance from its lack of movement. It is a body of mythic significance, be it the myths of female heroines or 'actual' heroines made mythic by their attachment to the signifier of the national body. Across the surface of this body run the bodies of men. Produced by ascetic training and assiduous regulation, these bodies serve to defend the female woman-nation and to institute the necessary processes for its permanent sanctity.

This attention to bodily matters is carried into the writings of the *Bulletin* pertaining to morality and literary culture. Immoral literature is a foreign 'pestilence' and alien infection. In the first issue a short article entitled 'A Crying Evil' (*Catholic Bulletin* 1911: 216–18) expresses concern at the 'delinquencies of our maids' caused by the poor-quality literature at their disposal. The author writes of the 'sensation of horror upon reflecting that the young, ignorant and practically unsupervised of the humbler classes have at their disposal a means of reaching and gathering the most unsavoury fruits of the Tree of Knowledge'. This is a literature that will awaken in readers' minds a feeling 'as enervating as it is wrong', a feeling of 'longings only too frequently realised through sin'. Immoral literature stimulates the body but it stimulates the wrong bodies –

women, children, the lower classes – and it stimulates them in the wrong way. This literature, imported by the enemy, then becomes regarded as a terrible attack on the Irish body – the social body – and becomes an exemplary case of the degeneration caused by colonial rule. The cure, however, is not absent: 'we are not without an antidote to the insidious poison with which the English Press is flooding us. The Irish Press has a high standard of purity, thank God, even that branch of it which is non-sectarian and caters only for the amusement of the multitude' (*Catholic Bulletin* 1911: 218). In returning to the purity of Irish products, the body can be protected.

This crusade for decent literature is not merely that. In the way in which it is constructed, it crosses over into discourses about morality, health and national culture. The drive for morality through control is clearly embedded in sexual concerns, in a concern that sometimes comes across as ridiculous in its portrayal of other nations and cultures. An article on 'Some Traits of the Catholic Gael' (*Catholic Bulletin* 1916: 99–105) informs us that the Irish, though friendly to strangers, are an aloof and private people when it comes to their affection, both personal and religious. Indeed, 'near relatives among us refrain from lavishing caresses on each other in public' (1916: 101). Other nations reveal their degeneracy through the improper, uncontrolled, use of their bodies, allowing them to be vehicles for the expression of love in inappropriate, public, spaces. The Irish body must be controlled – controlled by the self to ward off sin, controlled by the correct physical training, controlled by confinement in the home, controlled so as to defy the debilitating influence of foreigners. The only place for public expression of physicality is in the ordered exertion of the playing field or in the expression of physical force, where the body becomes a symbol of defence and defiance and where its blood is shed in the name of the land of Erin.

Consequences

The *Catholic Bulletin* was not the only place in which such discourses could be found during the pre-independence period. Mythic symbolism was central, not incidental, to the mobilisation of the nationalist movement after the mythic sacrifice of the Dublin 'rising' of 1916 against the British. The Proclamation delivered by Patrick Pearse from the steps of the General Post Office in Dublin is itself alive with this kind of imagery. It begins: 'Irishmen and Irishwomen: In the name of God and of the dead generations from which she receives her old tradition of nationhood, Ireland through us, summons her children to her flag and strikes for freedom.' Ireland is anthropomorphised as a mother, while the rebels and those who support them are but children called to her defence. Interestingly, in this passage, Ireland is held to invoke itself, through the prism of the rebels, and does so in the name of God *and* in the name of past ideas and ancient tradition. Ireland is invoked via the two poles of religion and Gaelicism, the two functioning as fixing points and articulated together in discourse such that each can invoke the other.

The connection between this sort of religious/maternal imagery and the masculinity of the heroes who will protect her is in evidence throughout Pearse's writings. In *The Coming Revolution* he wrote: 'we may make mistakes in the beginning and shoot the wrong people; but bloodshed is a cleansing and sanctifying thing, and the nation which regards it as the final horror has lost its *manhood*' (Pearse 1966, my emphasis).

This sort of discourse did not cease having effects once independence was achieved. De Valera regularly spoke in this way, referring, for example, to 'we the children of a race that has never ceased to strive, that endured for ages the blights of war and the disappointments of peace', and urging Irish America to 'band yourselves together to use your united strength to help break the chains that bind our sad sweet mother' (Moynihan 1980: 35). One of the most famous of De Valera's pronouncements on the national culture is that given in his St Patrick's Day broadcast in 1943. The Ireland that he says he and everyone else dreams of would be the home of a people who valued material wealth only as the basis of right living, of a people who were satisfied with frugal comfort and devoted their leisure to the things of the spirit – a land whose countryside would be bright with cosy homesteads, whose fields and villages would be joyous with the sounds of industry, with the romping of sturdy children, the contests of athletic youths and the laughter of comely maidens, whose firesides would be forums for the wisdom of serene old age. It would, in a word, be the home of a people living the life that God desires that man should live (Moynihan 1980: 466–9). This is a vision of a rural past that again evokes the gender roles that sustain it – the athletic youths and the comely maidens.

One way of clarifying the form and functioning of these discourses is by recognising them as revolving round two sets of binary oppositions, where the crucial distinction is that between inside and outside (Chatterjee 1990; Radhakrishnan 1992). The two sets are as follows:

A	B
Outside – Inside	Outside – Inside
Male – Female	Male – Female
English – Irish	State – Nation
Modern – Traditional	Modern – Traditional
Immoral – Moral	Active – Passive
Material – Spiritual	Material – Spiritual
Cultural – Natural	Urban – Rural
Global – Local	Public – Private

In constructing an essential notion of the true and good Irish people, nationalist discourse constructs a vision of the pre-administered, natural way of the Gael. It becomes concerned with a pre-modern, in one sense literally prehistoric, concept of the people and attendant imaginings of homeland. This homeland, while presented as still viable and recoverable, is under threat from outside, from the intervention of the coloniser. A duality is founded between this homeland, as inside (traditional, earthy, spiritual, moral and Irish) and the external coloniser, outside (modern, cultured, material, immoral and English).

The way in which the Irish is to be protected, that is to say the way in which the discourse of Irish nationalism is maintained, is not by the destruction of this dichotomy but by a refiguring of it and a shift in sets of oppositions. The language of statehood, of national autonomy, is a discourse that is not indigenous to the colonised nation but derives from the modern, the Enlightenment, and the 'foreign'. The 'English' cannot simply be banished, rather the 'Irish' has to be revived in order to displace it. This entails the acquisition of state power by the indigenous people. The possibility that such transplanting, moving to occupy the position of the occupier, would undermine Irishness, shifting the 'natural' and 'traditional' to the outer pole, is avoided by a shift in oppositions revolving around this inside/outside public/private distinction. In the present case we see that the state introduces the public/private dichotomy, between that concerned with matters of state, and the 'private', familial realm. The state becomes the terrain of the public sphere, an institution maintained as 'outside' in order to prevent it from interfering with the indigenous 'inside'. The nation then becomes cast as the private sphere, of nature, the home, etc., autonomous but only in as much as it is maintained and administered by the state. Thus the state emerges as both the protector and guarantor of the nation, yet at the same time ideologically legitimated as inferior to the nation, for it is the nation that is the progenitor and justification of the state.

When we map gender distinctions onto this a clear picture emerges. The state is the masculine machine that defends and controls the woman-nation, while the woman-nation is confined to the private and homely – the source of the physical and cultural regeneration and reproduction of the nation. Women have the duty of bearing new Irish children and constituting them as properly Irish by training them in the ways of the Gael. Women are cast as 'inside' while men are cast as 'outside'. This produces the paradox that women are more important and essential than men yet deprives them of power. The woman-nation is both goddess (source of power, object of veneration) and victim (assaulted by colonialism, in need of guidance from the state). Men can never 'be' the nation – they can only 'have' it – while women can never 'have' the nation, because they 'are' it.

This leads the state to take on a role in interfering with the 'natural' sphere in order to regulate it. Article 41 of the Irish Constitution adopted by the state in 1937 casts this ideological position in the law. Here the state 'recognises the Family as the natural primary and fundamental unit group of Society, and as a moral institution possessing inalienable rights, antecedent and superior to all positive law' (Article 41, 1, 1) – that is, it is subject to a natural law that predates and is higher than the law of the state, part of the private, natural, spiritual realm. The state 'guarantees to protect the Family in its constitution and authority, as the necessary basis of social order and indispensable to the welfare of the Nation and the State' (Article 41, 1, 2).

This entails a constitutional position on women and the claim that 'by her life within the home, woman gives the State support without which the common good cannot be achieved' (Article 41, 2, 1). 'The State shall, therefore, endeavour to ensure that mothers shall not be obliged by economic necessity to engage in labour to the neglect of their duties in the home' (Article 41, 2, 2). This in turn led to the constitutional bar on divorce, as the State will 'guard with special care the institution of Marriage, on which the Family is founded and to protect it against attack' (Article 41, 3, 1). This prohibition stood until overturned by referendum in 1995.

The implications of this in terms of sexual politics are obvious. It justifies religio-nationalist patriarchy making Irishness and womanhood inextricable. Indeed the Irish state has periodically gone into convulsions when confronted with issues regarding the status of women, unborn children, marriage and divorce, because the law and the Constitution stand as the definitive expression of the identity of the state as conferred on it by God and the Nation. Yet that nation is itself defined in terms of woman, hence the two come into conflict, and central signifiers of the State, 'Irishness' and 'Family' begin to collapse.

The only way for the state to maintain this sort of discourse is to reduce the significance of one or other of the signifiers. Hence it reduces women to their reproductive/sexual functions – that is, their function in relation to the reproduction of the population, subordinating them to the 'good' of the nation. The apotheosis of this is the crises over abortion experienced in Ireland in the 1980s: the 1983 constitutional referendum that resulted in the addition of a pro-life clause and subsequently the infamous 'X-case', in which a 14-year-old rape victim was prevented from leaving Ireland for Britain in order to undergo an abortion. In this case the rights of actual women were overridden in the name of protecting the sanctity of the reproductive activity of archetypal woman.

But the impact of these frames of thought is not only to be observed in reactionary political discourse. In some variants of feminist thinking in Ireland the association between the status of the nation and the status of women is also maintained. This leads to the belief that women can only be free if the nation is made free from the state – that is, the establishment of a full thirty-two-county republic. Thus, for example, Anne Speed (Smyth 1992: 85–98) links the liberation of women to a republican-nationalist, anti-European politics that joins the fight for independence in the North to the fight for a progressive Ireland and women's rights. The settlement of 1922 and the hegemony of conservative elements is identified as related to the deformation of the nation-state and the incompletion of independence as manifested by partition. Thus Ireland was never made free, is still oppressed by capitalism and colonial forces, and the fight must continue. In winning that fight, the rights of women will also be won, and in fighting for women's rights, one is fighting against the deformed state and for a 'free' Ireland (the real Ireland, of course, would never oppress women). The link between women and Irishness/Irish independence is maintained, and there cannot be any autonomy to a campaign for women's rights. Despite a modified articulation, the identitarian logic of nationalism remains intact.

Conclusions

As a form of discourse, nationalism is not confined to those countries under-going major conflict or containing secessionary movements. Billig (1995) draws attention to 'banal nationalism', the myriad ways in which a sense of nation-ness is routinely reinforced in Western states through the media, everyday language, symbols and so forth. The presence of discourses of nationality within popular and political discourse is often ignored, as is the way in which such discourse can contribute to other modes of discourse, such as those regarding the regulation of sexuality, morality, gender roles and bodily behaviour. In this respect there is nothing unique about Irish nationalism, although the configurations of discourse within it are specific to the circumstances and context of its development.

Discourses of nationality are not reducible to debates about the state of the nation or the meaning of nationhood, but rather nation is a category that circu-lates within the frame of this discourse, modifying it in its articulation, working to add support to an argument (for example, 'something is wrong because it will corrupt the national soul') and to earn support for itself (for example, 'people support this who want to destroy the nation, therefore if you oppose them you should support your nation'). Nation is a central articulating signifier within these discourses in the double sense of articulating a worldview and joining together differing elements.

This is not to say that nation necessarily takes a primacy within these discourses. Whether it is nation or sexuality that takes primacy within a discur-sive intervention is a matter of the specific strategies in play at any one moment, and it is for analysis to specify more precisely the nature of the configuration. Analysis of the discourses of nationalism can uncover the ways in which it inter-acts with other modes of discourse and can open up for scrutiny the ways in which, when we say one thing, we may also be saying another. This is part of the ideological institution of modern societies. The role of ideology, suggests Claude Lefort, is to obscure the fact the society is historical and self-instituting, to contin-ually cover over the divisions and historicity of the social order (Lefort 1984: 190–1). Our task is to uncover the ways in which these dense discourses operate and expose the manner in which they can inflect political discourse, be it of the Left or Right, and develop an adequate critique of these fictions, uproot the mythic anchoring of the social, and destabilise essentialist identitarianism.

References

Anderson, B. 1992. *Imagined Communities*. London: Verso.
Billig, M. 1995. *Banal Nationalism*. London: Sage.
Cairns, D., and Richards, S. 1988. *Writing Ireland*. Manchester: Manchester University Press.
Catholic Bulletin and Book Review. 1911–1939. Dublin: M.H. Gill.
Chatterjee, P. 1990. 'The nationalist resolution of the women's question'. In K. Sangari and S. Vaid (eds), *Recasting Women: Essays in Indian Colonial History*. New Brunswick NJ: Rutgers University Press.

Foucault, M. 1977. *Discipline and Punish: The Birth of the Prison*. London: Allen Lane.

—— 1989. *The Archaeology of Knowledge*. London: Routledge.

Laclau, E. 1979. *Politics and Ideology in Marxist Theory: Capitalism – Fascism – Populism*. London: Verso.

Lefort, C. 1984. *The Political Forms of Modern Society*. Cambridge: Polity Press.

Longley, E. 1990. *From Cathleen to Anorexia: The Breakdown of Irelands*. Dublin: Attic Press (LIP Pamphlet).

Meaney, G. 1991. *Sex and Nation: Women in Irish Culture and Politics*. Dublin: Attic Press (LIP Pamphlet).

Mosse, G. 1985. *Nationalism and Sexuality: Respectability and Abnormal Sexuality in Modern Europe*. New York: H. Fertig.

Moynihan, M. (ed.). 1980. *Speeches and Statements by Eamonn De Valera*. Dublin: Gill & Macmillan.

Parker, A., Russo, M., Sommer, D., and Yaeger, P. 1992. *Nationalisms and Sexualities*. London: Routledge.

Pearse, P. 1966. *Political Writings and Speeches*. Dublin: Talbot.

Radhakrishnan, R. 1992. 'Nationalism, gender and the narrative of identity'. In A. Parker, M. Russo, D. Sommer, and P. Yaeger, *Nationalisms and Sexualities*, pp. 77–95. London: Routledge.

Renan, E. 1897. *The Poetry of the Celtic Races*. London: Walter Scott.

Smyth, A. 1992. 'A sadistic farce – women and abortion in the Republic of Ireland, 1992'. In A. Smyth (ed.), *The Abortion Papers*, pp. 7–24. Dublin: Attic Press.

Speed, A. 1992. 'The struggle for reproductive rights: a brief history in its political context'. In A. Smyth (ed.), *The Abortion Papers*, pp. 85–98. Dublin: Attic Press.

9　Sexuality and civilisation

Weber and Freud

Gail Hawkes

The nineteenth century in Britain saw the culmination of a prolonged as well as steep rise in population, rapid urbanisation and technological developments in production. The inevitable disruption of traditional modes of work organisation and of the social relations that accompanied them, as well as the emergence of a fully fledged new ruling class, meant that this was truly the century of what Kumar has called 'the great transformation' (Kumar 1978). Yet it was not free of its insecurities and contradictions – particularly about the hegemonic status of the bourgeoisie, and of the effectiveness of their ideologies. As Peter Gay has reminded us: 'what the bourgeois had in common was the negative quality of being neither aristocrats nor labourer, and of being uneasy in their middle class skins' (Gay 1984: 3). While being principal actors and prime movers in the upheavals of old certainties associated with modernity, they were also at the vortex of its psychological consequences. A key feature of the great transformation was, therefore, the move to establish and disseminate new moral imperatives as the basis for a new social coherence. It is in the context of these imperatives of 'the civilising process' (Elias 1982) that the contributions of Weber and Freud will be examined.

For Weber, the hallmark of modernity is the rational organisation of human action, in the economic, political and social spheres. This 'means-end' orientation of human action requires the removal of all irrational and unpredictable elements. In presenting Calvinist beliefs as the key ideological input to the success of capitalism, Weber illustrates the impact of 'worldly asceticism' on sexual and erotic life. Freud's argument (see also Gibbins, Chapter 3 of this volume) about the relationship of 'civilisation' or modernity to sexual and erotic life is centred on the notion of the essential redirection and suppression of (original) polymorphous desires into the narrowed and ultimately unsatisfactory outlet of marital reproductive coitus. In the work of both men, modernity carries with it an inevitable loss of the richness and depth of human experience – no more so than in the experience of erotic desire and pleasure.

Freud, perverse pleasures and civilised sexual morality

By the end of the nineteenth century, scrutiny of 'the sexual' had moved outside the dominance of the Church. Increasingly, as a central if implicit element in public-health discourses and in pronouncements about the problem of the urban poor, sexual behaviour was subjected to secular scientific scrutiny (Keating 1972; Mort 1987). The science of sex was also essentially a post-Enlightenment project. The centrality of nature in its discourses; the faith in human reason to tame the 'beast within'; the commitment to observe, classify and record, rather than judge and punish; and the search to establish universal fixed paradigms of 'normal' and 'abnormal' are all features evident in this new endeavour (see also Mottier, Chapter 10 of this volume). The frames of reference as well as the outcomes of this scrutiny were consistent with and related to the central preoccupation of bourgeois ideology – stable, predictable ordered human behaviour in every sphere of life.

The conjunction of these factors produced an orthodoxy that underpinned the central pillars of bourgeois society. First, the endeavour provided a scientific basis for the naturalness of heterosexuality. Second, it legitimated the fiction of the 'asexual woman', or, at least, the erotic superiority of men. Third, through the preoccupation with the establishment of fixed categories, the science of sex simultaneously isolated and marginalised a wide range of erotic activities – specifically those that were non-reproductive and/or non-genital.

A key feature of sexology was the division of sexual behaviour into the binary distinction of 'normal' and 'perverse' – a distinction that represented a moral as well as scientific judgement. The notion of 'perverse' sexual practices demarcated certain expressions of desire and sources of pleasure as morally transgressive as well as injurious to health. The legitimation for the negative valuation of 'perverse sexual practices' – those that did not have reproduction as an outcome – was that they were 'unnatural'. The essentialist reading of nature that underwrote normality represents a flaw in the science of sex, and of the Enlightenment thinking from which it derived. It was within this assumption that nature was deployed to underwrite moral distinctions. Perverse sexual practices were thus not only unnatural but also wrong. Freud's work reflected its location in the paradigms of scientific enquiry, notably dispassionate classification and the commitment to isolate universal categories and causalities. Yet there were within his work significant challenges to the approaches and outcomes.

Sexual perversion is a central element in Freud's theories of sexuality. While in keeping with the science of sex he deploys the argument of the 'natural' equating to the 'normal', what constitutes these categories, and therefore what constitutes the perverse, is, in his work, reversed. Far from being evidence of an individual pathology, 'the disposition to perversions of every kind is a general and fundamental human characteristic', and 'something innate in everyone' (Freud 1986a: 87, 109). As Dollimore comments: 'the real conservative is the pervert...it is sexual perversion, not sexual normality, which is the given in

human nature' (Dollimore 1991: 176). All humans are born with polymor-
phously perverse potentials, which are demonstrable in the behaviour of the
infant at the breast, an original pleasure later rewritten in other autoerotic activities, including, though not exclusively involving, masturbation. This propensity
both illustrates and provides an outlet for 'uncivilised' – that is to say, socially
unregulated – sensory pleasures. In modernity, judgement about direction of the
sexual instinct, whether in children or adults, depends on whether the erotic
activity under scrutiny is directed towards reproduction (normal) or pleasure
(perverse) as the primary aim. Characterising these views, Freud comments:

> We actually describe a sexual activity as perverse if it has given up the aim
> of reproduction and pursues the attainment of pleasure as an aim indepen-
> dent of it...The breach and turning point of sexual life lies in it becoming
> subordinate to the purposes of reproduction. Everything which happens
> before this turn of events, and equally everything which disregards it and
> that aims solely at pleasure, is given the uncomplimentary name of
> 'perverse' and as such is proscribed.
>
> (Freud 1974: 258)

The distinction between the aims of the sexual instinct in terms of pleasure and
its eventual outcome in terms of reproduction is not a distinction that is chosen
but is rather one that is imposed by social norms. The sublimation of a primary
aim of pleasure within a reproductive imperative is, for Freud, the inescapable
consequence of civilisation through the imposition of what he calls 'civilised
sexual morality'. In his 1908 essay *'Civilised' Sexual Morality and Modern Nervous
Illness*, Freud (1986b) argues that 'the most injurious influence of civilisation
reduces itself, in the main, to the harmful suppression of the sexual life of
civilised people (or classes) through the civilised sexual morality prevalent in
them' (Freud 1986b: 185). Sexual life suffers this fate because the sex instinct is
constant, strongly developed and 'does not originally serve the purpose of reproduction at all, but has as its aim the gaining of particular kinds of pleasure'
(1986b: 188). For Freud, infantile pleasure from feeding, excreting and genital
stimulation are the original source and manifestation of erotic pleasure. The
sexual instinct in this 'uncivilised' state is directed towards the sole aim of
pleasure. The intervention of cultural influences is essential to redirect the sexual
instinct away from the primary aim of pleasure, and, in particular, autoerotic
pleasure. Failure to do so, he says, 'would make the sexual instinct uncontrollable
and unserviceable later on' (Freud 1986b: 188).

This view can be read as universal in its application, not directly associated
with or causally related to one specific historical period. Yet this was a man of
his time, who, despite his (still) startling proposals, is clearly situated within the
dominant bourgeois norms. In the context of modernity and of the social and
sexual norms that prevailed, the sexual instinct is redirected from pleasure to
aims that are 'serviceable to civilisation': reproductive marital heterosexual coitus
– the definitive features of 'normal' sexuality in the paradigms of the science of

sex. While located in a discourse of the individual, there are social consequences that are of particular resonance in the late nineteenth and early twentieth centuries.

In the late nineteenth century, forced late marriage (for economic reasons) and the construction of the asexual woman (for ideological reasons) were lodged in a discourse that promoted procreative marital sex as quintessentially natural and therefore normal, hence a high degree of sexual abstinence both before and after marriage is unavoidable. Freud points out that in the absence of adequate contraception and the discouragement of marital sex for pleasure, fleeting opportunities for the experience of legitimate sexual pleasure diminish and disappear within the first few years. Subsequently marital sexual life is characterised by 'spiritual disillusionment and bodily deprivation' (Freud 1986b: 194). The prevailing gendered sexuality, a key element in civilised sexual morality, produces women who are 'sexually anaesthetic'. The more 'civilised' their upbringing, the more this will be so. The stricter demands for chastity and virginity imposed on women by civilisation blight their ability to adjust to the limited sexual opportunities that marriage provides.

> When her capacity to love is awakened at the climax of her life as a woman, her relations to her husband have long been ruined; and as a reward for her previous docility she is left with a choice between unappeased desire, unfaithfulness or a neurosis.
>
> (Freud 1986b: 198)

Sexually unfulfilled marriages also impact on public morality, feeding male demand for prostitution:

> We need not enquire how far [men] frequently avail themselves of the degree of sexual freedom which is allowed them – although only with reluctance and under the veil of silence – by even the strictest sexual code. The 'double' sexual morality which is valid for men in our society is the plainest admission that society itself does not believe in the possibility of enforcing the precepts which it itself has laid down.
>
> (Freud 1986b: 195)

In his 1929 essay *Civilisation and its Discontents* (Freud 1986c: 64 ff.) Freud makes more explicit the interconnections between the historical context and the direction of the instinct to pleasure. In modernity, 'economic necessity' demands that energies previously expended in sex for pleasure be redirected into more appropriate political and social channels. This project is, however, inherently unstable and requires rigorous monitoring at the earliest stage, for 'there would be no prospect of curbing the lusts of an adult if the ground had not been prepared in childhood' (Freud 1986c: 104).

The redirection of the polymorphous pleasures with which we are born is a necessary element in the progression from child to adulthood. Civilisation demands that 'the choice of an object [of desire] is restricted to the opposite sex, and most extra-genital satisfactions are forbidden as perversions' (Freud 1986c: 104). It is required 'that there be a single kind of sexual life for everyone; disregarding the dissimilarities whether innate or acquired in the sexual constitution of human beings' (1986c: 104). This normative direction of desires suggests the acknowledgement rather than the denial of possible variations in sexual choice. It is also a recognition of the threat that these tendencies pose to the fragile 'order' of civilisation. 'Society believes that no greater threat to its civilisation could arise than if the sexual instincts were to be liberated and returned to their original aims' (Freud 1974: 48). The reality of this threat is illustrated in the further constriction of *legitimate* outlets of heterosexual coitus, and in particular of the possibilities for sexual pleasure:

> Present day civilisation makes it plain that it will only permit sexual relationships on the basis of a solitary indissoluble bond between one man and one woman, and that it does not like sexuality as a source of pleasure in its own right and is only prepared to tolerate it because there is so far no substitute for it as a means for propagating the human race.
>
> (Freud 1986c: 105)

Freud's account of the negative effects of civilisation on expressions of human sexual desire bears a striking resemblance to Weber's account of the impact of rationality on sexual life.

Weber, rationality and sexual asceticism

Rationality was the 'distinctive feature of modern Western social order' (Brubaker 1984: 9): a form of organisation of society characterised by the calculability of both the means and outcome of human action. Rationalisation demands the development and demarcation of bodies of specialised knowledge and the ascendancy of 'specialists'; the progressive erosion of traditional beliefs and practices: 'the development of increasingly powerful techniques for controlling men and nature' (Brubaker 1984: 37); and the extension of a means-end strategy to all spheres of life. A social order characterised by these features is one 'founded on the "dominion of conscienceless reason"' (Weber quoted in Brubaker 1984: 44). For the process of rationalisation 'demands the complete elimination from official business of love, hatred and all purely personal irrational and emotional elements which escape calculation' (Brubaker 1984: 2).

For Weber, the defining feature of modern Western culture is not just the existence of rationalisation but its intrusion into every sphere of human life. The original purpose behind the choice of means was their 'orientation towards man and his needs' (Brubaker 1984: 68). But the extent to which the 'arrangements, institutions and activities' of modern life are rationalised constrains rather than enables the expression of human needs and the orientation of action to serve them. 'That which was originally a mere means becomes an end itself. In this way, means as ends make themselves independent and thus lose their original purpose' (Brubaker 1984: 68). The framework that once guaranteed human freedom comes to 'enclose and determine humanity like an iron cage' (Brubaker 1984: 68). Humans are left with the remnants of 'freedom', the freedom to adjust to the creation that has escaped the control of its creator.

The calculability and predictability of the modern social order was not established nor assured solely in the administrative and economic spheres of modern Western capitalism. Nor, Weber argues, are the social features of capitalism to be explained in these terms alone. In *The Protestant Ethic and the Spirit of Capitalism*, he examines two related and key elements in the teachings of English Puritanism that link ascetic Protestantism with the calculability that is the essence of rational economic life: the 'calling' and 'worldly asceticism'. In previous teachings of medieval religion, work was valued as a means to 'preserve the life of the individual and the community' (Weber in Runciman 1994: 144). To work was to worship God, an obligation that was not just an act of worship but a sign of being one of the chosen faithful. There were two further requirements. First, that work should be 'unceasing, constant and systematic' (Weber in Runciman 1994: 161). Idleness and time-wasting were the worst of all sins. Second, to increase the fruits of labour is both a sign of grace and a duty to God. Accumulation of wealth is 'not only permissible but positively commended' (Weber in Runciman 1994: 148). The two obligations thus positively value, even require, the rational organisation of work: the structuring of the working day, advanced division of labour and keeping of accounts and ledgers, and the background of dispassionate bureaucratic administration.

The second and related key belief is 'worldly asceticism'. While the accumulation of wealth is a sign of grace ('to wish to be poor is the same as to wish to be ill'), the enjoyment of such riches in 'idle repose and sinful enjoyment of life' is a sign of moral turpitude. The eternal hazard of the possession of property and of wealth is that it might result in 'sloth and lusts of the flesh' (Weber in Runciman 1994: 140). Worldly asceticism thus recognises and confronts the human tendency to surrender to pleasures of the flesh. This belief distinguishes itself from monasticism, which demands the withdrawal of the vulnerable soul from the possibility of temptation. Worldly asceticism offers no such refuge. Its efficacy depends on believers being exposed to the ever-present temptations of the flesh, requiring denial *within* the context of the everyday world. The rational management of pleasure is moved, through these religious teachings, into the secular sphere as a key moral precept in every aspect of life. In relation to physical exercise, sustenance, sleep and even cultural pursuits, 'asceticism lay like a frost over Merry England' (Weber in Runciman 1994: 156). Unruly pleasures, 'superfluous, vain ostentations' undertaken for their own sake, were 'purposeless' and thus irrational.

The net of rationality underpinned by asceticism extends also to erotic life. 'The struggle against fleshly lust' was 'the struggle against the irrational use of possessions' (Weber in Runciman 1994: 160). Sexual desire was a 'possession', but not one that implied freedom of use (or of denial). It was, like the capacity to work, a gift from God. Thus, 'even in marriage, sexual intercourse is permitted only as the means willed by God to increase His glory, in accordance with the commandment to "be fruitful and multiply" ' (Weber in Runciman 1994: 143). Sexual asceticism requires the rational ordering of sexual desire, in reproductive marital union:

> This type of marriage is accepted as one of the divine ordinations given to man as a creature who is hopelessly wretched by virtue of his 'concupiscence'. Within this divine order it is given to man to live according to the rational purposes laid down by it and only according to them: to procreate and to rear children.
>
> (Weber in Gerth and Mills 1970: 349)

In *The Religious Rejections of the World and their Directions* (in Gerth and Mills 1970: 344), Weber discusses a dimension of sexual desire and pleasure that provides respite from the bleakness of the teaching of salvation religion. He contrasts the 'naive naturalism of sex' – unsublimated and unregulated sexual desire – with a conscious expression in 'the erotic sphere'. The former, he argues, is not consistent with advanced cultural development, yet is amenable to rational ordering. 'Inner-worldly rational asceticism…gathers the primal, naturalist, and *un*sublimated sexuality of the peasant into a rational order of man as creature' (Weber in Gerth and Mills 1970: 349). The 'untidy ends' of desire that fall outside this containing framework may be tolerated as unavoidable 'residues of the Fall'. 'According to Luther, God, in order to prevent worse, peeks at and is lenient to these [residual] elements of passion' (Weber in Gerth and Mills 1970: 49).

Weber's account of the 'erotic sphere' stands in opposition to this process. Eroticism, for Weber, is the outcome of the stylised sublimation of natural sexual instincts. 'The extraordinary quality of eroticism has consisted precisely in the gradual turning away from the naive naturalism of sex' (Weber in Gerth and Mills 1970: 344). The erotic sphere is impermeable to the strategies of rationality. It is a domain in which 'the greatest irrational force of life: sexual love' (1970: 343) is subject to regulation but is crucially *unroutinised*. The sublimation of natural desires into stylised pleasures thus elevated the erotic sphere beyond the confines of rationalism. Because of this elevation, eroticism appeared to be 'like a gate into the most irrational and therefore the real kernel of life, as compared with the mechanisms of rationalisation' (1970: 345).

The trajectory of the development of the erotic sphere has a history that far predates the ascendance of sexual asceticism. Weber argues that from the Hellenic period, through the Middle Ages to the Renaissance, sexuality in one form or another was sublimated in a variety of manifestations of 'the erotic sphere'. In the 'exclusively masculine character' of the Hellenic period, the 'deadly earnestness of love' was recognised in the ceremony of the love of boys. Later the 'cultural conditioning of feudal notions of honour…carried over the symbols of knightly vassalship into the erotically sublimated sexual relation'

(Weber in Gerth and Mills 1970: 345). The casting off of the 'sexual asceticism of the Christian knighthood', in the context of the Renaissance, conferred upon social and political intercourse both an 'overt and latent' sexual significance. But, he points out, 'the last accentuation of the erotic sphere...occurred when [it] collided with the unavoidably ascetic trait of the vocational specialist type of man' (1970: 349) – the quintessentially rational individual.

The valuations of desire in the erotic sphere and in sexual asceticism stand at opposite poles. For the former, the rejection of the passionate character and the pleasurable potential of eroticism is 'blasphemy'. For the latter, the 'reinterpretation and glorification of the animality of sex' (Weber in Gerth and Mills 1970: 347) represents an 'undignified' loss of control [and the] loss of orientation towards either rationalisation and wisdom of 'norms' willed by God, or the mystic 'having of godliness' (1970: 349). Weber argues that the principles of asceticism and the routinisation of the erotic in marriage meant that 'extramarital sexual life...could appear as the only tie which still linked man with the natural fountain of life' (1970: 346).

Under the specific conditions of sexual asceticism, the erotic sphere represented a 'joyous triumph over rationality'. In place of the 'lifelessness' that rationality inevitably engenders, the erotic sphere offers a powerful context in which the pleasures of 'irrationality' can be experienced – the possibility of the 'boundless giving of oneself' in 'opposition to all functionality, rationality and generality' (Weber in Gerth and Mills 1970: 347). 'The lover realises himself to be rooted in the kernel of the truly living, which is eternally inaccessible to any rational endeavour. He knows himself to be free from the cold skeletal hands of rational orders just as completely as from the banalities of everyday routine' (1970: 347).

Conclusion: common themes and outcomes

From one point of view, the views expressed by Weber and Freud about the impact of civilisation come from divergent standpoints. Freud's preoccupation with the taming of the instincts draws on the spheres of the subconscious and of psychoanalysis. Read one way, Freud's arguments about the troubled acquisition of 'civilised sexual morality' places the individual, and in particular the neurotic individual, at the centre of his analysis of the 'discontents of civilisation'. Weber, on the other hand, charts and evaluates the impact of rationalisation in primarily social terms. Yet despite these distinctions in approach, there are a number of demonstrable commonalities. On a general level, both thinkers share a profound ambivalence, even pessimism, about the impact of modernity in both an individual and a social sense. Both see the civilising process as inexorable and all-encompassing. In the work of both there is an acknowledgement that the Enlightenment belief in the capacity of human reason to liberate human potential was (retrospectively) naïve. Less obvious in Freud's writings, but made explicit in those of Weber, is the correlation between the project to mould 'hearts and minds' and the imperatives of bourgeois capitalism.

At a more specific level, there is a common theme that the process of civilisation directly (and negatively) impacts on the experience and direction of sexual desire and pleasure. In this respect the two are perhaps unique as commentators of modernity. Once again, there are differences that reflect the authors' principal preoccupations. Freud's conception of the disruptive potential of sexual desire centres on his notion of 'original perversity' – the innate polymorphous erotic potential – shaped and severely proscribed in the transition from the egoistic child to the social adult. The disruptive potential has a twofold presence. On the one hand, there is the ever-present threat that such a transition will be partial or distorted at an individual level, delivering the neurotic, socially and culturally incompetent adult onto the social stage. On the other hand, the negative consequences of this containment of erotic potential extend beyond the individual to the social dimension in the imposition of 'civilised sexual morality'. There are implications that go beyond the realm of psychoanalysis.

For the constraints placed on erotic potential are directly linked with the imperative for reproductive coitus, and the gendered moulding (or distortion) of desire in ways that suit it more fully to the demands of the bourgeois era. This cultural and political context is made more explicit in Weber's work, both in *The Protestant Ethic and the Spirit of Capitalism* and *Religious Rejections of the World and their Directions*. The extension of rationalisation, legitimated and driven by the teachings of salvation religion into the sexual sphere, illuminates the problematic of desire at two levels. First, it indicates that the rationalisation of desires and pleasures was a crucial component in the successful establishment of the bourgeois hegemony and of its linchpin – modern Western capitalism. Second, in the closing passages of *The Protestant Ethic*, Weber argues that the 'original spirit of capitalism', the notion of the 'calling' that directed and shaped attitudes to rational economic activity, atrophied once this ethic was internalised and established in the secular context. 'It might indeed be true to say of the "last men" of this cultural development: "specialists without soul, hedonists without heart": this cipher flatters itself that it has reached a stage of humanity never before attained' (Weber in Runciman 1994: 171). This process is equally evident in the impact of the ethic of asceticism on the shaping of sexual desires. While this original logic may have atrophied, the centrality of heterosexual reproductive sex remained, while its unruly counterparts, expressions of desire directed primarily towards pleasure not procreation, were marginalised, even silenced.

There is a more subtle process at work here that extends beyond the primary promotion of heterosexual coitus. Both Weber and Freud recognise, in their accounts of the ordering of desires, the disruptive potential that pleasure, and specifically sexual pleasure, represents for the modern Western social order. This notion of the threat posed by sexual pleasure is not one that is confined to modernity. The disruptive elements of sexual desire have been acknowledged in one form or another throughout the development of Western sexual culture (Foucault 1985). In classical Greece the proper use of desire and sources of pleasure lay at the heart of the construction of a balanced individual. In early Christianity this positive valuation of desire and pleasure was reversed. Sexual desire and pleasure were constructed as an alien, non-human force representing danger and destruction to those who succumbed to temptation. The Old Testament fall from the Garden of Eden vividly underlines the view that sexual desire is an ever-present threat to and weakness in humanity, a disruptive element that must be excluded since it cannot be managed (Gilman 1989; Hawkes 1996).

In the work of Weber and Freud, both located firmly in the tradition of secular scientism, there is an account of an alternative strategy in the context of the establishment of the modern Western social order. The specific relationship between the routinisation of pleasure associated with civilised sexual morality and sexual asceticism emphasises the imperatives placed on unruly pleasures in the context of modernity and bourgeois hegemony. Both civilised sexual morality and sexual asceticism recognise that the routinisation of desires and pleasures is a fragile and unstable component of the modernising process. In the late twentieth century, vestiges of these anxieties about the unruliness of desire persist. In the British context these can be demonstrated in the continuing and unresolved debates about the age of homosexual consent (see Waites, Chapter 2 of this volume), about the 'problem' of the sexuality of the young in the areas of contraceptive provision and the decriminalisation of prostitution (see also Gorjanicyn, Chapter 16, and Outshoorn, Chapter 17 of this volume). In all these areas, the social and political opposition argues that promiscuity will be the inevitable result of extending erotic democracy. The self-constructed individual of late modernity cannot, it seems, be allowed the full smorgasbord of choice. In the post-permissive decades of the late twentieth century, anxieties about uncontrollable desires illustrate the continued viability of connections between individual pleasures and the maintenance of social order (see also Gibbins, Chapter 3 of this volume). The potentially subversive force of non-routinised desires and pleasures so clearly recognised in the work of Weber and Freud remains a shadowy presence in the wings of late modernity.

References

Brubaker, R. 1984. *The Limits of Rationality: An Essay on the Social and Moral Thought of Max Weber*. London: Allen & Unwin.

Dollimore, J. 1991. *Sexual Dissidence: Augustine to Wilde, Freud to Foucault*. Oxford: Clarendon Press

Elias, N. 1982. *The Civilising Process*, vol. 1: *A History of Manners*. Oxford: Basil Blackwell.

Foucault, M. 1985. *The History of Sexuality*, vol. 2: *The Use of Pleasure*. Harmondsworth: Penguin.

Freud, S. 1974. *The Pelican Freud Library*, trans. J. Strachey, vol. 1: *Introductory Lectures on Psychoanalysis*. Harmondsworth: Penguin Books.

—— 1986a. *The Penguin Freud Library*, trans. J. Strachey, vol 7: *Three Essays on the Theory of Sexuality and Other Works*. Harmondsworth: Penguin Books.

—— 1986b. *The Standard Edition of the Complete Psychological Works of Sigmund Freud*, trans. J. Strachey, vol. ix (1906–1908): *'Civilised' Sexual Morality and Modern Nervous Illness*. London: Hogarth Press.

112   *Gail Hawkes*

—— 1986c. *The Standard Edition of the Complete Psychological Works of Sigmund Freud*, trans. J. Strachey, vol. xxi (1927–1931): *Civilisation and its Discontents*. London: Hogarth Press.

Gay, P. 1984. *The Bourgeois Experience: Victoria to Freud*, vol. 1: *Educating the Senses*. Oxford: Oxford University Press.

Gerth, H.H., and Mills, C.W. (eds). 1970. *From Max Weber: Essays in Sociology*. London: Routledge & Kegan Paul.

Gilman, S. 1989. *Sexuality: An Illustrated History: Representing the Sexual in Medicine and Art*. New York: Wiley.

Hawkes, G. 1996. *A Sociology of Sex and Sexuality*. Buckingham: Open University Press.

Keating, P. (ed.). 1972. *Into Unknown England 1866–1913: Selections from the Social Explorers*. London: Fontana.

Kumar, K. 1978. *Prophecy and Progress: The Sociology of Industrial and Post-Industrial Society*. Harmondsworth: Penguin.

Mort, F. 1987. *Dangerous Sexualities: Medico-moral Politics in England since 1830*. London: Routledge & Kegan Paul.

Runciman, W.G. (ed.) 1994. *Max Weber: Selections in Translation*. Cambridge: Cambridge University Press.

10 Sexuality and sexology

Michel Foucault

Véronique Mottier

Sexuality and sexual identities have become an important domain for political struggles over the past two decades. These struggles raise crucial issues, especially around the discourse of rights in the context of the liberal democratic state. However, in this chapter I examine the politicisation of sexuality from a more structural perspective. In particular, I focus on the connections between power and sexuality in late modernity, understood as 'the current phase of development of modern institutions, marked by the radicalising and globalising of basic traits of modernity' (Giddens 1991: 243).

The politicisation of sexuality

Sexual identities are politically relevant since they are constituted within fields of power. They are not merely the expression of natural instincts, but are social as well as political constructs. With the differentiation of sexuality from reproduction, anatomy has ceased to be destiny. The consequences of this change are profound, not least for women (see also Amir and Benjamin, Chapter 14 of this volume). As a result, and against the backdrop of individualisation and detraditionalisation processes, sexuality is not a predefined 'given' any more. It has become an empty signifier, opening up to plural meanings and interpretations. In this context, sexual identities are the outcome of individual as well as collective formation processes (see also Lloyd, Chapter 11 of this volume), which, in turn, connect in important ways to relations of power.

The connections between power and sexuality are all the more important because our relation to ourselves as sexual beings constitutes such a central component of modern identity. As Foucault puts it, 'Sexuality has always been the site where the future of our species, and at the same time our truth as human subjects, are formed' (Foucault 1994: 257; my translation). A similar point is made by Giddens, who argues: 'Somehow...sexuality functions as a malleable feature of self, a prime connecting point between body, self-identity and social norms' (Giddens 1992: 15). The two authors disagree, however, on the political implications of the centrality of sexuality to modern self-identity. For Foucault, sexuality is the prime target of 'bio-power' and as such fundamental to disciplinary processes. Giddens on the other hand, similarly to Beck and

Beck-Gernsheim (1995), interprets current transformations of intimacy more optimistically as processes that have potential ramifications towards a democratisation of the public sphere. While both Giddens's and Foucault's insights will form the backdrop against which I shall develop my argument, my concern here is to examine the political implications of identity-formation mechanisms from a somewhat different focus.

Under conditions of late modernity, social life is characterised by high levels of reflexivity. New knowledge or information is routinely incorporated both by lay agents and by institutional environments of action that are thereby reconstituted or reorganised (Giddens 1990, 1991; Beck *et al.* 1994). Like the self and the body, sexuality has become heavily infused with reflexivity (Giddens 1992: 31). The constitution of identity in late modernity is thus closely bound up with religious, medical and especially scientific truth-claims, and accordingly with the production and incorporation of knowledge. It is therefore important to analyse how the discursive shaping of sexual identities is embedded in relations of knowledge as well as fields of power.

In this chapter, I shall take a closer look at one of the discourses that shapes sexual identities, namely that of sexology (see also Hawkes, Chapter 9 of this volume). Sex research is especially relevant from the viewpoint of connections between power and sexuality, in that it produces truth-claims that are legitimised by the particular prestige of scientific discourse. More precisely, this essay will explore two questions. First, what are the discursive strategies through which sexology constructs sexuality? It is frequently argued – following Foucault – that sex research naturalises sexuality and sexual identities and that political counterstrategies should be based on the deconstruction of this essentialist discourse. I do not take issue with the critique of essentialist discourse. I want to argue, however, that the history of sex research is far more complex than its critics are willing to admit. Sexology houses a multiplicity of contradictory voices and viewpoints. The resulting discourse is far from homogeneous. Scientific discourses on sexuality are based on both essentialist and constructionist discursive strategies. Both types of strategies have been articulated within discourses that either marginalise, or legitimise sexual diversity. In short, it is not so much the type of discursive strategy – essentialist or constructionist – but rather the specific value-orientations connected to these strategies that determine the political consequences of a particular discourse on sexuality.

The second question that I want to raise is: how should we interpret the discursive construction of sexuality? Should the scientific discourses on sexuality that I deal with in this chapter be analysed primarily in terms of confessionary techniques of power/knowledge and discipline, as Foucault proposes, or not? Although I broadly share Foucault's critique of sexology, I suggest that his account of sex research is too one-sided, as it neglects the fundamental ambivalence that characterises scientific discourse on sexuality. Sexological discourse is not exclusively constraining; it can also be a reflexive resource for the active shaping of the sexual self.

In what follows, I start with a brief discussion of prevailing views on the connections between sexuality and power. I shall outline in more detail the Foucauldian problematisation of scientific discourse on sexuality, before suggesting a different interpretation of the relations between power and sexuality, emphasising the ambivalence of discursive mechanisms of identity formation.

The sexual liberation paradigm

Sex is on display in our everyday life. The emergence of the 'permissive' society over the past thirty or forty years in Western societies has been accompanied by the sexualisation of the media. There is a cacophony of discourses on sexuality – medical, religious, therapeutic, juridical and others – that tell us how to categorise our sex life, its problems and its prohibitions.

At the same time, the naïve belief in the subversive character of sexuality is dead (Duyvendak and Prins 1994: 3). The hope that the so-called sexual revolution would not only liberate sexuality but also subvert wider repressive structures of power, as Fromm, Reich or Marcuse believed, has faded. The reasons for this scepticism are practical as well as theoretical, and can be outlined briefly.

Following Giddens (1992: 28), the sexual revolution involved not only an advance in sexual permissiveness but also two basic elements. First, the development of reproductive technologies – the precondition of the sexual revolution – meant that conception could now not only be artificially prevented but also artificially produced. The differentiation of female sexuality from reproduction implies a radical transformation of female sexuality with, in turn, profound consequences for male sexuality. Second, there has been a flourishing of sexual diversity that has resulted in a 'decline of perversion' (Giddens 1992; Weeks 1986). The hegemonic narrative of sexual normalcy that constructed the concept of the pervert during the nineteenth century, described by Foucault (1990), has been undermined by the public proliferation of sexual diversity. As Weeks (1995: 27) formulates it: 'The sexual order, with its fixing of sexual identifications under the banner of Nature, Science and Truth, has all but gone…The contemporary sexual world appears as irrevocably pluralistic.'

Both elements can be framed in a narrative of sexual liberation. But they can also be articulated within a more sceptical perspective. The advance in sexual permissiveness may have been in itself 'gender-neutral', as Giddens (1992: 29) claims. Feminists have nonetheless pointed out that men have primarily benefited from its consequences. As one author puts it:

> The permissive era permitted sex for women too. What it did not do was defend women against the differential effects of permissiveness on men and women…It was about the affirmation of young men's sexuality and promiscuity…The very affirmation of sexuality was a celebration of male sexuality.
> (Beatrix Campbell, quoted in Gilfoyle *et al.* 1993: 184)

(For similar views, see Hite 1976; Jeffreys 1990.) Seen from this perspective, what constitutes for Giddens a revolution in 'female sexual autonomy' is for many feminists less an increase in sexual freedom for women than the fulfilment of male fantasies about female sexual availability. The rhetoric of sexual liberation legitimises male control of women's sexuality, it was argued (Millett 1970; Firestone 1972).

As for Giddens's second element of the sexual revolution, the celebratory image associated with the rise of sexual diversity has been modified by AIDS. As Duyvendak and Prins put it, sexuality is not undermining sexual norms any more, but its own participants (1994: 3). The flourishing of sexual identities and communities of choice in the 1960s and 1970s, especially those of lesbians and gay men, publicly demonstrated the profound transformations of the sexual order that were related to the sexual revolution. AIDS, as Weeks (1989, 1995) points out, has revealed the unfinished character of this revolution. Whereas lesbians and gays have been successful in establishing new public identities, the AIDS crisis has shown that they have not managed to suppress traditional associations of homosexuality with disease (Weeks 1989: 302). In a historic parallel with earlier fears of venereal disease and pregnancies, sexuality has moved away from its connection with liberation to become once again fraught with anxieties and risks.

From a theoretical angle, the idea that discourse on sexuality and in particular that of sexology is liberating has been challenged in particular by Foucault (1990). Sexuality, he argues, is not simply the ahistorical expression of natural instincts. It is a historical experience – relatively recent in its current form – that is constructed through various discourses. Since there is no such thing as an original, essential sexuality that is repressed by society, there is nothing to liberate (see also Lloyd, Chapter 11 of this volume).

It follows that discourses on sexuality cannot simply be pitted against power. This does not mean, of course, that sexuality has no connections to power. On the contrary, sexuality 'appears rather as an especially dense transfer point for relations of power' (Foucault 1990: 103). In contrast to the idea that discourse on sexuality is liberating, Foucault argues that power operates through the discourses that constitute sexual meanings and identities. Sexuality is regulated not through repressive but rather through productive power mechanisms.

Discourse, identity, truth

In the three published volumes of *The History of Sexuality*, Foucault shows how the discursive constitution of sexuality and sexual identities is, in modernity, intertwined with the problematics of truth. In the first volume, he challenges what he terms the 'repressive hypothesis' – the customary interpretation of the history of sexuality that sees a growing repression of sex since the seventeenth century, halted only recently (Foucault 1990). According to Foucault, discourses on sex have, on the contrary, been submitted to institutional mechanisms that increasingly incite discursive production. Sex becomes an object of knowledge, a 'truth issue'. The avowal of the 'truth' on sex is provoked through confession in all its various modes and sites, which Foucault considers as the essential procedure for the production of truth in the West.

With the birth of the human sciences, Foucault argues, sexual truth becomes elaborated in the scientific knowledge on these experiences. The confessionary techniques of power/knowledge that the human sciences employ are in Foucault's view closely connected to the disciplinary mechanisms that characterise modern societies. The human sciences, he argues in *Discipline and Punish* (1979), have developed in the same matrix of power/knowledge technologies such as the prison, where individuals become objects of knowledge as well as disciplined bodies.

Sexuality is a key element in Foucault's account of the rise of the disciplinary society. Sex became a crucial target of 'bio-power', the type of power that characterises the society of surveillance and control and that is organised around the regulation of the biological processes of the population (health, hygiene, birth control, etc.). As the focus of the technologies of the body, as well as of the control and regulation of the population, sex became central to the establishment of the disciplinary society. Sexuality, Foucault claims, became a matrix of disciplines, as well as a principle of regulation (Foucault 1990: 146). It follows that the confessionary mode of production of sexual truths is closely connected with mechanisms of surveillance.

In this context, sexology is seen in terms of naturalisation and fixation of identities. Resistance to normalising discourses is notoriously undertheorised in Foucault's work. Scattered passages in the *History of Sexuality*, vol. 1, do not override the overall suggestion of powerlessness against the normalising and disciplinary mechanisms of confession. Despite Foucault's oft-quoted assertion that 'Where there is power, there is resistance' (1990: 95), this theoretical claim is not in fact incorporated in the historical analysis in this work. The general mechanism that he stresses is subjection and normalisation, not resistant subjectivity.

Notwithstanding its empirical neglect, resistance does have a central importance in Foucault's framework, at least on a theoretical level. Asymmetrical relations of power, he argues, form complex strategic situations that are always localised and unstable. Power relations do not represent a permanent structure but rather a given moment of a continuing process. The distribution of power and the appropriation of knowledge are thus fundamentally unstable. Relations of power/knowledge are constantly shifting, forming 'matrices of transformation' where power and knowledge are constantly redistributed, rather than static arrangements.

Within this perspective, discourses are not only the products of power, but in turn produce power themselves. They are elements or tactical blocks within the field of power relations. Discourses can support foci of power, or foci of resistance. Truth-claims are possible instruments within power struggles against normalising discourses that define normal and deviant identities. 'The political question,' Foucault argues, 'is not error, illusion, alienated consciousness or ideology; it is truth itself' (Foucault, in Gordon 1980: 133).

In what follows, I shall look at some of the shifting truth-claims within sex research, while taking into account Foucault's insights into power and resistance. I shall not develop a systematic analysis of sexological discourse, but discuss some elements of the history of sexology, in order to illustrate my argument. My aim is not to assess whether the truth-claims that sexological discourse contains are actually, scientifically, 'correct'. Rather, I want to identify what discursive strategies are followed in formulating these truth-claims, and how the meanings and identities that they construct connect with the play of power and resistance.

Sexology and ambivalence

The birth of modern conceptualisations of sexuality can be traced back to the end of the nineteenth and to the early twentieth century, when sex emerged as an object of study within the social sciences (see Bullough 1994; Weeks 1989). During the preceding century, Darwinian theory had been the main focus of debate in the social sciences. Darwin's view of sexual selection as the key to evolution became a major impetus for the development of modern sex research. Through the concept of sexual selection, scientific investigations of sexuality were, from their beginnings, concerned with questions of heredity, degeneracy and race. These preoccupations were articulated in the rise of eugenics, a term that was coined in 1885 by Darwin's cousin, Sir Francis Galton (see Bullough 1994: 5).

A second major impetus for sex research was the growing concern with public health, in particular with prostitution, personal hygiene and venereal disease. Against this background, sex research became closely intertwined with growing state intervention in sexual matters. While sexual behaviour had been traditionally addressed in terms of morality, it became the object of a process of medicalisation (Weeks 1989; Tiefer 1995).

Early sex research thus focused on the social effects of sex, as well as on its nature. Indeed, modern sexology differs from older preoccupations with sexual morality primarily by its construction of sexuality as an object of study in its own right. As Weeks puts it, 'Sexology was simultaneously constituting and exploring a new continent of knowledge, assigning thereby a new significance to the "sexual" ' (1989: 142).

The central preoccupation of early sex research was the definition of the nature of sexuality. Sexuality was predominantly conceptualised in terms of natural instincts, which formed the basis for a variety of social experiences. This variety of sexual types was, accordingly, submitted to (as well as constituted by) a zealous labelling and classification effort by authors such as Krafft-Ebing, Westphal, Féré, Lasègue, Rohleder, Moll, Thoinot and Ellis. A narrative of sexual normalcy and deviations from the norm emerged, based on the biological 'naturalness' of essential human instincts. An important component of this narrative was the assumption that the biological differences between men and women, which justified their assignment to different social roles, also led to differences in sexual behaviour and needs. Related to this was the idea that natural sexual behaviour includes heterosexual acts and desires only.

Many of the pioneers of sex research were themselves actively involved in contemporary and highly politicised debates on sex reform. Ironically, their ideas were also used to organise and intensify the emerging disciplining of sexuality. As Weeks puts it, 'The paradox was that the early sexologists, who by and large were also conscious sex reformers, were simultaneously powerful agents in the organisation, and potential control, of the sexual behaviours they sought to describe' (1989: 145).

Although most early sexologists concentrated on the various deviations from sexual normalcy, others, in particular Ellis, studied 'normal' sexual behaviour itself. While research on deviations and on normalcy focused mostly on the nature of sexual instincts, the latter type of research led to the partial problematisation of biological naturalness itself (see Weeks 1989: 144). Sex was still understood in terms of a biological essence, but some sexologists, such as Geddes and Thomson, could not help noticing that even 'normal' sexual instincts were in fact quite diverse. The naturalising discursive strategies that composed the narrative of sexual orthodoxy thus simultaneously led to a partial problematisation of that very narrative, even among the first generation of sexologists. The suggestion by Ellis that normality itself was the result of social definitions rather than of natural instincts opened up the path of non-essentialist constructions of sexuality.

From the moment of its constitution, sexology's construction of sexuality was therefore far from homogeneous. In their common focus on biological instincts, early definitions of sexuality were mostly based on the idea of nature. However, the tension between essentialist and constructionist views that was to divide future generations of sexologists began to emerge at the very beginnings of scientific discourse on sexuality. In the following decades, the relative unity of early sexological discourse was shattered, giving way to disagreements about practically every aspect of the narrative of sexual orthodoxy, including the nature of sexuality and sexual identity. The objects of knowledge around which the controversies were strongest were female sexuality and homosexuality. On both these issues, the Kinsey reports on *Sexual Behaviour in the Human Male* (1948) and *Sexual Behaviour in the Human Female* (1953) were particularly important in opening up the debate. Kinsey's concept of a sexual 'outlet' involved a behavioural definition of sexual identity, which profoundly called into question the naturalising perspective.

The essentialist construction of sexuality and sexual identity was thus challenged from within the sexological discourse that had formulated it in the first place. This is not to deny that essentialist views of sexuality remained dominant for a long time. My point is rather that scientific discourse on sexuality has not been, for that matter, homogeneous. Its discursive strategies are ambivalent in that they are based upon both essentialist and constructionist sexual meanings.

This does not mean, of course, that the problematisation of the narrative of sexual orthodoxy has taken place within sexology only. Powerful challenges to sexology's truth-claims have come from gay and feminist counter-discourses. My argument is rather that the play of definition and resistance is not most fruitfully conceptualised as the binary opposition between scientific sexology that proposes reform from above and a grassroots sexology that proposes community organisation from below, as, for example, Weeks (1995: 27) implies. I suggest instead that the play of defining discourses and of resisting counter-discourses is less clear cut, more complex. As I have argued above, the construction of sexual identities has not been a straightforward unfolding of a narrative, but rather the result of struggles and disagreements within sexology itself. Furthermore, the discursive strategies that gay and feminist problematisations of scientific truth-claims on sexuality develop are not necessarily anti-essentialist. On the contrary, they are often based on the very identities that sexology constructed.

For example, until recently, medical discourse routinely defined homosexuality as an illness that might be subjected to normalising, 'corrective' treatment. Scientific discourse has suggested since that homosexuality may in fact have a genetic origin. Both these discourses have been taken over by at least some gay activists, and articulated within a counter-discourse along the lines of 'if homosexuality is an illness, or the result of a person's genetic make-up, rather than a perverse life-style choice as conservative moralists argue, then that means that we can't help the way we are and shouldn't be discriminated against' (see also Waites, Jackson and Rahman, Chapters 2, 6 and 7 of this volume, respectively).

It follows that it is not the essentialist or constructionist character of a particular discursive strategy that determines the political transformation of sexual meanings, but rather the values that orient these strategies. Furthermore, counter-discourses have occasionally adopted the discursive form of 'scientific' investigations of sexuality, most famously in the case of the Hite reports (Hite 1976, 1981, 1987; see also Mottier 1994, 1995; Stanley 1995). This makes it problematic to distinguish in any clear-cut way between sexology on the one hand and critique on the other.

Consequently, Foucault's account of the intertwining of sexological discourse with confessionary techniques of discipline and surveillance appears too one-sided. Regarding the relations between power and sexuality, scientific discourse is in fact ambivalent. It is at the same time the focus of definitions of sexuality and a possible site of resistance.

Ambivalence and the reflexive shaping of sexuality

The domain of sexuality, as well as its connections to power, has undergone profound changes over the past decades. The scientific investigation of sexuality with its accompanying large-scale sex surveys has contributed to the spectacle of sex, documenting these everyday experiments. Somewhat ironically, the primary agents in the transformation of sexual truths and power are those that were marginal in relation to hegemonic male heterosexuality, namely women, and homosexuals of both sexes.

The view that the transformations of male sexuality are largely a result of women's struggles to change their lives is shared by Giddens, as well as Beck and Beck-Gernsheim, for whom 'men seem to engage in self-liberation as spectators'

(Beck and Beck-Gernsheim 1995: 153). Leaving aside the question of whether current transformations of everyday personal life should be conceptualised in terms of liberation at all, the claim that 'men's liberation is a passive affair' (Beck and Beck-Gernsheim 1995: 152) underestimates, I think, the extent to which men actively engage in the reflexive shaping of their own sexuality. Nonetheless, there is little doubt that women indeed are in many ways the vanguard of the current transformations of sexuality and intimacy.

Whereas Giddens's analysis is primarily, and Beck and Beck-Gernsheim's account exclusively, concerned with heterosexual relationships, it is also within what Foucault (1990) terms the 'peripheral sexualities' that sexual meanings are experimented on and contested. 'The speaking perverts,' Weeks writes, 'first given a carefully shaded public platform in the volumes of early sexologists, have become highly vocal on their behalf...They speak for themselves in street politics and lobbying, through pamphlets, journals and books, via the semiotics of highly sexualised settings, with their elaborate codes of keys, colours and clothes, in the popular media, and in the more mundane details of domestic life' (Weeks 1985: 21). Contrary to claims that hegemonic sexual meanings have been left unexamined (for example, Rich 1983; Wilkinson and Kitzinger 1993), the current transformations and politics of sexuality have started to problematise the hegemony as well as the forms of 'normality'.

It is important to stress that while deconstruction can be a useful political strategy in the politics of sexuality by revealing the contingency of sexual meanings and arrangements, this does not make it intrinsically progressive or conservative. With regard to sexuality, the domain of moral values has been largely monopolised by right-wing discourses that reject sexual diversity in the name of 'family values', although an important attempt to articulate the problem of values within a discourse that legitimises sexual pluralism has been made notably by Weeks (1995). In the face of recurring moral fundamentalisms and sexual conservatisms there is a need for 'progressive forces' to elaborate strategies for reoccupying this discursive space. The political ambivalence of the discourses that establish sexual meanings and identities (see also Lloyd, Chapter 11 of this volume), in particular sexology, which has been crucial in regulating sexual truths, indicates that both constructionist and essentialist discursive strategies can provide a basis for transformative agency.

At the same time, this political ambivalence also suggests that our relation as subjects to the discourses that define us cannot satisfyingly be conceptualised as a passive one-way process. Living in conditions of late modernity means living in a world without intrinsic meaning. There is an impossibility of discursive closure, and therefore the potential possibility to problematise any construction of identity will always exist. Individuals have a reflexive relation to discourses that organise sexual meanings and identities. In the context of these discourses, sexuality and sexual identity are being actively constructed by agents, not imposed on passive bodies.

As Giddens (1992), Beck and Beck-Gernsheim (1995) and Weeks (1995) point out, the domain of sexuality and intimacy has thus become a privileged site for the reflexive project of the self. In the highly reflexive society that we live in today, self-identity has become fundamentally open and has to be actively constructed through everyday experiments (Giddens 1991). A similar argument is outlined by Foucault in the second and third volume of his history of sexuality, *The Use of Pleasure* (1985) and *The Care of the Self* (1986). Whereas Foucault's exploration of identity in his early writings stresses how discourses and practices define us, his later work on sexuality – cut short by his death in 1984 – begins to outline the enabling aspects of modern subjectivity from a more positive perspective. More precisely, initially framing identity indirectly through the exclusion of 'others' – the insane, criminals, etc. – Foucault shifts in his later work to a related question: how do we form our identity directly through 'practices of the self', in particular in the domain of sexuality?

From this angle, I want to invert Foucault's argument by suggesting that the knowledge produced by confessionary techniques in sexology could play the role of reflexive resources for the active shaping of the sexual self. The development of sexology has accelerated the reflexivity of sexuality. This very reflexivity means that sexuality is the locus not just of disciplinary power/knowledge mechanisms but also of active practices of self-fashioning. The truths that sexology produces can be articulated within normalising discourses. They can also present points of departure for essentialist self-definitions and identities. Finally, they can be points of anchorage for the reflexive shaping of the self.

This emphasis on the reflexive shaping of sexuality does not, in my view, disconnect this process from the power relations that partially condition it. It suggests, however, relations between power and sexuality that are far removed from the paradigm of sexual liberation.

References

Beck, U., and Beck-Gernsheim, E. 1995. *The Normal Chaos of Love*. Cambridge: Polity Press.
Beck, U., Giddens, A., and Lash, S. 1994. *Reflexive Modernisation*. Cambridge: Polity Press.
Bullough, V.L. 1994. *Science in the Bedroom: A History of Sex Research*. New York: Basic Books.
Duyvendak, J.W., and Prins, B. 1994. 'Subversieve seksualiteit'. *Krisis* 57: 3–9.
Firestone, S. 1972. *The Dialectic of Sex*. New York: Bantam Books.
Foucault, M. 1979. *Discipline and Punish: The Birth of the Prison*. New York: Vintage.
—— 1985. *The Use of Pleasure: The History of Sexuality*, vol. 2. New York: Random House.
—— 1986. *The Care of the Self: The History of Sexuality*, vol. 3. New York: Pantheon Books.
—— 1990. *The History of Sexuality*, vol. I, *An Introduction*. Harmondsworth: Penguin.
—— 1994. 'Non au sexe roi'. In D. Defert, and F. Ewald (eds), *Dits et écrits 1954–1988 par Michel Foucault*, vol. 3, pp. 256–69. Paris: Gallimard.
Giddens, A. 1990. *The Consequences of Modernity*. Cambridge: Polity Press.
—— 1991. *Modernity and Self-identity: Self and Society in the Late Modern Age*. Cambridge: Polity Press.
—— 1992. *The Transformation of Intimacy: Sexuality, Love and Eroticism in Modern Societies*. Cambridge: Polity Press.

Gilfoyle, J., Wilson, J., and Brown. 1993. 'Sex, organs and audiotape: a discourse analytic approach to talking about heterosexual sex and relationships'. In S. Wilkinson, and C. Kitzinger (eds), *Heterosexuality: A Feminism and Psychology Reader*, pp. 181–202. London: Sage.

Gordon, C. (ed.). 1980. *Power/Knowledge: Selected Interviews and other Writings by Michel Foucault 1972–1977*. Brighton: Harvester.

Hite, S. 1976. *The Hite Report on Female Sexuality*. New York: Dell.

—— 1981. *The Hite Report on Male Sexuality*. New York: Ballantine.

—— 1987. *Women and Love: The Hite Report on Love, Passion and Emotional Violence*. New York: St. Martin's Press.

Jeffreys, S. 1990. *Anticlimax: A Feminist Perspective on the Sexual Revolution*. London: The Women's Press.

Kinsey, A. 1948. *Sexual Behaviour in the Human Male*. Philadelphia: Saunders.

—— 1953. *Sexual Behaviour in the Human Female*. Philadelphia: Saunders.

Millett, K. 1970. *Sexual Politics*. London: Virago.

Mottier, V. 1994. 'La mise en discours de la sexualité: le féminisme à la recherche de stratégies.' *Swiss Yearbook of Political Science* 34: 79–98.

—— 1995. 'The politics of sex: truth games and the Hite reports.' *Economy and Society* 24: 520–39.

Rich, A. 1983. 'Compulsory heterosexuality and lesbian existence'. In E. Abel, and E.K. Abel (eds), *The Signs Reader: Women, Gender and Scholarship*. Chicago: University of Chicago Press.

Stanley, L. 1995. *Sex Surveyed 1949–1994*. London: Taylor & Francis.

Tiefer, L. 1995. *Sex is Not a Natural Act and other Essays*. Oxford: Westview Press.

Weeks, J. 1985. *Sexuality and its Discontents: Meanings, Myths and Modern Sexualities*. London: Routledge & Kegan Paul.

—— 1986. *Sexuality*. Chichester: Ellis Horwood and Tavistock.

—— 1989. *Sex, Politics and Society: The Regulation of Sexuality since 1800*, 2nd edn. London/New York: Longman.

—— 1995. *Invented Moralities: Sexual Values in an Age of Uncertainty*. Cambridge: Polity Press.

Wilkinson, S., and Kitzinger, C. (eds). 1993. *Heterosexuality. A Feminism and Psychology Reader*. London: Sage.

11 Sexual politics, performativity, parody
Judith Butler

Moya Lloyd

Judith Butler's work demonstrates that coherent gender identity is organised by dominant discourses. In this chapter I focus on three issues: the relationship between performance and performativity; the shift in argument from *Gender Trouble* (1990) to *Bodies That Matter* (1993b); and the form of politics entailed by understanding gender in performative terms. I argue that far from entailing the ludic politics argued for by some adherents of her theory – where the playful disruption of the signifiers (especially sartorial signifiers) of sex and gender suggests a politics where queer is good, queerer is better, but queerest is best of all – performativity/performance entails a politics that is ambivalent. This is not to say either that her work is apolitical or that it advocates a hyper-voluntarist politics, but that politics is reconstituted as a realm of uncertainty, making it impossible to prefigure its effects. In rethinking gender, Butler also rethinks the political.

Theorising gender

One of the most insightful and provocative facets of Butler's writing is the way in which she theorises gender. Gender, in many feminist accounts, is taken to be a social relation that is mapped onto the pre-existing biological categories of sex. For Jane Flax, this means that: '[e]ach culture identifies and sorts out somewhat differently a possible range of human attributes and activities and assigns some to one group and some to another' (Flax 1990: 26). Gender, in this sense, is understood in constative terms. It signals 'what we are': subjects of a discernible and given set of characteristics. Despite cultural and historical variability, the world remains organised into asymmetrical gender relations that have been '(more) defined and (imperfectly) controlled by one of its interrelated parts – the male' (Flax 1990: 23).

Implicit in this conceptualisation of gender relations is an invariant feature: that male and female, masculinity and femininity, are oppositional and mutually exclusive categories. To be female is not to be male. One can only be one or the other. Indeed, femininity might be regarded as the very condition of possibility for, or the constitutive outside of, the perpetuation of masculinity: the profane other that must be legislated against. Together, male and female are bound in hetero-logic: male not only assumes female but requires her for (heterosexual) completeness. This structure, in turn, has its own constitutive outside – homosexuality. For that which is included (heterosexual) can only be defined against that which is excluded (homosexual). As Fuss observes, it is an 'interior exclusion' (1991: 3). Although feminists have spent time criticising and revealing the ways in which women are oppressed, or discriminated against, by men, they have frequently left intact the binary structure that underpins their understanding of gender relations. This occurs, in part, because of the way in which gender identity is understood. Many theorists, as Butler reveals, rely upon the idea that there is a *something* that is regarded as fundamental to gender identity: a maternal nature, a specific mode of reasoning, natural passivity, a specific erotic nature, a developmental trajectory. Even when advocating that gender is socially scripted and acquired (rather than essential or natural), they themselves set up regulative fictions delimiting what counts as 'intelligible sex', positing the kinds of identity that are permitted to exist and those that are not (Butler 1990: 148).

These ontologies of gender, alongside the binary pairing noted above, generate an account of identity that claims to be descriptive, a simple enumeration of the relevant features of identity, but this account is, in fact, normalising (Butler 1992; Norval 1994: 117, 121). By setting out boundaries and markers around specific gender identities, these feminist explanations of gender operate as another (literal and figurative) mode of containment. They produce other versions of the disciplinary and regulatory strategies discussed by Foucault (see Mottier, Chapter 10 in this volume), establishing, to echo Canguilhem, categories of the normal and the pathological. Gender norms operate in this way to regulate and police the acceptable and the licit.

In the place of this substantialist account of gender, Judith Butler proposes the idea of gender performativity: gender not as an expression of what one is, but gender as something that one does (1990: 141). The emphasis shifts from the spatial to the temporal. Space does not disappear but is reconstituted: gone is metaphorical space – the continents of subjectivity habitable only by authentic substantive identities – and in its place is social space: the symbolic realm in which subjects interpellate and hail other subjects, in which the performative enactment of gender occurs.

In developing her account of performativity, Butler echoes both Austin and Derrida in asserting that the performative 'enacts or produces that which it names' (Butler 1993b: 23). She differs from Austin in repudiating any possibility of an autonomous agent as the author of performative utterances, following instead Derrida, for whom intentionality is always limited by the iterability of the sign. Repetition is fundamental to performativity. Performative utterances are, therefore, not simply singular events but effects of 'citational doubling' (Derrida 1991: 103). In place of language and signification, Butler talks primarily of discourses *à la* Foucault. Performativity, for Butler, operates through the 'reiterative power of discourse to produce the phenomena that it regulates and constrains' (1993b: 2). There is no single act of constitution or invention that produces the gendered subject; she/he is brought into being via recitation and repetition. Since there can be no possibility of recovering or recollecting previous acts and thus no chance of identical re-enactment, recitation and repetition remain reiterative: they reiterate the practices and norms that produce those regulatory sexual regimes through which gender is instantiated. Gender, for Butler, is a 'constituted *social temporality*' that in its 'occasional *dis*continuity' exposes the 'temporal and contingent ground-lessness of...[the] "ground"' (1990: 141).

Contrary to the substantialist conceptualisation(s) of identity noted above, Butler denies that gender is grounded in any way. She refuses the possibility of an internal essence or presence that precedes 'social and linguistic coding' (Poovey 1992: 241), attacking it as an instance of the metaphysics of substance (Butler 1990). Instead, she asserts that gender identity should be 'reconceived as a personal/cultural history of received meanings subject to a set of imitative practices which refer laterally to other imitations and which, jointly, construct the illusion of a primary and interior gendered self or parody the mechanism of that construction' (1990: 138). The gendered self has no ontological status apart from the acts that compose it; only 'bodily gestures, movements and styles constitute the illusion of an abiding gendered self' (1990: 139–40).

Gender identity comprehended in these terms is not a fixed category; it does not identify nor represent particular groups of subjects. One 'is' never one's gender, merely in a condition of 'doing' it. Rather than the foreclosure of the category of gender, there is only ever incompleteness and uncertainty.

The aim of Butler's analysis is to denaturalise what Janice Raymond has called 'hetero-reality': 'the ideology that woman is for man' (Raymond 1986: 11). The discourses that constitute compulsory heterosexuality have been instrumental in constructing a phantasmic, but severely regulated, notion of gender identity. Heterosexual subjectivity is the effect of the production of a specific relationship between sex, gender and desire (where gender follows from sex, and desire follows from gender). Heterosexuality is merely a truth effect of discourse that occludes, Butler proposes, the panoply of 'gender discontinuities' that challenge the naturalness of these connections where 'gender does not necessarily follow from sex, and desire, or sexuality generally, does not seem to follow from gender' (Butler 1990: 135–6). Revealing 'gender discontinuities' exposes hetero-sexuality as a regulative fiction. This can be demonstrated, Butler suggests, by analysing the practice of drag or female impersonation.

What is specifically important about drag, avers Butler, is that it is a cultural practice that belies the belief in an original/primary gender identity. In drag, three distinct 'contingent dimensions of significant corporeality' are discernible, and played up(on): anatomical sex (contingent maleness), gender performance (the feminine figure displayed in the impersonation), and gender identity (hetero-versus homosexuality). That drag can produce a coherent picture of woman, however misogynous that picture may be, discloses the '*imitative structure of gender itself*' (Butler 1990: 137). It demonstrates that there is no original to imitate. As a consequence, drag denaturalises, divulging the culturally fabricated nature of gender coherence. It reveals all gender as only ever parody, and gendered beings as simulacra. This leads Butler to contend that the recitation of 'heterosexual constructs in non-heterosexual frames brings into relief the utterly constructed status of the heterosexual original', exposing 'gay to straight *not* as a copy to the original, but, rather, as copy is to copy' (1990: 31). There is no original from which gay, lesbian or transvestite subjects deviate; the original is itself a mythical figuration. Echoing Lacan, Butler declares that all gender enactment comprises a failure to 'become "real" and to embody "the natural"' (1990: 146). The resulting 'parodic proliferation', she alleges, 'deprives hegemonic culture and its critics of the claim to naturalized or essentialist gender identities' (1990: 138). On this argument, parody seems to be inherently subversive (1990: 100). Indeed, so strong is this sense that parody, sending up gendered identities, has the power to undermine compulsory heterosexuality that Gail Hawkes states:

> If 'drag' is the verbal shorthand for the performative use of gendered dress codes to subvert the hegemonic twinning of gender and sexuality, then we can speak, in this sense, of dress as performance, of women 'dragging up as women'. Or of men 'dragging up as men'...Dressing-up as performance allows rereading of all dressing-up as playful...[where] the readings of the male/masculine/heterosexual, female/butch/lesbian, male/camp/homo-sexual, are not reversed but deliberately scrambled.
>
> (Hawkes 1995: 269)

As dressing up proliferates (lipstick lesbians, butch cowboys and so on) it will inaugurate, Hawkes intimates, a game of 'guess the sexuality(ies)', where all gendered meanings will be queered (Hawkes 1995: 269; see also Martin 1992: 107). Drag, in Butler's sense, is not simply about dressing up, however. To produce a coherent figuration of 'woman' necessitates more than wearing women's clothing (as drag testifies). Aside, perhaps, from the ordinary sense in which drag may be regarded as transgressive – that is, as cross-dressing – in what other ways does it operate? How, for instance, does it expose the fashioned nature of all gender identity? Is all 'drag' politically subversive of compulsory heterosexuality?

Performativity and performance

Butler contends (throughout her work) that the practices that produce gendered subjects are also the sites where critical agency is possible. Gender is simultaneously a mechanism of constraint (a set of norms that define us as normal/abnormal) and a locus for productive activity. This doubled relation draws on three sets of claims. The first is Lacanian: that failure to embody the ideal is inevitable, that subjects are unable to achieve a stable gendered identity. The second is Derridean: that the repetition central to the maintenance and constitution of gender is always repetition with a difference (or a *différance*). The last is Foucauldian: that this repetition creates the space for transformation. Gender performativity may be inevitable, but gender identity is always open and incomplete. Or, as Hawkes puts it, compliance with internalised codes (in her case, dress codes) 'is at one and the same time unconscious and profoundly managed' (Hawkes 1995: 262). In *Gender Trouble*, Butler observes that the option is not 'whether to repeat, but how to repeat or, indeed, to repeat and, through a radical proliferation of gender, *to displace* the very norms that enable the repetition itself' (Butler 1990: 148; see also 141). It is in the interstices between the impossibility of identical recitation and necessary reiteration, in the 'failure to repeat, a deformity, or a parodic repetition' (1990: 141), that critical feminist practice and the opportunity for 'gender transformation' becomes possible. The task is 'to locate strategies of subversive repetition...to affirm the local possibilities of intervention through participating in precisely those practices of repetition that constitute identity and, therefore, present the immanent possibility of contesting them' (1990: 147).

It is in this context that Butler asks: 'what kind of gender *performance* will enact and reveal the *performativity* of gender itself in a way that destabilizes the naturalized categories of identity and desire?' (1990: 139, my emphasis). Here she points to a distinction, though does not elaborate it, between performance and performativity. Performances reveal the discontinuity and incoherence beneath gender and desire. The question is how? She illustrates this relation through the example of drag, which operates through a disjunction, and rewriting, of the connections between sex, gender identity and gender performance. This means that constituted subjects can 'act out' fictional gender roles. If this is understood in a theatrical or filmic sense (where men can play women and women can play men), then there would seem to be no problem.

However, it is not clear from the examples that Butler uses that this is necessarily the case. Since she abandons the Austinian distinction between pure speech acts and parasitic speech acts, where the former refer to utterances issued in 'ordinary circumstances' (Austin 1962: 22), and the latter to theatrical, poetic uses of the same words (or, here, actions), an easy distinction between performance and performativity is difficult to sustain. Rather, Butler follows Derrida in arguing that both ordinary speech-acts and theatrical performances are underpinned by the same citatory practices, and that the distinction between theatre and 'real life' cannot be upheld. Thus, the same linguistic conventions are recited in a 'real' wedding and a stage wedding. They have to be, in order to create the effect of marriage (see Butler 1995: 134–5). However, if performativity produces that which it names, then what is it that prevents a performance operating performatively? What is it that prevents Butler being read as the advocate of a 'you-can-have-any-gender-you-like' theory? This ambiguity is further exacerbated by the assertion in *Bodies That Matter* that drag is 'an example of performativity' (Butler 1993b: 230). So, can performance and performativity be separated analytically?

Butler provides one answer to the question of the distinctions between performance and performativity in 'Critically queer' (reprinted with revisions in *Bodies That Matter*). A performance is a 'bounded "act"' that is differentiated from performativity on the grounds that performativity *'consists in a reiteration of norms which precede, constrain, and exceed the performer and in that sense cannot be taken as the fabrication of the performer's "will" or "choice"'* (Butler 1993a: 24). In the context of performativity there is no subject that precedes or enacts the repetition of norms. The subject is the effect of their compulsory repetition. This 'subject-effect', as Spivak calls her/him, is nothing more than the 'effect of an effect'; a metalepsis, 'the substitution of an effect for a cause' (Spivak 1988: 204).

This repetition of gender norms therefore repudiates any notion of voluntarism. 'There is no "one" who takes on a gender norm'; the 'one' is produced through reiteration of the discursive norms that precede and are in excess of her/him (Butler 1993a: 23). Even though performativity may acquire 'act-like status', it is only ever a repetition of discursive conventions (however dissimulated). It is not a matter of deciding who one wants to be today that is at the core of performativity but compulsory repetition. No one can evade the recitation of gender norms.

But where does that leave performance? Performance is defined by Butler as a 'bounded "act"'. What does this mean? In what sense is the 'act' bounded? Butler aligns performance with 'theatricality' (seeming, thereby, to blur the Derridean idea that everything is in some sense theatrical). By this she means that a performance is a kind of citation that *'mimes and renders hyperbolic'* the discursive convention that it draws upon (1993b: 232; see also Butler in Osborne and Segal 1994: 38). This is not theatre as self-creation or as pure invention. Performance takes up and reiterates the signs and outward codifiers that discourse performatively produces as the attributes of gender. It is a process, then, of *re*-signification and not signification *ab initio*. As Cindy Patton puts it: performance 'involves deployment of signs which have already attained meaning and/or standard usage within the legitimated discourse and crystallized practices of a "social", understood as a place of contestation' (Patton 1995: 182). But it is hyperbolic performance: 'to be excessively excessive, to flaunt one's performance as performance, is to unmask all identity as drag' (Fuss 1995: 81n.). Drawing on Irigaray's distinction between 'mimicry' (parody) and 'masquerade' (passing or imitation), this implies, for Fuss, that a performance cannot be read as parodic if it is not excessive. It is not enough, for example, to repeat or recite the codes of hetero-masculinity; it is necessary to turn them into a 'hyperbolic display' (Butler 1993a: 24). But is such a distinction sufficient? What, for example, represents evidence of excess – a certain walk? particular clothes? a voice pitched too high or too low? Performance as hyperbole suggests that it is merely the degree of excess that will determine the political effectiveness and subversiveness of any performance. Is this enough, however, to shatter the heterosexual matrix?

Far from a performance allowing one to have the gender of one's choice, the purpose is to reveal all gender as performance. This still does not clarify how a performance may be a bounded act, particularly as the material upon which performance draws itself might be said to exceed, constrain and precede the performer. One obvious way might be to say that a performance expresses the 'will', or is the 'choice' of the performer. That is, gendered subjects decide for themselves how they are going to act up, how they are going to exaggerate the gestures of femininity, masculinity, lesbianism or whatever. This indicates that a performance expresses its author's intentions. The drag performer scripts his act in certain ways. So, one can apparently have any gender one likes in the context of performance.

However, it is a mistake to reduce the performativity of gender to parodic performance understood in this way. It is easy to do, because, as Butler herself admits, her discussion of drag was ambiguous (1993a: 21). It opened the way to readings that presumed that cross-dressing of any kind created new forms of gender identity. So when is dressing up 'theatrical' and when, if ever, is it constitutive of gender identity?

The difficulty with distinguishing performance and performativity, as Butler uses them, arises in part from the ambivalence of the term 'performance'. For it stands both for the ensemble of dramatic and artistic practices and conventions of the theatre/stage, and for performance apprehended as a much looser set of actions and practices that produce the effect of gendered identity. Drag, in this respect, is also a multifaceted concept. It resonates with the theatrical tradition of the drag artist, the practice of cross-dressing in a general sense, and, more complicatedly, with the idea that drag is the allegory for all gender. In this regard, then, all gender is a matter of performance, of enacting the signs of gender. Nevertheless, it is not always clear how these terms operate. Furthermore, there is often blurring of the line between performance and performativity. Thus, the statement that 'gender performativity is not a question of instrumentally deploying a "masquerade"' is offered in refutation of a criticism concerning performance (Butler 1995: 136; see Benhabib 1995). Although generally performativity appears to relate to discourse (or language) and performance to practices (including those articulated by discourse), there are occasions when this distinction becomes muddied. Either way, what Butler is clear about is that neither the discourses that performatively produce gender nor the practices through which it is performed derive from the intentions of a preconstituted subject that stands outside these conventions. In this respect, neither performance nor performatives are prior to power and discourse. There is no voluntarist or autonomous subject.

As an explanation of the ways in which gender identity is lived out on a day-by-day basis, Butler's argument is persuasive. The idea that occasional gaps open up within contemporary culture where norms (both dominant and annihilating) can be mimed, reworked, resignified and, of course, reincorporated is suggestive. Where Butler differs from the advocates of 'feel-good' gender discourses is in recognising that individuated subjects are constituted within the constraints of normative heterosexuality. Gender is a performatively produced effect. Although there may be some latitude for transgressing gender norms, these reworkings principally function endogamously. What does this imply about the transgressive potential of drag?

Transgression and/or recuperation?

Butler concedes that there is no necessary relation between drag and subversion. At best, drag is a 'site of ambivalence' (1993b: 125). It is a product of the regime of power that it, at the same time, opposes and denaturalises. The difficulty is that, while at a theoretical level Butler's argument is persuasive, at times it underplays the significance of the material structures within which parody occurs. There is implicit in Butler's discussion of drag a sense that it will only have any impact (albeit a small one) if it is performed by someone on the margins of society. Although the privileges of heterosexuality tend to accrue from its naturalisation and from the ascription of originality and normalcy to it, this privilege is such that, at times, heterosexuality can afford to reveal its own mimetic nature without losing any of its power. Straight drag is a case in point. Of such examples, Butler announces, 'I would be reticent to call them subversive' (1993b: 126). Alongside all the other qualifications she has made, Butler now implicitly proposes that only gay drag can be subversive. What distinguishes films like *Tootsie* and *Some Like it Hot* from the drag performed in a club or at a ball is left largely unexplained. The effect, for me, is to suggest that Butler believes that marginality is what Fuss terms 'a privileged site of radicality' (1991: 5). That is, Butler is not saying that being in a marginalised position is a good thing, because clearly it is precisely marginalisation that enables hegemonic discourses to perpetuate particular versions of normality. It is, rather, that only those refused or abjected by heteronormativity can act parodically to displace it. This implies, as Osborne and Segal contend, that it is 'within critical subcultures that transgressive reinscriptions are going to make a difference' (1994: 38). If this is what Butler intends, then she needs to spell out how marginality functions in this way, and who can legitimately call themselves a marginalised group or critical subculture. Where, for instance, do straight women fit?

Conclusions

Butler's greater stress on the non-subversive effects of drag in *Bodies That Matter* is a shift from her earlier position. It highlights more visibly the power cartography upon which subjects are positioned differentially. It indicates that no performance has the ability to undermine the heterosexual edifice completely or automatically. At best the politics of parody is uncertain, incremental: 'subversiveness is the kind of effect', she asserts, 'that *resists calculation*' (1993a: 29) and that requires a challenge to 'the capacity to read' what is going on (Butler in Osborne and Segal 1994: 38). Subversion, therefore, is predicated upon the impossibility of predicting the outcome of any parodic political practice. It is precisely the absence of any guarantee that it will bring about the intended outcome, or any outcome at all, that seems to draw Butler. This is partly an attribute of the fact that the effects of discourse are not bounded by particular acts of legislation, the utterance of statements, authorial intentions or specific events. They are, to some degree at least, always indeterminate (see also Mottier,

Chapter 10 in this volume). This means that politics is neither fettered nor predetermined by the parameters of any specific discourse; its results cannot be forecast (for a different view see Martin 1992: 104). Consequently, it is impossible to plot the range or forms of subversion (and their opposites) that might emanate from specific discourses, acts or practices, or to assess the extent to which challenges to the 'heterosexual nation' might succeed. Butler's conceptualisation of performativity suggests the possibility for continual resignification (both transgressive and complicit), but in so doing it nullifies some of the ways in which all performances of gender are curtailed by material circumstance. Only some performances in some contexts impel the categorial rethinking of gender. Others may result in death or ignominy.

Any form of parody may thus provoke a number of simultaneous yet contradictory responses. It may be both transgressive and recuperable at the same time. Since parodic performances are parasitic on normalised practice, it cannot be otherwise. Effects are, as a result, ultimately incalculable: responses cannot be predicted in advance, and neither can the various ways in which particular 'acts' may be imitated by others. This depends upon hyperbolic performances by specific people in specific places at specific times (albeit not those with heterosexual privilege). It does not capture, however, the extent to which it matters with whom we 'do our genders' or to whom we 'do our genders', nor does it gauge how this bears on the political effectiveness of 'radical' practices. It does not forefront sufficiently the lateral relations between bodies. It is easy to neglect or to underestimate the importance of the space within which performance occurs: the others involved in or implicated by the production, and how they receive, interpret and respond to what they see. Inasmuch as Butler does mention others, it is with respect to their position as readers of allegedly transgressive activities. They are, in this regard, reduced to the level of passive recipients (Butler in Osborne and Segal 1994). This is not enough.

It is in the nature of the performativity–performance nexus that it promises two different, even contradictory, sets of effects. On the one hand, it charts a landscape of transgression, of resignification, of catachresis. On the other hand, it evokes a world that regards only some subjects as legible and legitimate, namely heterosexual subjects. Taking the first scenario, the heterosexual matrix appears fragile. The necessity of performative repetition conjures the potential for productive crises that induce its decomposition. Heterosexuality is revealed as an edifice built (literally and figuratively) upon insubstantial foundations. Examples that expose the proximate relationship between homo- and heterosexuality enable the latter's reconceptualisation as itself a copy of a copy. In this manner, cross-dressing becomes a mechanism that reveals the artifice of all gender. This is closer to the position that Butler indicates in *Gender Trouble*, where the possibilities for change are more optimistically presented. By contrast, the alternative sketch presumes the at best possible and at worst likely consolidation of the heterosexual matrix, where abjects reinforce this hegemony through the way in which their dissident performances necessarily reflect patterns constitutive of heterosexuality. Cross-dressing is, after all, only comprehensible because the categories of male/masculine and female/feminine are understood as simple, mutually exclusive binaries. Here heteronormativity is seen as so tenacious that even shifting, mobile power relations cannot critically undermine it; they cannot effect a substantial reconfiguration of the gendered world. Rather, heterosexuality is elastic enough to re-encompass or re-envelop 'queer' politics – to domesticate it, to reintegrate all dissonant performances. This accords more with Butler's revised (or clarified) understanding of drag in *Bodies That Matter*. Acknowledging theoretically the performative underpinnings of gender suggests that a more permissive reading is possible. Contemplating its operation in a world riven by economic disparity, racism, homophobia and sexism sways me in favour of a more circumspect reading. This is not to say that the theatricalisation of politics is ineffectual nor that an aestheticisation of politics cannot have some impact. It cannot, however, be all that politics consists in. As Butler herself notes, 'The Foucauldian in me says there is no one site from which to struggle effectively' (in Osborne and Segal 1994: 38). The Foucauldian in *me* would agree.

References

Austin, J.L. 1962. *How to Do Things with Words*, 2nd edn. Oxford: Oxford University Press.

Benhabib, S. 1995. 'Feminism and postmodernism: an uneasy alliance'. In S. Benhabib *et al.*, *Feminist Contentions: A Philosophical Exchange*, pp. 17–34. New York and London: Routledge.

Butler, J. 1990. *Gender Trouble: Feminism and the Subversion of Identity*. London: Routledge.

—— 1991. 'Imitation and gender insubordination'. In D. Fuss (ed.), *Inside/Out: Lesbian Theories, Gay Theories*, pp. 13–31. London: Routledge.

—— 1992. 'Contingent foundations: feminism and the question of "postmodernism"'. In J. Butler, and J.W. Scott (eds), *Feminists Theorize the Political*, pp. 3–21. London: Routledge.

—— 1993a. 'Critically queer'. *GLQ: A Journal of Lesbian and Gay Studies* 1: 17–32.

—— 1993b. *Bodies That Matter: On the Discursive Limits of 'Sex'*. London: Routledge.

—— 1995. 'For a careful reading'. In S. Benhabib *et al.*, *Feminist Contentions: A Philosophical Exchange*, pp. 127–43. New York and London: Routledge.

Derrida, J. 1991. 'Signature/event/context'. In P. Kamuf (ed.). *Between the Blinds: A Derrida Reader*, pp. 82–111. Hemel Hempstead: Harvester Wheatsheaf.

Flax, J. 1990. *Thinking Fragments: Psychoanalysis, Feminism and Postmodernism in the Contemporary West*. Berkeley CA: University of California Press.

Fuss, D. 1991. 'Inside/out'. In D. Fuss (ed.), *Inside/Out: Lesbian Theories, Gay Theories*, pp. 1–10. London: Routledge.

—— 1995. *Identification Papers*. London: Routledge.

Hawkes, G. 1995. 'Dressing-up – cross dressing and sexual dissonance'. *Journal of Gender Studies* 4: 261–70.

Martin, B. 1992. 'Sexual practice and changing lesbian identities'. In M. Barrett, and A. Phillips (eds), *Destabilising Theory: Contemporary Feminist Debates*, pp. 93–119. Cambridge: Polity Press.

Norval, A. 1994. 'Social ambiguity and the crisis of apartheid'. In E. Laclau (ed.), *The Making of Political Identities*, pp. 115–37. London: Verso.

Osborne, P., and Segal, L. 1994. 'Gender as performance: an interview with Judith Butler'. *Radical Philosophy* 67: 32–9.

Patton, C. 1995. ' "Performativity" and spatial distinction: the end of AIDS epidemiology'. In A. Parker and E.K. Sedgwick (eds), *Performativity and Performance*, pp. 173–96. London: Routledge.

Poovey, M. 1992. 'The abortion question and the death of man'. In J. Butler, and J.W. Scott (eds), *Feminists Theorize the Political*, pp. 239–56. London: Routledge.

Raymond, J. 1986. *A Passion for Friends: Towards a Philosophy of Female Affection*. Boston MA: Beacon Press.

Spivak, G. 1988. 'Subaltern studies: deconstructing historiography'. In *In Other Worlds: Essays in Cultural Politics*, pp. 197–221. New York and London: Routledge.

12 Sexual politics and sexual difference

Luce Irigaray

David Boothroyd

Ever since Marx declared that 'the point' was to change the world rather than merely to interpret it, philosophers have been whipped with the popular understanding of this thesis: namely, that thinking is a deficient mode of being political compared to action; thinking is less real and less effective with respect to the transformation of society. I open this chapter on the politics of sexual difference on this note because I wish to make it clear at the outset that, whatever the 'political implications' of Irigaray's feminism may be, we must resist the supposition that what it is to be political has already been decided in principle, in advance, and is *the same* in the cases of both sexes. We are invited by Irigaray to consider whether the political has been determined, as such, according to a masculine schema, and, if so, what this implies for a politics of sexual difference and for feminism.

Politics and otherness

Modern feminism has sought to counter the predominance of male agency by prioritising gender over sexual difference (see also Carver, Chapter 1, and Lloyd, Chapter 11 of this volume). Irigaray's view is that this comes at the price of abandoning the question of sexual difference to the discourse of biology and sexual politics to variants of the discourse of sociobiology, and that we should see that such a position exhibits a degree of complicity with male power (see also Gibbins, Chapter 3 of this volume). It is the strategic value (for feminism) of such a move that Irigaray's insistence on sexual difference seeks to question and challenge. She argues that the continued allegiance to the ideal of universality will always work against women's true desires and therefore against their political interests, too.

Women's *otherness*, it could be said, is the climate of Irigaray's political thought. Within what she sees as a general global masculinist economy, both of concepts and of generic violence, rethinking and reprioritising sexual difference is not undertaken at the expense of 'local' solutions to local issues: the successes of the traditional politics of egalitarian feminism are neither denied nor disparaged. Hers is a feminism dedicated to finding ways to continue to challenge the limits of the masculinist framework in which all feminisms have always had to find their voice, and within which the restriction it imposes upon the female imaginary is encountered.

In attempting to understand the complexity and subtlety of Irigaray's account and refusal of this restriction, it is important to bear in mind how her position is subtended by her critical engagements with the Western philosophical tradition, as interpreted by Nietzsche, Heidegger, Derrida and Levinas, and others, and how they inform the general re-evaluation of Freudian psychoanalysis and her critique of Lacan. Tina Chanter's recent *Ethics of Eros: Irigaray's Re-writing of the Philosophers* (1995) contributes enormously to redressing the tendency to put Irigaray's political thought on trial in the court of Anglo-American feminism to answer the charge of 'essentialism', linked directly, in several influential critical assessments of her work, with her emphasis on sexed incarnation, or *the body*. Chanter shows in great detail how Irigaray's thinking is informed throughout by philosophical deconstructions of the essentialist metaphysic and remains constantly vigilant of the essentialising force of the language in which her thinking of the feminine, female identity, the female body and sexual difference is expressed. In doing so, Chanter demonstrates incontrovertibly the naïvety of concluding that Irigaray is seeking to supplant a masculinist essentialism (an essentialism that valorises 'male qualities' and takes the male body as its point of departure) with a feminist essentialism based on the female body. Irigaray has often been charged with appealing to a fixed and universal notion of the nature of the feminine, something that would preclude the possibility of changing the basic character of relations between the sexes.

Chanter's book decries the intellectual energy lost on the critical targeting of this essentialist Irigarayian straw woman. The point I wish to make here is that to ascribe to Irigaray any empiricism of the body misses even the most evident features of her rejection of the representational model of language. It is to empiricism, she complains, that the question of sexual difference is traditionally relegated (Irigaray 1996:13).

Of course, anyone not convinced of the importance of interrogating the relation between language and reality in the discussion of the political, and who believes that these questions obfuscate rather than aid the theorising of a reality (and the political realities) held to lie *behind* language, may decide to part company with Irigaray at this point. Chanter correctly stresses, in explanation and not apology, that it is 'the assumption of a pre-existent reality, prior to language [that] is precisely what Irigaray and Lacan, influenced in this respect by Hegel and Heidegger, want to overcome' (Chanter 1995: 3). Overcoming the metaphysic of a pre-existent reality is the indispensable condition for the 'peaceful cultural revolution' that Irigaray envisages, but this does not, she argues, exclude concrete political engagement in the present to 'create a politics of sexual difference that encompasses the most private life between persons as well as the organization of society or societies as a whole' (Irigaray 1994: xvi). This 'overcoming' encompasses both the refiguration of the symbolic and the experience of interpersonal relations, which are always sexed.

The body and language

At this point I shall turn to Irigaray's writings on and of the body; to how they must be read in the context of this philosophical rethinking of the language–reality relation; and to how the interpretative activity this engenders might also be understood as a political strategy for accomplishing real change in the phallocratic determination of both societal and personal relations. In an attempt to overcome the determination of women's subjectivity, on both concep-tual and practical levels, according to masculinist models of thought and by men themselves, Irigaray undertakes what is most readily described as a discursive reappropriation of the female body. This involves accounting for the female body's specificity otherwise than by reflecting it in a language that is structured according to the specificity of the male sex. The problem she identifies is: how to think femaleness without subordinating this thinking to what could be termed discursive *phallo-mimesis*. In the course of this process, it could fairly be said that Irigaray's discourse breaks with common sense and the apparently transparent, founding notions normally deployed to calculate the political value and impact of ideas. Theoretical notions such as consciousness, agency, autonomy, identity, freedom, etc., all of which figure in determining the meaningfulness and scope of *action* or *practice*, and all of which are thought on the basis of metaphysical *arché*-tropes of the male sex, namely, those of presence, unity and visibility, are subjected to a redetermination on the basis of the female sex (*sexe*). (I note here that the French word *sexe*, which straddles the conceptual distinction between sex, gender, genitalia and sex-membership, plays a far from insignificant role in Irigaray's usage.)

In undertaking this work, she aims to counter the knowledge that we claim of these notions on the basis of their current circulation in language. Appealing to a Saussurian model, we could say that the transparency of this common-sense or normal language (*parole*) is guaranteed by an underlying and pre-existing grammar (*langue*), and that what Irigaray is calling for in response to this state of affairs is 'an examination of the operation of the "grammar" of each figure of discourse, its syntactic laws or requirements, its imaginary configurations, its metaphoric networks' (Irigaray 1985a: 75; Chanter 1995: 240). This move aims to liberate our thinking of the body from the grasp of biological naturalism, which reduces the sexual difference of sexed bodies to their essential physical characteristics. The task then becomes that of the reappropriation of the female body on the basis of sexual difference, for a political revolution in thought, through a refoundation of conceptuality – otherwise than according to phallo-mimetic masculinism. In the absence of any conventional names for this project of writing, which Irigaray herself is evidently not so directly concerned to name, I have elsewhere proposed the term 'labia-tropocentrism' (Boothroyd 1996). This term represents an attempt to respond to her emphasis on the female sex/geni-tals (*sexe*), the 'lips' (*les lèvres*), and to their synechdochical and catachretic figuring in her account of the female sex (*sexe*) (Gallop 1990: 97).

The notion of discursive *constitution* is preferred to construction, which always bears with it a sense of transcendentality and makes the false assumption of a theoretical meta-language. Indeed this is a metaphysical conundrum that Irigaray's prose actively engages with. If 'construction' reflects a sense of the psychic *tabula rasa* fundamental to gender identity, then 'constitution' is intended to emphasise the somatic *corpus rasum*; the givenness of sexed embodiment as distinct from the attribution of meaning to it; or, as the body's *morphological* specificity prior to its gender determination (Irigaray 1985a; cf. Whitford 1991: 58; Butler 1993: 57 ff.). If 'constructionism' is generally held to counter any attempt to propose the (natural) givenness of gender, then Irigaray's notion of the sexed *bodymorph* is intended to bear the weight of a givenness of sex prior to its conceptual determination as natural, biological, anatomical, etc. The body is here considered as an unwritten blank, but one with a sexual morphology that is held to figure as the limit of its discursive inscription. The 'bodymorph' expresses a notion of the uninscribed or discursively undecided body. This way of thinking of the body unsettles any discourse that might claim to define it as this or that, or in terms of the notion of *essence*, or to think of it, precisely, in terms of its identity, as something that has a being expressible in terms of what it *is*. Furthermore, Irigaray places emphasis on the bodily *encounter* with the other (*corps-à-corps*), which is articulated on the basis of a *morphology* of sex difference (or sameness).

Implicit in this refusal of the language/phenomenon split (so difficult to express without slipping into the discourse of either one or the other) and of the representational model of language rejected along with it, is an acknowledgement and new notion of the givenness of sexual difference. The important effect of this move is to focus attention on sexual difference as an *aporia*: it exemplifies the relocation of the *work* of inscription away from the body's supposed unity to the bodily separation of *one* from *the other*. It shifts the focus of thinking from the identity of the one to the encounter with the other (body). References in Irigaray's account of the female sex to birthing, bleeding, lactating, the lips, the placenta, the mucus, etc., can be regarded neither as simply literal nor as simply metaphorical. They collectively work to recover the female specificity of self-origination (figured, for example, as the birth of the girl child) and thereby to inaugurate a thinking that will be able to counter the secondary of the female sex, in whatever discourse this is articulated – in biblical discourse, in eugenic discourse, in neurophysiological discourse, or in the discourse of politics, which traditionally conceives of women's emancipation in the compensatory terminology of *equality* of the sexes.

If this deconstructive refiguring of the female body can be called a political undertaking, it is perhaps, as Margaret Whitford has put it, a 'politics of the imaginary' (1994: 380). To this end, Irigaray's writing works at unsettling the series of conceptual oppositions supporting male privilege through systematic valorisation and association with maleness. But rather than writing in the style of philosophical abstraction, through the formulation of the idea or concept, she allows her discourse, in a sense, to emanate from the female body itself. Space permits just a few examples: she reinterprets Plato's Cave, 'the most famous fable about knowledge', on the basis of the figure of the womb (Irigaray 1985b: 265); she refigures the body fluids in tropical opposition to 'the solidity of the penis'; she says, for example, that the (tropical or discursive) properties of fluids have been abandoned to the feminine (1985a: 116) and that the trope of solidity symbolises the 'triumph of rationality' (1985a: 113). Consequently, she attempts to reappropriate the trope of elemental fluidity for the thinking of female origination and female pleasure: the 'marine element' figures and refigures the amniotic waters and the exploration of female '*jouissance*' (1991: 107); the mucus links the themes of love and language and is the 'condition of possibility' of both (1993a: 170). She counters the masculinist (and Freudian) presentation of the vagina as the 'horror of nothing to see' (1985a: 26) with a description of it as the 'envelope which men require for their identity' (1991: 107). Referring to sexual difference and the sex organs (*sexe*) in the same breath, she says that the 'failure to establish a sexual identity for both sexes, man and the race of men, has transformed the male organ into an instrument of power with which to master maternal power'. There remains, nonetheless, the possibility that men can rethink their penises as 'a masculine version of the umbilical cord' (Irigaray 1993: 17), in other words, rethink their relationship to their mothers – hence there can be a decisive change in relations between the sexes.

The forging of a new language, one might say a prose, of sexual difference, is not so much a strategy for firming up the philosophy *behind* the politics, the theory behind praxis, but an attempt, an experiment, that is *creative* and indeed involves the re-mythologising of the creation of sexual difference itself. This constitutive *poiesis* (Gallop 1990) is as correctly described as political as it is philosophical or figurative, as real as it is imaginary, because it aims to recover the origin of the differentiation that gives rise to the very distinction of one discursive type from another and the privileging of one as more 'realistic' than another. Irigaray resists the fetters of the real/figurative distinction and pursues what might be called a *surrealisation* of sexual difference in the service of a politics of the imaginary, a politics that 'contains the idea that imagination – the possibility of imagining that things might be different – could have a critical function in political thought' (Whitford 1994: 380). An integral feature of feminism must be the forging of such a new language, one that does not erase the body but that 'speaks the body' (Irigaray 1993b: 19). Such a language, Irigaray attempts to demonstrate throughout her corpus, would lead the way to a re-articulation and re-evaluation of the encounter between the sexes, which, she says, should become

> An encounter characterized by belonging to a sexed nature to which it is proper to be faithful; by the need for rights to incarnate this nature with respect; by the need for the recognition of another who will never be mine...by the reinterpretation of notable figures or events in our tradition...by turning the negative, that is, the limit of one gender in relation to the other, into a possibility of love and creation.
>
> (Irigaray 1996: 11)

Here we begin to see, perhaps, that when Irigaray describes herself as a militant for the impossible, the 'impossible' refers to the desire for and the impossibility of a return to the moment in which the distinction between the ethical and the political has not taken place: the impossible, original non-difference of the inter-personal and the political. But do these words betray an idealism of the difference engendering 'love and creation' and a rejection of the political?

From surreality back to reality: Irigaray and the Italian Left

The traditional notion of politics and the political is neither simply rejected nor simply adopted by Irigaray, as a basis for effectuating change. While most of her writings ostensibly aim to contribute to what she identifies as the task of 'changing the forms of symbolic mediation' (for example, on the basis of her refiguration of the female body recalled above), she at the very least indicates her commitment to 'short-term' political goals as these are ordinarily conceived, and which explicitly take the form of civil action: for example, that 'in the meantime, the civil laws must be changed to give both sexes their identification as citizens' (Irigaray 1994: xvi).

Four lectures on politics and sexual difference, delivered under the auspices of the Italian Communist Party (PCI) and the 'Italian Left', between 1986 and 1989, and published in 1989 with a preface as *Le temps de la différence: pour une révolution pacifique* (Irigaray 1994), provide an insight into the possible political implications of the thinking of sexual difference, undertaken substantively across Irigaray's philosophical, psychoanalytical and poetic body of work. It has often been in Italy, where her standing as an *ostensibly* political thinker is most strongly established, that she has expounded her ideas concerning the need to establish sexuate (*sexué*) rights and obligations as cultural norms.

Sexuate rights and obligations

Irigaray considers the limitations on female emancipation, as this is conceived within an egalitarian framework, to be straightforward: no matter how legitimate demands for equality may be, every such victory for women is in danger of sanctioning the continued submission of women to 'the imperatives of a culture that is not their own...of alienating their female identity' (Irigaray 1993c: 85). She emphasises the need to propose 'new values that would make it possible to live sexual difference in justice, civility and spiritual fertility' (1994: xiv). In her addresses to several women's groups and at political meetings of the left, she has suggested how 'law' and 'rights' might be changed to respect sexual difference. In her overt and direct references to the politics of sexual difference, she has indicated how sexuate rights and obligations – rights based on sexed incarnation – may be enshrined in the law. She identifies 'the need for objective laws to organise relations among women and between women and men', and says that, 'In the absence of civil laws positively defining their real rights and duties, the only criteria women have to refer to are subjective ones', and as long as this is the case, 'there can be no democracy, however attractive the immediate allegiance of a collectivity to a proposition may be' (Irigaray 1996: 2).

In several writings, particularly in the interviews and Congress addresses, Irigaray has attempted to articulate concrete examples of the everyday statutes and injunctions that may follow from such an incorporation of sexual difference into a 'new civil code' (1994: 84). In an interview conducted by Christina Lasagni, entitled 'Why define sexed rights?' she was asked to comment on how laws and rights might be created 'in accordance with sexual difference?' (Irigaray 1993c: 86). In response, she lists, in a very skeletal form, what are effectively 'sexed' versions of a set of recognisably liberal and leftist themes and feminist demands of one sort or another, formulated in the discourse of rights and obligations. For example, she invokes the right to 'human dignity', the rights of mothers in relation to their children, and to representation in civil authority in general and changes to laws on property. All of these are stated with little or no detail provided as to how these suggestions might be formulated in practice. As a political philosopher, she clearly sees her role in terms of explaining the need to undertake this 'revolution' and the nature of the ideas upon which it might ultimately be based. For example, she speaks at much greater length of women's alienation from the law 'from birth and by their genealogies'. Her proposals aimed at redressing this predicament are relatively programatic in tenor and briefly stated. She specifically suggests, for example, rights for 'everyone on the basis of sexual difference'; the reduction of 'the rights of groups or companies owned by one or only a few people'; the redefinition of 'adequate laws on housing and indeed private property'; redressing 'the infringement of space by pollution [and] enforced nomadism'; the reduction of 'the power of money' and the return to 'valid exchanges'; the questioning of 'the origins of the law'.

Such examples may seem extraordinarily naïve, simplistic, incomplete and certainly undeveloped in the ordinary sense, particularly in comparison to her textually subtle, linguistically and philosophically complex discussions of love, the body and mother–child relations. This brevity on practical matters, however, must always be set against the discursive breadth of the philosophical endeavour she is embarked upon. Her texts are suspicious of and resistant to any decision of the political whenever its demand threatens to limit their effect. They typically slide to and fro between philosophical reflection, psychoanalytic speculation and poetic discussion of the divine, while incorporating straightforward reference to and association with the daily life of sexed individuals in relation to one another. And although this might be taken as an indication of the simplicity of her political thinking, calculated in traditional scientific-political terms, it may also, more importantly, be taken to highlight the difficulty, or even the *impossibility*, of bridging the gap between the interpersonal and the political in general, or between psychoanalysis of individuals and the understanding of political culture at large. It must, in any case, be acknowledged that Irigaray goes out of her way to emphasise that this is precisely the terrain her thinking seeks to rework and work against: namely, *the epochal decision to think the politics of emancipation in terms of the struggle for equality.*

> [D]enying that women and men are different in the name of some hypo-
> thetical social equality is a delusion, a bias in favour of a split – an
> impossible split – between private life and social identity. Out of bed or
> away from home, we somehow mysteriously become unisexual or asexual.
>
> (Irigaray 1994: vii)

The practical struggle of identity politics across difference is here inversely represented as an 'impossible split' between the interpersonal and the political. It is
my contention that the new kind of political philosophy that Irigaray's work
develops emerges, precisely, out of its focus on this aporetic split. For Irigaray,
this moment of undecidability decisively corresponds to the encounter with the
other; *of the one (sex) with the (sexed) other,* and it is from within this encounter that
she articulates her 'argument' in favour of the contiguity of sexual difference
and the political, aiming to politically reorient her readers towards the 'politics of
sexual difference'. The apparent paucity of Irigaray's remarks on action and
policy, read in conjunction with the suggestions of the 'revolution' to come, must
always be weighed against the strength of her analysis of the current *impossibility*
of this revolution's expression in conventional political terms.

Conclusions

Irigaray's writing highlights and exploits the instability of the distinction between
the 'political' and the 'cultural', something evidenced in the fact that any 'short-
term' political aim must be informed by the more general cultural framework in
which it is conceived as such. Where there is a failure to think the
political/cultural relation (for example, in the form of prioritising the political),
then a political movement such as feminism is unwittingly prone to follow a
trajectory and 'agenda' that have parameters determined in advance by
masculinism. While Irigaray on many occasions acknowledges the strategic value
of the feminist politics of equality and its historical achievements, she is adamant
that its limitations are implicit in its conception of the political. As Whitford has
noted, Irigaray ultimately rejects the view that equality can even be an intelligible *goal* for women because 'the conditions for its intelligibility have not yet
been met' (Whitford 1994: 380). In other words, so long as sexual difference is
relegated to the discourse of the natural as opposed to the cultural, then it is not
even possible to think equality without appealing to a metaphysic that supports a
conceptual distinction between the female *gender* and the female *sex*. This is
precisely the metaphysic of the modern, phallocentric, 'political' or what
Irigaray calls the *masculine neutral*.

From a historical perspective, in its struggle against male power, the women's
movement has clearly had very real and immediate reasons to deny any significance to sexual difference. It has indeed sought to expose it as a weapon in the

hands of cynical male power, which is set on refusing to accept the political logic of modernity. Liberty, equality, fraternity, knowledge and reason are supposed to be guaranteed by the modern secular ethic. However, the promise of delivering the full benefits justly and to all are indisputably 'long term'. And it is somewhere between the present moment and an indefinitely postponed future that the rationalisation of violence towards the other – in the form of relatively benign prejudicial exclusions of *others*, or as the malignancy of torture – always takes place.

Much of what Irigaray says in the course of her Nietzschean re-evaluation of all (masculine) values appears at first to be based on a positive revaluation of ostensibly masculinist determinations of the feminine in relation to, for example, nature, maternity and feminine qualities, often precisely those motifs that the post-Beauvoirian women's movement, in its many variations, has long sought to reject and refute. On the one hand, Irigaray's writing is consequently, at the very least, in danger of playing into the hands of the masculinist conceptualisation of women. On the other, she has been suspected of overemphasising the space of women-among-themselves, of being a philosopher of lesbian separatism and of female-to-female relations, and consequently considered to say little of import with respect to the normative political project of women's appropriation of the public sphere (which, on this account, is to be regarded as essentially masculinist).

Irigaray's writing aims at the dismantling of patriarchy and at the same time sets out to accomplish its own distanciation from such a generic 'masculinism'. This is a discursive undertaking that involves a general strategy of avoidance of what could be called the traditional genre of political theorising, whether at the level of its literary style or in terms of its fundamental rejection of feminisms of equality, which historically have claimed the mantle of the political in feminism. While acknowledging the historical significance of the gains resulting from traditional 'political feminism' and its struggle for equality between the sexes, Irigaray continues to argue emphatically that the implicit understanding of the political on which it is based can never truly serve women's needs. Of necessity, these remain invisible in the conceptual light of the political culture to which it belongs. Her work undertakes to expose and redress the limits of this existing political culture and its failure to think sexual difference, and to promote a sexing of cultural politics that also, at the same time, serves as a form of feminine resistance to masculinist totality.

References

Boothroyd, D. 1996. 'Labial feminism: body against body with Luce Irigaray'. *Parallax* 3: 65–79.

Chanter, T. 1995. *The Ethics of Eros*. London: Routledge.

Gallop, J. 1990. *Thinking Through the Body*. New York: Columbia University Press.

pIrigaray, L. 1985a. *This Sex Which is Not One*. Ithaca NY: Cornell University Press.

—— 1985b. *Speculum of the Other Woman*. Ithaca NY: Cornell University Press.

—— 1991. *Marine Lover of Friedrich Nietzsche*. New York: Columbia University Press.
—— 1993a. *An Ethics of Sexual Difference*. Ithaca NY: Cornell University Press.
—— 1993b. *Sexes and Genealogies*. New York: Columbia University Press.
—— 1993c. *Je, Tu, Nous*. London: Routledge.
—— 1994. *Thinking the Difference*. London: Athlone.
—— 1996. *I Love to You*. London: Routledge.
Whitford, M. 1991. *Luce Irigaray: Philosophy in the Feminine*. London: Routledge.
—— 1994. 'Irigaray, Utopia and the death drive'. In C. Burke, N. Shaw and M. Whitford (eds). *Engaging with Irigaray*, pp. 379–400. New York: Columbia University Press.

Part III

Commodification of sexuality

Economic activity and public policy

13 Sexuality and the International Conference on Population and Development

The Catholic Church in international politics

Palena R. Neale

This chapter examines how the various bodies of Christ, such as the Church, the Holy See and the pope, have been used to define woman as wom(b)an, woman defined in relation to her body. Specifically, it will explore how the political and religious bodies of Christ engaged with the international community in an attempt to maintain control of wom(b)an's body at the International Conference on Population and Development (ICPD), sponsored by the United Nations and held in Cairo, 1994, particularly with respect to wom(b)an's roles, reproductive options and sexuality. I shall begin by reviewing briefly how the pope has been invested with a composite of authority, jurisdiction and sovereignty to direct the Universal/Catholic Church, the Holy See and the Vatican City State. I shall then examine how this power has been used to define, assign and confine woman as wom(b)an, and to develop doctrine presented as 'divine', such as that concerning marriage and the family, birth control, abortion and homosexuality. Each of these doctrines works on its own and in conjunction with the others to discipline, punish, regulate and control the bodies of 'the faithful', with particular consequences for 'woman'. Finally, I shall explore how the bodies of Christ operated within the international arena both prior to and during the conference in an attempt to preserve a specific, Catholic articulation of wom(b)an.

It is necessary to clarify several points at the outset. The first centres on the '(official) Catholic perspective', the 'hierarchical perspective', the 'official Church position' or the 'magisterial perspective'. Quite simply they all refer to the same process or stamp of approval whereby a certain issue has received papal and episcopal attention, known as 'hierarchical attention', and thus becomes the 'official line'. This does not refer to the multitude of the faithful and their respective views, which are neither unanimous nor easily ascertainable. It is a well-known fact that there often exists a gulf between the 'official' Catholic perspective and the practising Catholic in the pew.

The second point of clarification that I would like to offer concerns the concentration on woman. The point that should be remembered is that any discourse that moves to discipline, punish, regulate and control contains within it implications for both men and women. The primary focus on woman within this chapter is based on the disproportional interest on behalf of the Church hierarchy in the bodies of women. This interest has a 2,000 year history and is rich in regulatory imperatives that target specifically the bodies of women. That is not to say, however, that they bear no implications for the male population.

The power of the pope

The Bishop of Rome has had granted two principal doctrines inherent to the Petrine office: namely, papal primacy and the gift of infallibility. Put differently, the pope in the exercise of the Petrine function derives his supreme spiritual authority through the Spirit of God and receives doctrinal support from the doctrines of papal primacy and infallibility. It is also important to consider the temporal sovereignty and independence bestowed upon the papacy based on the 1929 Lateran Treaty.

Papal primacy refers to the primacy of the pope over the whole Church. The pope, by definition, is installed as the head of the Church, which would extend to all expressions of Christianity, not simply the Catholic Church. The doctrine of papal infallibility institutionalised the understanding that there has been and continues to be divine assistance bestowed upon the pope, thereby preventing the possibility and liability of papal error in teachings on faith and morals (Hebblethwaite 1986: 12–51). Thus, at the most general level, the papacy derives its spiritual authority from the Spirit of God and is operationalised through the doctrines of papal supremacy and infallibility.

Cardinale outlines what he terms the political means available to the pontiffs for the deployment of papal power: namely, papal diplomacy, arbitration, concordats and participation in intergovernmental organisations (Cardinale 1976: 25–34). Here I am going to focus on the first and last – or papal diplomacy and participation in intergovernmental organisations. Simply put, papal diplomacy is directed at regulating the mutual relations between Church and state to ensure peaceful harmony between the two powers and thereby advancing the religious, moral and social welfare of peoples (Cardinale 1976: 25–34). Among the primary aims of papal diplomacy are the promotion of closer relations between the Apostolic See and the local Churches, the protection of Church and the Holy See's interests within the country of operation, the advancement of universal goals such as the promotion of international order, and the creation of friendly relations among nations realised through peaceful coexistence. Papal diplomacy is not limited to the ecclesiastical and political spheres; papal commissions extend into the areas of development and ecumenism (Cardinale 1976: 37–56). Finally, as previously mentioned, the papacy ensures that active participation with intergovernmental and international organisations is maintained and cultivated. The Holy See has throughout history maintained an active diplomacy and currently maintains formal diplomatic relations with 157 countries where sixty-seven of these maintain permanent resident diplomatic missions to the Holy See in Rome. The remainder have missions located outside Italy with dual accreditation. The Holy See also maintains ninety-one permanent diplomatic missions abroad (Bremner 1995).

The papacy ensures that active participation with intergovernmental organisations is maintained and cultivated. For example, the Holy See has permanent observer status at the United Nations (UN): the office of the UN in Geneva and specialised institutes; the UN Food and Agriculture Organisation in Rome; the UN Educational, Scientific and Cultural Organisation in Paris. The Holy See also has a member delegate at the International Atomic Energy Agency and at the UN Industrial Development Organisation in Vienna. It maintains permanent observers at the Organisation of American States in Washington, DC, and the Council of Europe. In addition, the Holy See has diplomatic relations with the European Union in Brussels (Bremner 1995).

'Woman' in Catholicism

The official Catholic perspective of woman modelled after the blessed Virgin Mary finds her truest expression through the sincere gift of self most fully realised as some combination of the trinity, virgin–mother–spouse (see also Finlayson, Chapter 8 of this volume). The lowest common denominator of each – and required for the realisation of all – is the female body, or the biological difference (or uniqueness) detailed in Genesis. 'Woman' in Catholicism is designated as a site for Catholic investment, where the dignity and vocation of woman are realised most fully through the use or disuse of the female body. The following section examines briefly how woman's body is used as a site for Catholic investment, particularly through an examination of discourses on marriage and the family, birth control, abortion and sexuality.

> A man and a woman united in marriage, together with their children, form a family. This institution is prior to any recognition by public authority, which has an obligation to recognise it. It should be considered the normal reference point by which the different forms of family relationships are to be evaluated.
>
> (*Catechism of the Catholic Church*, 1994, no. 2202: 475)

The traditional view of marriage within the Catholic Church was clear. The primary purpose of marriage was procreation and the rearing of children; physical love between husband and wife was subordinate. This view, however, was modified in *Gaudium et Spes, Pastoral Constitution on the Church in the Modern World* (1965) under the title 'Some more urgent problems'. According to Davey (1991), there were two important developments reconceptualising marriage and sexuality: namely, the move to a covenant versus contractual marriage, and divorce, remarriage and the Eucharist. Very briefly, marriage as a covenant saw a move from marriage as a contractual device, the primary purpose of which was to protect sexual rights, to marriage as a covenant, whereby the whole of each life is embraced and is not simply a venue for procreation. This reconceptualisation bears considerable legal consequences. Specifically, a covenant, unlike a contract, is witnessed by God and therefore, in the eyes and laws of the Church, cannot be broken. Davey notes that this 'personalist' view of marriage was expanded and reinforced in Pope Paul VI's encyclical *Humanae Vitae* (1968), in which he speaks of marriage covenants as the special relationships whereby man and woman are equal companions in an everlasting friendship (Davey 1991: 267–71). Although it is not my intention to discuss in any detail divorce, remarriage and the Eucharist, it is worth noting that the Church finds it impossible in most cases to recognise the termination of a marriage. Specifically, divorce in the Catholic Church is a violation of the dominical command that states 'what God has joined together let no one separate' (Matthew 19:6; Mark 10:9). The Church regards divorce and remarriage without an annulment as an automatic forfeiting of the Eucharist, the most important and significant celebration in the Church's worship of Christ.

It is useful to draw attention to a few general considerations and implications regarding the Church's teaching with respect to marriage and the family. Intimately bound up in the Church's articulation of the family is a heterosexual imperative, a marital imperative and a procreative imperative. Further, this particular articulation is set up as the divine moral standard from which all else is gauged. More specifically, a heterosexual imperative is at work which targets individuals, partnerships and ultimately the family. This effectively excludes any alternative expressions of personal commitment in the form of partnerships outside the heterosexual imperative, such as gay and lesbian partnerships, as well as heterosexual partnerships that exist apart from marriage. The heterosexual imperative is further able to exclude and police alternative forms of expression by defining them as the other/deviant to the universal/Catholic norm. Therefore, by insisting on a heterosexual imperative, the Church is effectively able to deny matrimony and hence family to that which it defines as the 'other'. Furthermore, prescriptions calling for the unconditional commitment to the transmission of life work to regulate and control both the heterosexual and homosexual laity with respect to sexual activity. The procreative imperative is a theme that is developed further in the Church's position regarding birth control.

The Church's teaching on birth control and contraception is very clear. *Humanae Vitae, On Human Life* (1968), the papal encyclical on the regulation of birth, provided the definitive pronouncement on birth control and contraception, while implicitly encoding the Church's understanding on sexuality and morality. Birth control, as detailed by the Church magisterium and enshrined in doctrine, refers to an attempt to regulate human sexuality. This is permitted in the form of natural family planning or the use of a woman's infertile period for the marriage act, provided there are reasonable grounds for the couple's unwillingness to conceive or their desire to space out children (Pope Paul VI 1968: nos. 10–11, 16:12–13, 16–17). Contraception, often referred to as artificial contraception, refers to those methods – such as sterilisation, intrauterine devices, condoms, the pill and abortion – that are utilised with the specific intent of regulating and/or interrupting the generative process. Contraception has been, and still is, vehemently condemned by the Church magisterium (nos. 14:15–16).

Regardless of theological dissent, opposition expressed on behalf of the laity, and ministerial reluctance to *Humanae Vitae* (1968), as well as Church precedents for magisterial change, the traditional teaching regarding birth control and contraception was, and still is, enforced to regulate and control human sexuality in general, and women's bodies in particular. Except in the most limited of cases, women are not free to make contraceptive choices. This effectively instils one of two 'options': namely, abstinence from sexual activity or perpetual pregnancy. The Church magisterium denies women reproductive rights, and as Ruether asserts, reflects a 'patriarchal clericalism' that is unwilling to 'accept women's autonomous personhood' (Ruether 1991: 263). Furthermore, the legislative magisterium is able to discipline and punish dissenting bodies through the sacrament of penance directed at the laity. The Church hierarchy is further able to regulate and control the soldiers in the field, or the Catholic ministry, who are expected to perform according to plan or face disciplinary action ranging from intimidation to direct expulsion from the Church. Also falling under the broad category of birth control is abortion (see also Amir and Benjamin, Chapter 14 of this volume).

Abortion, or the intentional expulsion of the foetus from a woman's womb, is, according to Church doctrine, 'gravely contrary to the moral law'. According to the *Catechism of the Catholic Church*, the Church, since the first century, has maintained the 'moral evil' of all procured abortions. Similarly, formal co-operation in obtaining an abortion is tantamount to a 'grave offence'. Women who undergo an abortion, as well as those involved in the abortion procedure, are subject to the penalty of excommunication, as specified by *Canon Law* (1992: n. 2271–3, 489–90). The crime against human life in the particular form of abortion is, and has been, condemned through the legislative power of the Church, and it remains unchangeable, as detailed in documents ranging from *Apostolicae sedia* (1869), *Code of Canon Law* (1917), *Casti connubii* (1930), *Gaudium et Spes* (1965), *Humanae Vitae* (1968), *Declaration on Abortion* (1974), *Catechism of the Catholic Church* (1994), and *Evangelium Vitae* (1995), to list but a few. What is stressed according to each and every communication on behalf of the Church and papal pronouncement is that, from the moment of conception, the embryo must be treated as a person and must be defended, cared for and healed, analogous to any other human being. Further, this 'inalienable right to life' must be recognised and respected by civil society, as well as by political authorities (*Catechism of the Catholic Church* 1994, nos. 2270–5, 2319–23: 489–90, 498–9). Human rights must be extended to the innocent and vulnerable foetus in all but the most limited situations (Ratzinger 1991: 2–3).

Contrary to popular perception, the Catholic position on abortion does not reveal a monolithic theological, canonical or scholastic body of thought that has remained unchanged throughout the centuries. Theologians, canonists and priests have for centuries debated issues surrounding abortion, such as hominisation, or the point at which an embryo becomes a human being, the body–soul relationship, as well as the relationship between the Church's conceptualisation of sexuality and the condemnation of abortion (Hurst 1990: 1–3). As many scholars note, each of the issues contains a history rich in contemplation, which highlights diversity and inconsistency when reviewed throughout the centuries. Also of significance when examining abortion through history is the relationship between abortion and papal infallibility. Again, contrary to popular perception, abortion is not governed by papal infallibility, despite Church communications and papal pronouncements that often 'appear' as infallible teachings. Hence ecclesiological inconsistencies and the exclusion of abortion from the realm of infallibility provide an opening for discussion and moral contemplation regarding abortion, despite attempts to give the appearance of a debate long concluded. As Hurst maintains, 'The opinion of all church scholars and theologians has *never* been unanimous on abortion' (1990: 2).

Homosexuality and 'woman'

As numerous theologians note, homosexual activity within official Catholic teaching has been judged anywhere from unnatural and sinful to intrinsically evil (McBrien 1994: 993–1000; Porcile-Santiso 1990: 209–10; Potts 1991: 276–9; Ruether 1990: 221–31). Pronouncements ranging from Saint Paul and Thomas Aquinas through to the most recent statements on behalf of the Church hierarchy have all taken part in condemning homosexual activity as contrary to the laws of nature, as well as violating the fundamental purpose of sexual activity: namely, procreation. According to the *Catechism of the Catholic Church*, one of the most recent reference texts for the teaching of Catholic doctrine, homosexuality is understood as:

> ...relations between men or between women who experience an exclusive or predominant sexual attraction towards persons of the same sex. It has taken a great variety of forms through the centuries and in different cultures. Its psychological genesis remains largely unexplained. Basing itself on Sacred Scripture, which presents homosexual acts as acts of grave depravity, Tradition has always declared that 'homosexual acts are intrinsically disordered'. They are contrary to the natural law. They close the sexual act to the gift of life. They do not proceed from a genuine affective and sexual complementarity. Under no circumstances can they be approved.
>
> (*Catechism of the Catholic Church* 1994, no. 2357: 504–5)

Homosexuality is divided into the condition (disorder) and the activity (sin), with the former being tolerated and the latter inadmissible. Although there have been various attempts to justify the magisterium's position within Scripture and sacred texts, the official reasoning underpinning the ban on homosexual activity resides in the relationship between sexual activity and procreation. Specifically, the hierarchical magisterium's opposition towards homosexual activity is founded on the principle of finality, which insists that in order for sexual activity to have 'true meaning' and 'moral rectitude', it must be within a 'true' marriage and must always remain open to the possibility of the transmission of life (McBrien 1994:

995–1000). Homosexual activity is incapable of falling within the parameters of the principle of finality, as it simply cannot find expression in what the Church defines as a 'true' marriage and is further incapable of remaining open to the possibility of the transmission of life. Homosexual activity is denied expression and is deemed devoid of moral rectitude. Hence the heterosexual imperative operating in conjunction with the procreative imperative is used to condemn homosexuality in general and to forbid homosexual activity in particular.

The Holy See and international politics

What is important to consider now is how the particular or Catholic expression of 'woman', including doctrine(s) directly affecting women, is advanced as the universal/Catholic in international venues and events. An examination of the Holy See's position at the ICPD, particularly that pertaining to woman and the family, reproductive health and reproductive rights, reaffirms traditional Church teaching on 'woman', namely, woman as wife and mother, or wom(b)an. This further highlights the politics at stake in the articulation of woman and exposes the political battles being fought by the bodies of Christ in the name of 'woman'.

The ICPD evolved from a series of preliminary sessions and regional population conferences regarding issues such as population, development and sustainable economic growth, as well as national population reports prepared by over 150 countries. The conference itself, held 5–13 September 1994 in Cairo, was the largest meeting on population and development ever held, attracting over 10,000 participants from 180 countries, including 4,000 representatives from some 1,500 different NGOs and over 4,000 journalists (UNFPA 1994: A:2).

The Holy See, by virtue of its permanent observer status as a non-member state, was an active, vocal and some would argue obstructionist participant at the UN-sponsored conference. The Holy See brings with it the moral and religious teaching of the Catholic Church and specifically the agendas of the current papacy. John Paul II, representing the most authoritative body of Christ on earth, set into motion a vehement attack on the ICPD and the draft Programme of Action.

Five months prior to the actual conference, the Vatican embarked upon an unprecedented campaign in a final effort to market the moral visions of John Paul II. Included here are some of the major and/or public (ab)uses of the bodies of Christ, specifically the pope, the Holy See and the Vatican. Specifically, Pope John Paul II met privately with Dr Nafis Sadik, executive director of the UN Population Fund and Secretary-General of the ICPD, and criticised both the draft Programme of Action and her inability to steer this misconceived project back on track (18 March 1994, *L'Osservatore Romano*, English edn, 23 March 1994: 1–2). Shortly thereafter, he issued letters to every head of state asserting that the document promoted an individualistic lifestyle that was completely incompatible with marriage and would in fact work toward the obsolescence of marriage altogether (19 March 1994, *L'Osservatore Romano*, English edn, 20 April 1994: 1). In keeping with his 'educational' mission, he had summoned all the ambassadors assigned to the Vatican to review the Church's position on 'artificial' contraception and abortion (Vatican Information Service, 25 March 1994). He even made appeals to the Clinton administration, whereby he urged the United States to put an end to the 'war against the family' (*New York Times*, 24 April 1994: A18).

Throughout the spring and summer of 1994, Pope John Paul II continued to take advantage of every opportunity to publicly address audiences where he was able to denounce the conference and the draft Programme of Action, insisting that it was a 'plot to destroy the family' and represented the 'snare of the devil' that was working to promote a 'culture of death' (John Paul II, Addresses of 15, 24 April; 12, 19, 26 June; 3, 10, 17, 24, 31 July; 7, 14, 28 August; 4 September 1994).

In August 1994, just weeks before the conference was set to begin, it was reported that John Paul II had reached out to Islamic countries, particularly the repressive regimes of Libya and Iran, in a last-ditch attempt to form a pro-life coalition that strictly prohibited abortion, 'artificial' contraception, and sterilisation (*New York Times*, 18 August 1994: A1). Interestingly enough, a Libyan news agency later reported that in return for Libya's support in condemning the Cairo conference, Vatican diplomats were prepared to support Libyan efforts to resolve their differences with Western governments regarding the 1988 bombing of the Pan Am jet over Lockerbie (Gould 1994/95: 14–19; Ruether 1994/95: 20–1; *New York Times*, 18 August 1994: A1). However, Vatican officials have denied this.

The bodies of Christ did not stop at pre-conference media manipulation and sensationalism and were equally active within the conference itself. For example, the Vatican immediately seized upon the reference to abortion and was able to influence conference debate, and, as some delegates charged, impeded further progress and blocked the conference agenda (*New York Times*, 8 September 1994: A1). Abortion alone was not the sole area of contention between the Vatican and the majority of UN delegations in Cairo. The lowest common denominator regarding the Holy See's partial consensus and areas of objection appeared to be located in women's status and the sexual and reproductive rights of individuals and couples (Shannon 1994/95: 3–10).

The sixteen-chapter document, or the 'Programme of Action', adopted at the final session, calls for new strategies to address population issues by acknowledging and working within the mutually reinforcing relationships among population and development issues. Running throughout the document is the theme of empowerment of persons in general and women in particular, seen as the key to providing more options through expanded choices by opening access to education, health services, skill development and employment. The 'Programme of Action' maintains that attempts to slow population growth, reduce poverty, improve economic progress and environmental protection, and reduce unsustainable consumption and production are interrelated and mutually reinforcing (UN 1994, 1: 4).

Of particular importance for the purpose of this essay is the position of the Holy See with respect to the final document put forth at the ICPD. The reservations of the Holy See have been summarised as follows: those that involve a loss of control of the female body, as well as those initiatives that are ambiguous regarding the family, marriage and sexuality (Shannon 1994/95: 3–10). Specifically, initiatives containing or making reference to terminology such as 'sexual health', 'sexual rights', 'reproductive health', and 'reproductive rights' are completely unacceptable to the Holy See, as they are in violation of Church teaching on 'artificial' contraception as it relates to pregnancy prevention and education and protection from HIV, as well as to Church teaching on abortion. The second significant area of objection centres around the ambiguity in the 'Programme of Action' regarding the family. According to Catholic doctrine, the family must consist of a man/husband and a woman/wife, which serves as the basic unit of society; there is no room within Catholic doctrine for 'alternative' (read homosexual) family units.

Conclusions

It has been my intention to explore the issue of papal power and to review how the spiritual sovereignty, authority and jurisdiction assigned to the papacy has been used as political power and as a means to gain entrance to the international political arena. Specifically, I have attempted to highlight the political use of the spiritual by examining how spiritual power has been used to define the Catholic wom(b)an. I have also reviewed how this power was used at the ICPD in an attempt to enforce this particular articulation of wom(b)an.

I would like to offer two observations in conclusion. The first pertains to the Holy See's permanent observer status as a non-member state. Why does a religious body assume such a position, particularly when no other religious grouping enjoys similar status? The attempt by the Holy See to turn the ICPD into an international conference on abortion was met with much criticism from the majority of participating delegations, and it led one Egyptian delegate to ask 'if the Vatican rules the world?' (*New York Times*, 8 September 1994: A1). Similarly, the Vatican's permanent observer status as a non-member state was challenged by numerous NGOs that participated at the ICPD, and it has been challenged more recently at the World Conference on Women held in Beijing. Ultimately, the 'voice of God' was heard loud and clear when the Holy See attempted to advance a particular notion of what can and should be done with respect to population, development and sustainable economic growth: increase food planning, not family planning.

Perhaps, at the most basic level, the idea of increasing food planning as a potential solution to population problems appears logical. There is, however, more at stake. For instance, the insistence by the Holy See's delegation that food planning should remove, replace or somehow negate family planning (read 'artificial' family planning) devalues the suggestion of food planning. The Holy See's vocal proposals, including their obstinate behaviour surrounding abortion, resulted in the shaping of the conference agenda, and it is illustrative of a power performance that sought to advance a particular or Catholic solution as the universal one.

The second and final observation I would like to mention relates to sexuality. All the bodies of Christ, the pope, the Holy See and the Church are celibate males, whose power and control requires absolute sexual and reproductive renunciation. How is it that the celibate bodies of Christ exhibit a disproportional interest in the bodies of wom(b)an? Perhaps before that question can be addressed, the whole notion of clerical celibacy needs to be called into question. Surely the decrease in the number of women and men religious entering consecrated life, the number of 'persons religious' leaving the Church in favour of marriage and family, and the numerous instances of priestly sexual activity are symptomatic of a much larger problem. Has the celibate imperative, which requires a renunciation of sexuality and sexual activity, corrupted the fundamental goal of preaching the Gospel and saving souls by a desire to regulate and control? The bodies of Christ, after all, derive their position at one level from their biological specificity or male anatomy, and also derive hierarchical power based on a commitment to discipline, punish, regulate and control the corporeal body for the priestly ministry. Hence preaching the Gospel and saving souls is at one level dependant on rule – rules that deny sexual activity as well as an active ruling of the celibate body. Perhaps this sheds some light on the rules and ruling of wom(b)an, whose roles are defined and confined as wife and mother with extremely limited reproductive options.

References

Bremner, M.J. (ed). 1995. 'Background notes: the Holy See, September 1995'. *Bureau of Public Affairs*@gopher://dosfan.lib.uic.edu.

Cardinale, H.E. 1976. *The Holy See and the International Order*. London: Colin Smythe.

Catechism of the Catholic Church. 1994. London: Geoffrey Chapman.

Davey, T. 1991. 'Marriage and sexuality'. In A. Hastings (ed.), *Modern Catholicism: Vatican II and After*, pp. 267–71. Oxford: Oxford University Press.

Gould, C. 1994/95. 'Hellfire and diplomacy'. *Conscience* 15: 14–19.

Hebblethwaite, P. 1986. *In the Vatican*. Oxford: Oxford University Press.

Hurst, J. 1989. *The History of Abortion in the Catholic Church: The Untold Story*. Washington DC: Catholics For a Free Choice.

John Paul II. Address before the Regina Coeli, St. Peter's Square. 24 April 1994. Address before the Angelus, St. Peter's Square. 17 April; 12, 19, 26 June; 3, 10 July. Address at Castel Gandolfo: 17, 24, 31 July; 7, 14, 28 August, 4 September 1994.

McBrien, R.P. (ed.). 1994. *Catholicism*, 3rd edn. London: Geoffrey Chapman.

Paul VI. 1968. *On Human Life, Humanae Vitae*. London: Catholic Truth Society.

Porcile-Santiso, M.-T. 1990. 'Roman Catholic teachings on female sexuality'. In J. Bercher (ed.), *Women, Religion and Sexuality*, pp. 192–220. Geneva: World Council of Churches.

Potts, T.C. 1991. 'Homosexuality'. In A. Hastings (ed.), *Modern Catholicism: Vatican II and After*, pp. 276–9. Oxford: Oxford University Press.

Ratzinger, J.C. 1991. *Human Life Under Threat*. London: Catholic Truth Society.

Ruether, R.R. 1990. 'Catholicism, women, body and sexuality: a response'. In J. Bercher (ed.), *Women, Religion and Sexuality*, pp. 221–32. Geneva: World Council of Churches.

—— 1991. 'The place of women in the Church'. In A. Hastings (ed.), *Modern Catholicism: Vatican II and After*, pp. 260–6. Oxford: Oxford University Press.

—— 1994/95. 'The Vatican and Islam'. *Conscience* 15: 20–1.

Shannon, D. 1994/95. 'The Vatican and the Cairo Conference'. *Conscience* 15: 3–10.

UN 1994. Draft Programme of Action adopted at the International Conference on Population and Development, Cairo, 5–13 September 1994, A/CONF.171/L5.

UNFPA 1994. Press Summary of Key Recommendations from the International Conference on Population and Development, 13 September, pp. 1–14.

14 Sexuality and the female national subject

Contraception and abortion policy in Israel[*]

Delila Amir and Orly Benjamin

Until recently the issue of abortion has generally been dealt with from two main points of view. First, abortion was analysed as an issue of conflict between women and the political establishment (Lovenduski and Outshoorn 1986). Second, it was examined as an issue that triggers the exertion of social control on women in order to prevent the violation of the hegemonic moral order (Petchesky 1984). These two scholarly discussions have provided a framework for understanding sexual and reproductive behaviour in terms of its connections with the normative order around gender and the symbolic world of any collective. One question may be raised on the basis of the suggested link between sexual and reproductive behaviour and the collective's moral and gender order: what is the relevance of such behaviour to processes related to the constitution of the national subject in terms of its gendered affiliation? Furthermore, if we accept that women's sexual and reproductive behaviour consists of primary components of the moral order, a second question may be raised: to what extent is the constitution of women's affiliation to the national collective conditioned by their following the imperatives of the moral order? In this chapter we explore these questions within the Israeli context.

Conflict and control

The literature on political conflict contended that women's sexual and reproductive practices and behaviours have a high potential for tension on both the institutional and personal level. Abortion has been historically defined as a major arena for women's political struggle for rights over their bodies world-wide (Petchesky 1984; Berer 1993). A more recent source of tension is the issue of contraceptives. Although the availability of contraceptives has expanded women's options in controlling their fertility, paradoxically it has also created a new area of regulation and control regarding the sexual and reproductive behaviour of women (Nathanson 1987; Chilman 1987).

One explanation for the conflict potential of these issues links sexuality and reproduction to the core normative order and the symbolic world of any collective (Schur 1984; Davis 1985). It has also been claimed that a dominant group reacts in an extreme fashion to statements or behaviours that give an alternative interpretation of its 'symbolic world' (Berger and Luckmann 1966). Thus alternative sexual and reproductive conduct is viewed as a threat to and an attack on the moral and symbolic system of the dominant group or culture (Lauderdale 1976). This argument may be linked to the more general feminist contention regarding the universality of institutions that appropriate the privilege of defining normative behaviour and requiring women's sexual and reproductive practices to adhere to it (Lorber 1993). One of the central institutions that articulate, manage and impose such normative requirements in contemporary societies is the state and its various extensions (Henshaw 1990; Berer 1993; Lovenduski and Outshoorn 1986).

The feminist perspective has further highlighted the multidimensional meanings of these issues on both the personal and the political levels. Butler (1993), for example, introduced the notion of 'trouble' as experienced on both these levels (see Lloyd, Chapter 11 of this volume). An unwanted pregnancy is not only experienced as 'trouble' on the personal level – involving decision-making, pain and expense – but is often also perceived as 'trouble' on the political level – involving either tensions between opposing value systems or challenges to the hegemonic moral order. In exploring this 'trouble' at the political level, we have suggested (Amir and Benjamin 1992) that what is most troubling about a woman who chooses to terminate her pregnancy is her definition of it as 'unwanted'. Such a definition contradicts the social ethos still prevalent in Israel that perceives pregnancy and its outcome as unconditionally welcomed by the mother. Despite the increasing legitimacy of women's reproductive choices, the idea that women only choose motherhood under certain conditions does not fit with the social expectation that women are mothers first and foremost (Hutter and Williams 1981; Oakley 1981; Fisher 1987).

The maintenance of motherhood as a central criterion for women's commitment to the moral order has legitimised various institutional controlling practices (Braverman 1991; Gerson 1989). However, 'control' of women is interesting not only in terms of the punitive deprivation of those who 'deviate' or 'get in trouble' (Butler 1993). It is even more interesting in terms of the constitution of the national female subject. Yuval-Davis (1989: 106), for example, argues that 'Women and their sexuality are seen as the gate-keeping elements for the boundaries of the national collectivity.' In addition to the requirement that women perform the role of reproducing the members of the nation, argues Hintjens (1993: 3) – on the basis of her comparison of three national movements – women's sexual mores make up a major component of the 'gendered terrain on which all national battles are fought'.

Yuval-Davis and Anthias (1993: 6) point to the complex link between women and the state, involving a duality that enables gender as a category to be maintained as both powerful and silenced. This approach provides a point of departure for elaborating on the relationship between women's sexual and reproductive behaviour and the constitution of the female national subject who is embedded in controlling practices. Previous attempts to theorise this relationship focused on either women's contribution to the reproduction of the nation or on nationality and sexuality being two separate sources of identity (Mosse 1985; Parker *et al.* 1992). However, we have attempted to follow a line of argument that focuses on the way in which these two sources are derived from each other (see Finlayson, Chapter 8 of this volume) by drawing upon the argument that 'a nation can consolidate its identity by projecting beyond its own borders the sexual practices or gender behaviours it deems abhorrent' (Parker *et al.* 1992: 10). This suggestion is developed here in two directions: first, uncovering actual behaviours and characteristics that are deemed 'abhorrent'; second, examining the possibility that at times sexual behaviours that are deemed 'abhorrent' would also be visible within the nation itself. Under such circumstances it may be expected that difference will be emphasised not only in relation to the 'other' located beyond the border (Connolly 1991) but to categories of 'otherness' inside the nation.

Hence we suggest that in order to investigate the processes through which the female national subject is constituted, it is also necessary to ask how the *non-affiliated* female subject is constituted, and how her sexual and reproductive behaviour is defined *vis-à-vis* the moral order. This raises the possibility that controlling practices directed at women's sexual and reproductive behaviour bear two products. The first is the maintenance of normative boundaries; the second is the constitution of three differentiated subjects: the normative, the marginal and the 'other'.

The Israeli context

In Zionist rhetoric, much effort has been directed at constructing the woman soldier, the woman kibbutznik and pioneer, the working woman and the young woman as similar and equal to men in terms of her contribution to the collective and in terms of her entitlements (Fogel-Bijaoui 1997; Bloom 1991; Golan 1991; Safir 1991). However, most researchers looking at women in Israel tend to question the implied parallels between men and women in these contexts. This is true particularly for army service. For the Israeli man, the process of constituting his national identity is inseparable from his army service. At the same time it is widely agreed that, with regard to Israeli women, the army operates as a system emphasising their exclusion from the hegemonic national identity and from the experiences shaping it (Weinshall 1987; Bloom 1991; Bar-Yosef *et al.* 1978; Bloom and Bar-Yosef 1985; Bar-Yosef and Padan Eisenstadt 1977). Motherhood, rather than army service, has always been the necessary condition for social legitimation for Israeli women. It not only builds a sense of belonging, but is also an experience that creates a connection with the collective through institutions that provide care and education.

The Israeli abortion law

In Israel, as in most countries today, the sociopolitical stance toward abortion is legally formulated. The current law prohibits abortion except under specific circumstances, reflecting the broad public consensus that abortion is unacceptable as a contraceptive. Thus the law does not focus on abortion as a human right, but as a back-up procedure to correct technical and 'human' failures (Amir and Benjamin 1992). This legal device operates in the context of an open market for the purchase of contraceptives and a medical establishment that actively advocates their usage.

This supposedly pragmatic and accommodating rationale for abortion requires the discretionary decision of a medical committee composed of two physicians and a social worker, one of whom has to be a woman. The abortion committee is obliged to follow four guidelines as approval criteria:

- the pregnant woman's age – under 17 or over 40;
- the legal status of the future child – a product of incest, rape or out-of-wedlock pregnancy;
- hazard to the woman's physical or mental health;
- indications of defects or abnormality in the foetus's development.

These criteria can be seen as a compromise between four distinct political stances:

- the view of a small feminist group that introduced the concept of the woman's choice and right to her body;
- a secular welfare position emphasising the child's right to basic life chances;
- the religious attitude, which is primarily concerned with the legitimacy of the newborn, i.e. that it is born to a legitimately married couple;
- the demographic argument that until recently dominated Israeli nationalistic and sectarian ideology, which emphasises the importance of a high birth rate among Jewish families (Sabatello 1988; Amir and Navon 1989).

In this respect, the Israeli position towards abortion differs considerably from most other societies, where the rationale of abortion laws is linked to a broader socio-ethical principle, and where the state's position regarding the legitimacy of pregnancy termination and entitlement to privacy is clearly expressed. The absence of a voiced socio-ethical commitment in the law may be interpreted as a way of silencing political trouble and an effort towards depoliticisation of the issue (Lovenduski and Outshoorn 1986).

Defining encounters

In order to uncover the process through which the normative boundaries of the Israeli Jewish collective are constructed through encounters with women 'in trouble', we shall examine how the law is interpreted and applied by professionals. Following Joffe's understanding of professionals as 'front-line workers' (Joffe 1986), we suggest that their normalising practices are significant in normatively constituting national affiliation. The analysis of the discourse produced in 'defining encounters' reveals the way in which a politics of silencing appears when professionals are dealing with an individual woman in 'trouble'.

Specifically, our study is based on a secondary analysis of data collected in two studies:

1   Abortion Approval Committees (Amir and Benjamin 1992), when interviews were conducted with twenty-nine social workers serving on thirteen abortion approval committees out of the nineteen committees active at the time the study was carried out (1986–8).
2   Educating Immigrant Women (Amir and Elmelech 1992; Amir *et al.* 1995). This study was based on interviews of fifteen key people in twelve Israeli service organisations, which deal with immigrant women from the former USSR and also serve the general public. The issues addressed in the structured interviews concerned thoughts, perceptions and feelings about the sexual and reproductive behaviour of 'Russian' immigrants who arrived in Israel between 1989 and 1994 (about 600,000 immigrants entered Israel from the former USSR over that period).

The abortion approval committee: constituting the marginal

An abortion approval committee has permission to examine and assess not only the physical condition of the applicant and the circumstances of her pregnancy but also, and perhaps as an implicit agenda, her attitudes regarding sexual behaviour and commitment to motherhood. One striking statistic is that 95 per cent of applications are approved. This figure raises the possibility that the procedure is not so much concerned with decision-making as with performing educational and controlling functions.

Eighteen of the twenty-nine social workers reported that they, or the whole committee, discuss contraceptives with the woman, inquiring into what she has used and what she intends to use. Moreover, the applicant is often asked about her sexual behaviour, her relationship with the man involved in the pregnancy, and the extent to which she is determined to terminate her pregnancy. The applicant is thus compelled to discuss intimate issues in her life. In the context of this exposé, the woman is told that abortion can be detrimental to her future fertility and that emotional trauma may ensue (both these points are not substantiated by existing empirical evidence; Amir forthcoming; Teichman *et al.* 1993). Such information, apparently, is often transmitted in a disciplinary tone and form.

When social workers were asked why they think the pregnant woman should have to appear before the approval committee, many indicated that they considered the meeting an educational opportunity. First, it is a means of convincing her to use contraceptives regularly. Second, appearance before the committee teaches the woman a lesson in terms of assuming responsibility for her body and actions. Many of the social workers perceive their role primarily in terms of collecting information from the abortion candidate. This information serves two purposes. First, the social worker examines the extent of the woman's determination to forgo the pregnancy. Where determination is lacking, she is likely to encourage the woman to continue it to term. That kind of ambivalence is the declared justification of the committee mechanism itself: the prevention of 'unnecessary abortions', as defined by policy-makers (Amir and Navon 1989). Second, she examines the candidate's eligibility on the basis of the criteria that permit the committee to approve a termination of pregnancy. This probing for information usually focuses on the circumstances under which the pregnancy developed. Even young, unmarried women, who are clearly eligible for the abortion (both because they fit the age criteria and because of their out-of-wedlock pregnancy) are required to describe the nature of the relationship within which the sexual event occurred and to explain why they cannot build a family together with the man who is a partner to the pregnancy. While the issue of a relationship with a partner is only raised in the treatment of unmarried women, information regarding the use of contraceptives is required from women of all social categories. The women are treated as if all other sources of their identity – profession, socio-economic status, education – are all less important than their wayward contraceptive behaviour.

The study reveals a defining and constituting mechanism whereby the abortion candidate is covertly scolded for her actions, labelled as a deviant, warned not to repeat the behaviour, and 'educated' in the usage of contraceptives. She is held accountable for what is defined as her 'failure' to avoid 'trouble' by means of which she is constituted as marginal. The fact that a woman finds herself in a situation where she defines her pregnancy as unwanted is attributed to her surrender to spontaneous urges and seen as evidence of irresponsible sexual behaviour.

The educational focus of the approval committees raises the possibility that what is actually constituted throughout the process is the marginality of women who define their pregnancy as unwanted. In the very same process, the professionals involved constitute, via negation, the definition of the normative requirements of Israeli women in the realms of sexual and reproductive behaviour. That is, by confronting applicants with the 'norms', they clearly indicate the non-normative nature of these women's behaviour.

The procedure followed by the approval committee and the discourse produced by professionals in it has shown that three characteristics are attributed to the women: irresponsibility, lack of commitment, lack of good sense. In this context we then enquired about the socio-demographic characteristics of the applicants in comparison to the non-applicant. In their responses the interviewees from abortion approval committees consistently attributed to applicants a marginal familial status, emphasising that these women do not maintain long-term formal or legitimate intimate relationships, and claiming that most applicants are either adolescent, single, widowed or divorced – an opinion that is not substantiated by empirical evidence, as more than half of the applicants seeking abortion are married (*Israeli Monthly Statistical Supplement* 1992).

Educating immigrant women

Most Israeli service organisations have joined the national effort aimed at absorbing the mass immigration from the former Soviet Union. One of the major focuses of this national enterprise was found to be the intensive introduction of immigrant women to the use of medical contraceptives (Amir and Elmelech 1992; Amir *et al.* 1996). The basic working assumption was a total negation of the new immigrants' previous practice, i.e. the use of abortion as a common form of contraceptive. The social service establishment views ex-USSR women and their reproductive practices not only as different but as unacceptable. They expect Russian women to adapt quickly to Israeli 'norms' and to acquire reproductive and contraceptive practices supposedly characteristic of Israeli society and Western culture.

Among service organisations, health and medical services expressed the highest level of distress and anxiety about the potential dangers posed by the Russian women's 'deviant' behaviour, reflecting a panic reaction with moral overtones (Ben-Yehuda 1985; Cohen 1972). However, labelling the immigrant women and their behaviour as deviant cut across all the organisations. Even those that recognised the cultural and experiential differences spoke of the women as having to 'cross the gulf'. Understanding the difference mainly served an instrumental purpose, as a means of ensuring and enhancing the success of education and socialisation, and as a necessary condition in the process of absorption and integration.

Predominant in the professional discourse produced in the encounter between the absorbing establishment and the immigrants is the construction of the women as 'others': 'they don't use contraception'; 'their sexual behaviour is irresponsible and promiscuous'; 'they are different, they can't speak about sex at all'. Additionally, an explanation for this implied otherness is constructed: they are educated Ashkenazi, but behave like *'frechot'* because they didn't have any contraception 'there'. *'Frechot'* is a derogatory slang term often used to refer to inane Sephardic girls as part of the social construction of the difference between 'Ashkenazi' – Jews of European or Anglo-Saxon origins – and 'Sephardim' – Jews of Asian or African origin.

Such explanations about what 'really' happened 'there', in places where immigrant women come from, are articulated at various levels of knowledge and awareness. For example, the administrators and professionals interviewed completely ignored the fact that abortion in the USSR was a legal and normative behaviour, and that the procedure was neutralised of all its value-laden Western associations, being constructed as a completely instrumental and technical procedure, with no massive risk, similar to that of a tooth extraction (Gray-DuPlessix 1990; Remennik 1991). Yet, despite the accessibility of information and evidence regarding the Soviet reproductive reality, the absorbing establishment discourse continues to maintain its 'situational' explanation, i.e. 'they used abortion because they didn't have a choice'. On the basis of such assumptions embedded in the professional discourse, an expectation is constructed that, with the change in circumstances and the availability of contraception in Israel, immigrant women will soon become 'responsible and sensible'. One interviewee said forgivingly: 'It takes time to become an Israeli woman committed to the "nation" [*Am Israel*].'

However, the discourse is much less forgiving when discussing the sexual and reproductive behaviour of the immigrant women who have been in the country a longer while. At this stage, professionals express disappointment that these women continue to use abortion as a major means of family planning, saying: 'they overwhelm the [abortion approval] committees'. This disappointment is accompanied by an attack on the sexual behaviour of the immigrant women, which is, according to the interviewees, 'unbridled' and 'verging on promiscuity'.

This commitment to educate immigrant women has been legitimised by expressions of a paternalistic concern for women's health, and by an instrumental concern for the financial burden incurred by the host society in supporting an 'abortion industry'. Furthermore, massive mobilisation and involvement is justified as a necessary part of 'absorbing' the immigrants and helping them become 'Israeli women'. This image is discursively constituted through the presentation of 'us' as educated women who use contraceptives, who follow the 'Western way', and the immigrant women as the 'un-Western other'. The professionals involved in the encounter between the new immigrants and Israeli society appear to be holding a presumptuous stance that delegitimises difference ('it is not done here'). At the same time, emphasising the 'otherness' of new immigrants creates a clear normative image of the female who properly belongs to the Israeli collective.

Conclusions

In this chapter we used as our theoretical point of departure the feminist argument linking women's sexual and reproductive behaviour to the boundaries of national collectives (Yuval-Davis and Anthias 1993). We have elaborated on this framework to join scholars currently attempting to break with prevailing academic paradigms that treat nation and sexuality as discrete and autonomous constructs (Mosse 1985; Parker *et al.* 1992). Our focus on abortion-related controlling practices that depart from both the conflict-management approach and the social-control approach enabled us to analyse the way in which the practices that regulate sexual and reproductive behaviour not only constitute the 'normal' female subject (Amir and Benjamin 1992) but also normatively constitute the national female subject. Sexual normalisation, in our analysis, emerges as a primary component of discourses that create affiliation to the national collective.

What we find, then, is a contraceptive-focused normalising practice. The gatekeeping condition for joining in the Jewish collective is that abortion should not be used as a contraceptive, and that the 'trouble' of an unwanted pregnancy should be avoided in order to confine any possible challenge to the notion of committed motherhood. This condition, which is obviously specific to women, substantiates the argument in Yuval-Davis and Anthias (1993) regarding the dual position of women in the constitution of national collective boundaries. They are perceived both as equal members of the collective and as a special category in it defined by their reproductive roles. In Israel, we have shown, the reproductive role is understood as a commitment to legitimate motherhood. However, an integral part of this commitment is the expectation that women will join the national effort to silence the 'trouble' involved in any suggestion that pregnancy is unwanted. This politics of silencing is directed at keeping motherhood 'private'.

On the political level, silencing this 'trouble' is a major concern of legislators and policy-makers. This can be seen as a means of reducing internal political conflict and of blurring differences between ideological stances. One interesting point regarding the Russian women is that their past experiences serve as a source of knowledge and of resistance to attempts made by Israeli professionals to maintain their hegemony over the definition of sexual and reproductive behaviour. Their resources and practices continue to disrupt the silencing while further reinforcing their 'otherness'.

* The full version of this chapter is 'Defining encounters: who are the women entitled to join the Israeli collective?', in *Women's Studies International Forum* 20 (5/6): 639–50. Used with permission of Elsevier Science.

References

Amir, D. (forthcoming). *Abortion in Israel: Rhetoric and Reality.* Jerusalem: The Jerusalem Institute for Research on Israel. (Hebrew).

Amir, D., and Benjamin, O. 1992. 'Abortion approval as a ritual of symbolic control'. In C. Feinman, *The Criminalization of a Woman's Body*, pp. 5–26. New York: The Hayworth Press.

Amir, D., and Elmelech, Y. 1992. 'Educating Lenna: Israeli Organizations and Services Mobilize to Educate Women Immigrants from the Ex-USSR in Proper Sexual, Reproductive and Contraceptive Behaviour'. Research Report 13. Tel-Aviv: Institute for Social Research, Tel-Aviv University. (Hebrew).

Amir, D., and Navon, D. 1989. 'The Politics of Abortion In Israel'. Research Report 13–69. Tel-Aviv: Pinchas Sapir Research Institute, Tel-Aviv University. (Hebrew).

Amir, D., Remennick, L.I. and Elmelech, Y. 1996. 'Educating Lenna: women immigrants and 'integration' policies in Israel – the politics of reproduction and family planning'. In N. Lewin-Epstein, Y. Ro'i and P. Ritterband (eds), *Russian Jews on Three Continents: Migration and Resettlement*, pp. 495–509. London: Frank Cass Publishers.

Bar-Yosef, W.R., and Padan Eisenstadt, D. 1977. 'Role system under stress: sex roles in war'. *Social Problems* 25: 45–135.

Bar-Yosef, R., Bloom, R.A., and Tzivia, L. 1978. *Role Ideology of Young Israeli Women.* Jerusalem: Work and Welfare Research Institute, The Hebrew University of Jerusalem.

Ben-Yehuda, N. 1985. *Deviance and Moral Boundaries.* Chicago: University of Chicago Press.

Berer, M. 1993. 'Making abortion safe and legal: the ethics and dynamics of change'. *Reproductive Health Matters* 2: 5–10.

Berger, P.L., and Luckmann, T. 1966. *The Social Construction of Reality*. New York: Doubleday.

Bloom, R.A. 1991. 'Women in the defence forces'. In B. Swirski, and M. Safir (eds), *Calling the Equality Bluff: Women in Israel*, pp. 128–38. New York: Pergamon Press.

Bloom, R.A., and Bar-Yosef, R. 1985. 'Israeli women and military service: a socialization experience'. In M.P. Safir, M.P. Mednick, D.N. Izraeli, and J. Bernard (eds), *Women's Worlds: From the New Scholarship*, pp. 260–9. New York: Pergamon Press.

Braverman, L. 1991. 'Beyond the myth of motherhood'. In M. McGoldrick, M. Anderson, and F. Walsh (eds), *Women in Families: A Framework for Family Therapy*, pp. 227–43. New York: Norton.

Butler, J. 1993. *Gender Trouble: Feminism and the Subversion of Identity*. New York: Routledge.

Chilman, S.C. 1987. 'Reproduction norms and social control of women'. In J. Figueira-McDonough and R.C. Sarri (eds), *The Trapped Woman: Catch-22 in Deviance and Control*, pp. 34–52. Beverly Hills CA: Sage.

Cohen, S. 1972. *Folk Devils and Moral Panics*. London: MacGibbon & Kee.

Connolly, W.E. 1991. *Identity/Difference: Democratic Negotiations of Political Paradox*. Ithaca NY: Cornell University Press.

Davis, N. 1985. *From Crime to Choice: The Transformation of Abortion in America*. Westport CT: Greenwood Press.

Fisher, S. 1987. 'Good women after all: cultural definitions and social control'. In J. Figueira-McDonough, and R.C. Sarri (eds), *The Trapped Woman: Catch-22 in Deviance and Control*, pp. 318–47. Beverly Hills CA: Sage.

Fogiel-Bijaoui, S. (forthcoming). 'Women in Israel: the social construction of citizenship as a non-issue'. *Israeli Social Science Research* (Special Issue on Women in Israel).

Gerson, K. 1989. 'Reluctant mothers: employed women in the 80s'. In B.J. Risman, and P. Schwartz (eds), *Gender in Intimate Relationships: A Microstructural Approach*, pp. 205–19. Belmont CA: Wadsworth Inc.

Golan, A. 1991. 'Musings of an Israeli superwoman'. In B. Swirski, and M. Safir (eds), *Calling the Equality Bluff: Women in Israel*, pp. 99–101. New York: Pergamon Press.

Gray-DuPlessix, F. 1990. *Soviet Women Walking the Tightrope*. New York: Doubleday.

Henshaw, S.K. 1990. 'Induced abortion: a world review'. *Family Planning Perspective* 22: 76–89.

Hintjens, M.H. 1993. 'The place of women in nationalist discourse: three case studies'. In M.H. Hintjens (ed.), *Women in Nationalist Discourse*, pp. 1–16. Swansea: University College.

Hutter, B., and Williams, G. 1981. 'Controlling women: the normal and the deviant'. In B. Hutter, and G. Williams (eds), *Controlling Women*, pp. 9–39. London: Croom Helm. (Oxford Women's Series).

Israeli Monthly Statistical Supplement. 1992. Demographic Characteristics of Women Applying to the Abortion Approval Committees. 11. (Hebrew).

Joffe, C. 1986. *The Regulation of Sexuality*. Philadelphia PA: Temple University Press.

Lauderdale, P. 1976. 'Deviance and moral boundaries'. *American Sociological Review* 41: 660–4.

Lorber, J. 1993. *Paradoxes of Gender*. New Haven CT: Yale University Press.

Lovenduski, J., and Outshoorn, J. 1986. *The New Politics of Abortion*. London: Sage.

Mosse, L.G. 1985. *Nationalism and Sexuality: Middle-Class Morality and Sexual Norms in Modern Europe*. Madison WI: University of Wisconsin Press.

Nathanson, C. 1987. 'Family planning and contraceptive responsibility'. In S.F. Spicker, W.B. Bondeson, and H.T. Engelhardt, Jr. (eds), *The Contraceptive Ethos*, pp. 183–99. Dordrecht: Reidel.

Oakley, A. 1981. 'Normal motherhood: an exercise in self-control?' In B. Hutter and G. Williams (eds), *Controlling Women*, pp. 9–39. London: Croom Helm. (Oxford Women's Series).

Parker, A., Russo, M., Sommer, D., and Yeager, P. 1992. 'Introduction'. In A. Parker, M. Russo, D. Sommer, and P. Yeager (eds), *Nationalism and Sexualities*, pp. 1–18. New York: Routledge.

Petchesky, R. 1984. *Abortion and Woman's Choice: The State, Sexuality, and Reproductive Freedom.* Boston MA: Northeastern University Press.

Remennik, L. 1991. 'Birth control patterns in the USSR: abortion still dominant'. *Journal of Social Science and Medicine* 33: 841–8.

Sabatello, F.E. 1988. 'Abortion and the demographic issue in Israel'. *Welfare and Society.* 10: 69–75. (Hebrew).

Safir, M. 1991. 'Was the kibbutz an experiment in social and sex equality?' In B. Swirski, and M. Safir (eds), *Calling the Equality Bluff: Women in Israel*, pp. 251–60. New York: Pergamon Press.

Schur, M.E. 1984. *Labeling Women Deviant: Gender Stigma and Social Control.* New York: Random House.

Teichman, Y., Senhar, S., and Segal, S. 1993. 'Emotional reactions of Israeli women to abortion'. *American Journal of Orthopsychiatry* 63: 277–88.

Weinshall, D.T. 1987. 'Does military service help women into management?' *Women Management Review* 3: 38–45.

Yuval-Davis, N. 1989. 'National reproduction and 'the demographic race' in Israel'. In N. Yuval-Davis and F. Anthias (eds), *Women–Nation–State*, pp. 92–109. London: Macmillan Press.

Yuval-Davis, N., and Anthias, F. 1989. 'Introduction'. In N. Yuval-Davis and F. Anthias (eds), *Women–Nation–State*, pp. 1–15. London: Macmillan Press.

15 Sexual harassment in the workplace

Equality policies in post-authoritarian Spain

Celia Valiente

This chapter explores the role of the Spanish state in one domain of citizens' sexualities, namely sexual harassment in the workplace, which is at present an offence punishable under the labour law and the Penal Code. This chapter traces how unwanted sexual behaviour at work was first defined as a public problem in the mid-1980s by state feminists (see Stetson *et al.* 1995) and feminists within trade unions, and how the matter was placed on the government agenda (see Kingdom 1984: 3), and legislated and implemented in 1989 and 1995.

The example of sexual-harassment legislation in Spain demonstrates that the political battle around the establishment of state regulation of citizens' sexualities is in some cases a struggle over 'naming'. A social interaction (such as undesired sexual moves in the workplace) is identified as an unacceptable problem. Different actors then try to impose different conceptualisations of what constitutes sexual harassment, and different ways of regulating the issue according to their definitions of the country's cultural and historical identity. The policy that is eventually established incorporates both the winning definition of the problem and the accurate solution.

This chapter examines the elaboration of sexual harassment regulation through distinctive policy stages: problem definition and agenda setting; policy formulation; and policy implementation.

Problem definition and agenda setting

In order to establish a public policy, it is necessary for political élites to conceptualise a situation as a 'problem' requiring governmental intervention (Dery 1984). This stage of the policy-making process is called problem definition. It is particularly important in the case of sexual harassment, since the behaviour encompassed within this term had always existed but had never been seen as a serious issue that necessitated action by authorities (Stockdale 1991: 53). No specific legal definition of sexual harassment in the workplace existed in Spanish law up to 1989. To fight against unwanted sexual advances was more difficult at that time than later on, when a 'name' existed in the law to designate and punish this behaviour.

The task of defining sexual harassment as a problem that deserved state attention (and solutions) was undertaken from the mid-1980s mainly by feminists within the main trade unions – Unión General de Trabajadores (UGT) and Comisiones Obreras (CCOO) – and state feminists of the main women's machinery at the central state level – Instituto de la Mujer. Inspired by international examples, sexual-harassment activists promoted research both about the extent of unwanted sexual advances in Spain and about the difficulties of prosecuting the perpetrators.

The Madrid section of the UGT women's department commissioned a study about sexual harassment in the city of Madrid (Calle *et al.* 1988). The study was based on interviews with a non-representative sample of air hostesses, female administrative assistants and female workers in the hotel and catering industry and in chemical and metal factories. The study showed that in the three months preceding the interviews, the overwhelming majority of the interviewed declared they had suffered 'slight' sexual harassment, which occurred when a man in the enterprise behaved towards a female worker as follows: whistling at her 'in a provocative manner'; directing unwanted sexual comments, conversations or dirty jokes to her; and/or making flirtatious comments during work time. Half of those interviewed declared that they had received unwanted sexual glances, expressions or gestures. One out of four respondents reported receiving undesired phone calls or letters of a sexual content, or unwanted propositions to go out for dinner, to have a drink, or to join in parties 'with erotic intentions'. Also one out of four interviewed reported being intentionally pinched, touched or cornered without her consent. Finally, 4 per cent affirmed that they had 'been pressurised by a man in the workplace to maintain intimate contacts'.

The study also showed that the most frequent reactions by victims were (in this order): to offer resistance against the harasser, or to ignore the unwanted sexual advances in the hope that the perpetrator would stop (Calle *et al.* 1988: 57–8, 127). The findings of this and other studies showed that sexual harassment was widespread in Spain, a phenomenon already observed in studies of other countries (Carter 1992: 433; Fitzgerald 1993: 1071; Husbands 1993: 112; Stockdale 1991: 54).

With respect to state feminists, the Instituto de la Mujer also commissioned a study (INNER 1987). This was based on open-ended interviews with a non-representative sample of female workers in private firms in Madrid, Barcelona, Seville and Valencia, in hotels and catering, banking and insurance, textile and clothing industries, commerce, factories and offices. It showed that hardly any victims denounced their harasser. When victims rejected the harasser's advances, they were penalised in job promotions, continuously received reprimands for insignificant mistakes, or were assigned the most unpleasant jobs (INNER 1987: 36–7).

In the second half of the 1980s, most feminist trade unionists and femocrats agreed on two points: that sexual harassment was as widespread in Spain as elsewhere; and that no adequate mechanisms in the law or within the firms existed for preventing or prosecuting unwanted sexual advances (if victims dared to denounce them). Nevertheless, femocrats and feminist trade unionists disagreed over a crucial issue: the exact definition of sexual harassment.

Advocates of sexual-harassment policy agreed that the word 'harassment' meant unwanted sexual advances. Nevertheless, disagreements arose about which concrete acts constituted sexual harassment. A minority of femocrats and feminist trade unionists argued that a comprehensive range of behaviour had to be included in an official definition of sexual harassment, such as lascivious glances, and verbal and physical advances, although actions had to be punished differently in accordance with their seriousness. This broad definition was thought to be the prevalent definition in the United States.

The majority of Spanish sexual-harassment activists thought that such broad definition was exaggerated, typical of 'Anglo-Saxon puritanism', and completely alien to 'Mediterranean' (also described as 'Latin', 'South European' or 'Spanish') culture. Interestingly, the same arguments against what was thought of as 'Anglo-Saxon puritanism' were advanced in the discussion of sexual-harassment policies in other countries – for example, in France (Mazur 1993, 1996; Smith 1996). In Spain, this South European culture was seen in very positive terms, as a liberating culture in which people can express without obstacles an important dimension of the self – sexuality. Spanish culture was described as one in which people often tell jokes, frequently touch each other, accept consensual sexual relations at work, and publicly perform sexual behaviours (for instance, openly courting, or kissing and hugging in the street, to the amazement of foreigners). In such a culture, it is especially hard to assess whether people behave naturally according to their cultural patterns or harass. In contrast, the Anglo-Saxon culture was described in negative terms, as one in which people have to behave as prudes due to social control, guilty feelings of religious origin, or simply because of an inability to enjoy life and one of its pleasures (sex). Most Spanish advocates of sexual-harassment policy thus preferred a narrower definition that excluded acts considered 'less serious' (or not serious at all), for instance, lascivious glances or light innuendo. These were thought to be an inevitable component of Latin idiosyncrasy.

Feminists in the state and in the unions agreed that sexual blackmail by superiors had to be punished, because they were taking advantage of their higher positions within companies to harass female subordinates. Nevertheless, agreement broke down as soon as the harassment perpetrated by colleagues was discussed (that perpetrated by subordinates was hardly debated). For the majority of feminists within the state and trade unions, harassment by co-workers was radically different from that perpetrated by superiors, because it was believed that only the latter could seriously endanger female subordinates' careers within the company or in the labour market in general. Subsequently, it was thought that women could stop the unwanted advances from male colleagues. Spanish feminists knew that both types of harassment were offences in the United States and other countries, but again most of them argued that such a solution was exaggerated and alien to Mediterranean cultures. Consequently, the majority of

Spanish advocates of sexual-harassment policy demanded punishment only for harassers who were superiors.

Most of the sexual-harassment activists that I interviewed affirmed that sexual harassment is about power, not about sex. Therefore, they identified a situation of harassment only when unwanted sexual moves happen in a clear context of unequal power relations (for instance, that of a male boss and a female subordinate). Only in that case did they call for state policy.

In order to understand the way in which the majority of activists were mobilised in this policy area, it is important to note that from 1939 until 1975 Spain was governed by a right-wing authoritarian regime that actively repressed citizens' sexualities (especially female citizens' sexualities). The last thing that activists wanted was that sexual-harassment regulation should be associated with the repressive authoritarian policies of the former regime. In order to distinguish sexual-harassment reform clearly from the past policies, they insisted that the former was not an intrusion of the state in the sexual privacy of citizens but an official treatment of unequal power relations unrelated to sex.

In contrast, a minority of Spanish feminists argued that all unwanted sexual advances (regardless of the type of act and the position of the perpetrator) were discriminatory against women. For the mere fact of being women, women were seen in the workplace and everywhere else by perpetrators as sexual objects to be used without having to ask for consent. All unwanted sexual advances had therefore to be termed 'harassment' and had to be penalised, although differently according to the gravity of the offence.

These and other dilemmas and disagreements were overcome without additional theoretical thinking on the occasion of the opening of a 'policy window' (see Kingdom 1984: 173–4). The government was preparing a bill that contained the following gender equality reforms: an extension of paid maternity leave, the possibility that fathers could take the last weeks of this paid leave, and the extension of unpaid parental leave. Femocrats and feminist trade unionists decided to take advantage of this governmental move to reform legislation in order to enhance the position of women. Thus, sexual-harassment activists placed pressure on the government to include the regulation of sexual harassment in this legislative reform. Their demands did not contain any provision that could have meant a significant extra cost for employers, such as the obligation to establish internal mechanisms in their firms to combat sexual harassment. Probably for this reason, and because their demands were framed in accordance with majoritarian views of the Spanish cultural and historical context, their demands were rapidly included in the governmental agenda.

Policy formulation

The first legislative step was Act 3/89 of 3 March. When the bill was discussed in Parliament, the main party in opposition, the conservative Partido Popular (PP), opposed any state action in this area of feminist policy (*Diario de Sesiones del Congreso de los Diputados, Comisión de Política Social y de Empleo*, III legislatura, 16

November 1988: 12795–817; *Diario de Sesiones del Senado*, 22 February 1989: 5101–7). The conservative MP Celia Villalobos Talero argued that any measures against sexual harassment had to be negotiated between employers and trade unions in collective bargaining. She also defended the view that public policy would be useless, because sexual harassment would only decline when sexist attitudes disappeared in Spanish society and not when a bill is passed in Parliament. The conservative MP Juan Carlos Aparicio Pérez affirmed that women were already protected against unwanted sexual advances by general legislation, and that no specific regulation was required.

Advocates of sexual-harassment reform – for instance, the PSOE MP Francisco Arnau Navarro – emphasised the 'pedagogical character' of the bill, because it would send society a clear message that sexual blackmail in the workplace would no longer be tolerated. In the context of the strong social and political support for integrating Spain into the group of economically developed and politically democratic countries, sexual-harassment advocates convincingly argued that policy on sexual harassment was necessary, because the matter was already regulated in the countries Spain sought to emulate. In fact this argument was false, since the first legal definition of sexual harassment was elaborated in Spain in 1989, earlier than in other Western countries, e.g. Sweden or France in 1992 (Elman 1996: 111; Mazur 1993: 11). Nevertheless, Spanish advocates argued that Spain was behind other countries in this matter, and it never occurred to anybody that the opposite could be true.

When the bill was being discussed in the Senate, the mass media amply covered the polemic around the so-called 'miniskirt ruling', given by the Lérida provincial court. An employer was fined 40,000 pesetas (approx. £200), because he suggested to a sixteen-year-old female employee that she should have sexual relations with him in return for extending her fixed-term contract, while putting his hands on her breast and buttocks. According to the magistrate who made the ruling, Rodrigo Pita, the employer had committed an offence of non-violent indecent assault (*delito de abusos deshonestos no violentos*). Nevertheless, the magistrate also wrote in the court ruling that the employee 'had provoked her employer with her specific clothing [a miniskirt], perhaps innocently, and that he could not control himself in her presence' (*El País*, 19 February 1989: 27). In a subsequent statement to the radio, the magistrate declared that the employer could not have resisted the provocation, 'because [the episode] happened in summer and he perhaps had eaten too much'. He also affirmed that the employee had provoked 'a biological or psychological' reaction in her employer, because 'it all depended on the miniskirt. It was a matter of centimetres, and of course if the miniskirt measured very few centimetres and was made by economising on fabric, it was more provocative than another piece of clothing using more fabric' (*El País* 22 February 1989: 26). The polemic around the 'miniskirt ruling' gave sexual-harassment activists further proof of how difficult it was to punish unwanted sexual advances in Spain at a time when there was still no specific regulation of the matter.

Because the social-democratic Partido Socialista Obrero Español (PSOE) (the party in office which presented the bill) had the absolute majority of the seats in Parliament, the bill was approved as Act 3/89 of 3 March, which contains the first specific legal definition of sexual harassment. The Act reformed the Workers' Statute, article 4.2.e of which was modified to read that 'in their work, workers have the right…to respect for their intimacy and dignity, which includes the protection against verbal or physical attacks of a sexual nature'. Article 63 of the Civil Service Act of 7 February 1964 was similarly modified. Thus employers' acts against the intimacy and dignity of workers (sexual harassment included) are considered a very grave infraction in labour matters, to be penalised with a fine of 500,000 to 15,000,000 pesetas (approx. £2,400 to £71,500).

The second legislative step was the 1995 Penal Code (see Delgado-Iribarren 1996). In 1994 the PSOE government presented a new penal code as a legislative project. The existing code was a substantially modified version of that instituted in 1848. This PSOE project did not contain any references to sexual harassment. Advocates of sexual harassment reform came this time mainly from the trade union CCOO and from Izquierda Unida (IU), an electoral coalition of left-wing parties which was the second main opposition force. Sexual harassment activists joined efforts and put pressure on the IU congressperson, who was actively participating in the preparatory works for the penal code, to present an amendment to the government project to include an article prohibiting sexual harassment in the workplace. This person happened to be a male MP, Diego López Garrido. He defended the amendment in Parliament, where nobody said anything against the opportunity to include the prohibition of sexual harassment in the new penal code.

The new Penal Code was approved by Act 10/1995 of 23 November by the votes of MPs from all parties except those from the Partido Popular, who abstained from voting for reasons that were unrelated to sexual harassment. Article 184 of the new Penal Code states that sexual harassment occurs when a person 'demands favours of a sexual nature, for his/her benefit or for the benefit of someone else; taking advantage of a situation of superiority of professional, educational or similar nature; announcing to the other person explicitly or tacitly some harm to his/her expectations in his/her professional, educational or similar situation'. Sexual harassment is punished with prison for twelve to twenty-four week-ends, or with a fine of 36,000 to 18,000,000 pesetas (approx. £180 to £86,400).

It is worth remembering that the legal structure in Spain is a codified system. In common-law systems (for instance, those of the UK and the USA) judges build case law, and great importance is placed on precedent. In contrast, in code-law systems, judges are supposed to apply the principles of the code and laws in each particular case. The source of law is therefore not the precedent but what is written in the codes and other pieces of legislation. This is why it was so important in Spain to reform the labour law and later the penal code with the inclusion of a clause banning sexual harassment.

Policy implementation

Regarding sexual harassment, an efficient policy would make episodes of this type happen less frequently than previously, when regulation did not exist. Unfortunately, it is not possible to know whether the incidence of sexual harassment in Spain is higher or lower in the late 1990s than before 1989. The studies commissioned in the mid-1980s by the Instituto de la Mujer and feminist trade unionists described above were based on non-representative samples, and have not been replicated since then. To my knowledge, no other monographic study on the incidence of unwanted sexual moves in the workplace has been made.

An effective sexual-harassment policy establishes legal mechanisms that are often used to punish perpetrators and to provide victims with compensation. This is preferable to situations in which, for whatever reason, victims do not rely on the law to seek redress. It is important to understand that in Spain sexual-harassment victims can either start litigation or try to stop the harasser by themselves. What they cannot do is to use internal mechanisms in the private firms or state departments where they work (such as mediators or procedures for investigation and punishment) to stop unwanted sexual behaviour, because in general these mechanisms hardly exist. Nevertheless, secondary sources and the interviews conducted for this chapter reveal that the number of legal complaints has been extremely low (*El País* 13 May 1997: 2; Escudero 1993: 468; Pérez 1995: 55; UGT-Departamento de la Mujer 1994: 11).

The people interviewed for this research gave me one reason that explains why many women do not file a complaint. Many victims do not conceptualise unwanted sexual advances as attacks against their intimacy or their sexual freedom, nor as episodes of gender discrimination. Rather, these victims consider such sexual harassing behaviours as 'facts of life', which are certainly unpleasant but to a certain extent inevitable.

The apparent characteristics of Spanish legal culture may also discourage victims of any offence (including sexual harassment) to go to court to seek redress. Surveys suggest that, generally speaking, Spanish citizens are in favour of negotiation and compromise, and opposed to litigation. Many Spaniards believe that it is better to reach a bad compromise between two contending parties than a good result after litigation. The majority of the population has never had any contact with the legal system, and believes that the courts function badly, and that in criminal trials judges proceed with partiality (Toharia 1994).

With regard to sexual-harassment activists, Instituto de la Mujer femocrats and feminists within trade unions (and to a lesser extent within some political parties) have been the main actors involved in this policy area before and after the elaboration of the 1989 and 1995 reforms. No other social or political actors (for instance, employers, mainstream trade unionists, or state units other than the Instituto de la Mujer) have been active in the fight against unwanted sexual moves.

As for employers, their position on sexual harassment and its regulation is a combination of ignorance and indifference, but not opposition, as in other countries. The majority of Spanish employers are of the belief that sexual harass-ment does not take place in their companies. Most employers also consider that it is a minor problem that does not require any investment or effort on their part. Similarly, employers' organisations have not included the fight against sexual harassment among their priorities.

Like the majority of employers, the majority of trade union delegates behave as if sexual harassment were not a problem in the companies and sectors where they represent workers. Accordingly, most collective agreements do not contain any reference to sexual harassment (*El País*, 14 May 1997: 25; Pérez 1995: 57; UGT-Departamento de la Mujer 1994: 38).

Lastly, the approval of Act 3/89 and of the new penal code has not led to the mobilisation of more resources and efforts against sexual harassment within the state. The public service is not an outstanding actor in this battle. For instance, in 1992 only four ministries (Industry and Energy; Economy; Social Affairs and Agriculture; Fishing and Food) made reference to the matter in their collective agreements (*El País*, 12 March 1992: 24).

Two main outcomes of the regulation of sexual harassment can be identified. First of all, in the late 1990s, public awareness of the existence of unwanted sexual behaviour at work is slightly higher than a decade earlier. There is some evidence to support this point. For instance, some newspapers publish reports on the matter now but did not do it ten years earlier. Reports and debates about sexual harassment have appeared in most mass media. Of course, this media attention has been produced not only by sexual harassment reforms and by court decisions but also by special events such as the US Senate hearings concerning Clarence Thomas and Anita Hill in 1992, and the publication in 1994 of the translation into Spanish of the best-seller *Disclosure* by Michael Crichton, and the première of the film based on this book. Second, although the level of litigation is low, litigation indeed takes place and some harassers have been punished.

While interviewing advocates of sexual-harassment policy, I asked them if the two outcomes of the reforms (the slight increase in public awareness and the few court rulings) are so modest that we are led to conclude that the official treat-ment of sexual harassment has been useless. I also asked them what would happen, if anything, if the prohibition on sexual harassment were suppressed in the labour law and the penal code.

All activists consider that the reforms are a significant policy, because these are (or might be) a first step in the fight against unwanted sexual behaviour in the workplace. It was very important that the laws were passed, since the official debate about the importance and gravity of sexual harassment is now closed. The inclusion of sexual harassment in the penal code was particularly important in this regard, because the penal code defines the most reprehensible behaviour in a modern society (such as killing, raping or stealing, and since 1995 also sexu-ally harassing) and assigns punishments for perpetrators. The battle over the recognition of the problem of unwanted sexual behaviour was fought and won. By approving the 1989 and 1995 reforms, lawmakers publicly stated that activists were right to argue that sexual harassment substantially contributed to women's inferior status in labour. Lawmakers indicated that detractors of sexual-harassment regulation clearly underestimated the prevalence and gravity of the phenomenon. This was a political victory for activists. Law, which is a privileged discourse (Outshoorn 1996: 6), now contains statements derived from feminist discourse. Therefore, if the 1989 and 1995 reforms were now abolished, activists would have to do again what they have done since the mid-1980s: pressurise policy-makers to elaborate a sexual-harassment bill.

Conclusions

This chapter has shown that the formation of sexual harassment policy in Spain was mainly a battle around defining the issue. Feminist trade unionists and Instituto de la Mujer femocrats 'named' a common social interaction as an unacceptable problem. 'Naming' was in this case a crucial political action, because by giving a 'name' to a situation, activists converted a 'private' matter into a 'public' problem. As a consequence, important political and social actors and some sectors of public opinion began to conceptualise unwanted sexual moves at work not as 'facts of life' or as reflections of citizens' sexual preferences (belonging to the sphere of personal/private freedom), as they have done in the past, but as a social problem that deserves public attention (and solutions).

Sexual-harassment activists successfully put pressure on the government to initiate sexual-harassment reform because they 'named' the problem in a way that was consistent with majority views concerning Spanish cultural and historical idiosyncrasy. Most activists defined sexual harassment as a situation related to power and not to sex. Paradoxically enough, they effectively called for governmental policy in a domain of citizens' sexualities by insistently avoiding any talk about sex. In this way, they averted the potential association between the regulation of sexual harassment and the repressive sexual policies of the former authoritarian regime. However, with their definition of the problem, activists implied that behaviours that would be termed harassment in other countries – for instance, infrequent lascivious glances or dirty jokes – were acceptable in the Spanish context.

Activists skilfully articulated demands for government action on sexual harassment because they accurately perceived that a policy window had opened, and quickly took advantage of these propitious moments. Obviously, this finding has implications for feminist activism in the Spanish context. If feminists believe that public policies can help to improve women's status, some activists have to work within the state, and have intimate knowledge of the dynamics of the policy-making process, in order to identify the opening of policy windows.

The case of sexual-harassment policy in Spain also shows the limitations of state intervention in this matter. The reason is that very few victims rely on the law to find redress and compensation, and no important political and social actor (apart from state feminists and feminist trade unionists) is involved in this policy area in the late 1990s. The approval of the sexual-harassment bills was a victory for activists, but not a triumph in any sense for victims who suffered unwanted sexual advances but did not subsequently litigate. Activists recognise with dismay that this is the most common situation. Activists then know that a great deal has to be done in order to spread information about the reforms (which might possibly deter some harassers from further harassment), to support victims in their resistance to harassers, and to implicate other perpetrators in the battle against unwanted sex in the workplace, a fight that has just started with the definition of a problem and the elaboration of policy.

References

Calle, M., González, C., and Núñez, J.A. 1988. *Discriminación y acoso sexual a la mujer en el trabajo*. Madrid: Fundación Largo Caballero.

Carter, V.A. 1992. 'Working on dignity: EC initiatives on sexual harassment in the workplace'. *Northwestern Journal of International Law and Business* 12: 431–60.

Delgado-Iribarren, M. (ed.). 1996. *Ley Orgánica del Código Penal: trabajos parlamentarios*. Madrid: Cortes Generales.

Dery, D. 1984. *Problem Definition in Policy Analysis*. Lawrence KA: University Press of Kansas.

Diario de Sesiones del Congreso de los Diputados, Comisión de Política Social y de Empleo, III legislatura, 16 November 1988: 12795–817.

Diario de Sesiones del Senado, 22 February 1989: 5101–7.

Elman, A. 1996. *Sexual Subordination and State Intervention: Comparing Sweden and the United States*. Providence RI and Oxford: Berghahn.

Escudero, R. 1993. 'El acoso sexual en el trabajo'. *Relaciones Laborales* 24: 468–79.

Fitzgerald, L.F. 1993. 'Sexual harassment: violence against women in the workplace'. *American Psychologist* 48: 10, 1070–6.

Husbands, R. 1993. 'Análisis internacional de las leyes que sancionan el acoso sexual'. *Revista Internacional del Trabajo* 112: 109–37.

INNER. 1987. 'El acoso sexual en el puesto de trabajo'. Unpublished report.

Kingdom, J.W. 1984. *Agendas, Alternatives, and Public Policies*. Glenview IL and London: Scott, Forest & Company.

Mazur, A.G. 1993. 'The formation of sexual harassment policy in France: another case of French exceptionalism?' *French Politics and Society* 11: 11–32.

—— 1996. 'The interplay: the formation of sexual harassment legislation in France and EU policy initiatives'. In R. Elman (ed.), *Sexual Politics and the European Union: the New Feminist Challenge*, pp. 35–49. Providence RI and Oxford: Berghahn.

Outshoorn, J. 1996. 'The meaning of "woman" in abortion policy: a comparative approach'. Paper presented at the 1996 Annual Meeting of the American Political Science Association, San Francisco, August 29–September 1.

Pérez, M.T. 1995. 'Informe general 1995: nivel de aplicación del Derecho Comunitario en materia de igualdad'. Unpublished report.

Smith, A.C. 1996. 'National identity and sexual harassment'. Paper presented at the Tenth International Conference of Europeanists, Chicago, March 14–16.

Stetson, D. McBride, and Mazur, A.G. (eds). 1995. *Comparative State Feminism*. Thousand Oaks CA: Sage.

Stockdale, J.E. 1991. 'Sexual harassment at work'. In J. Firth-Cozens, and A.W. Michael (eds), *Women and Work: Psychological and Organizational Perspectives.* Milton Keynes and Philadelphia PA: Open University Press.

Toharia, J.J. 1994. *Actitudes de los españoles ante la Administración de Justicia.* Madrid: Centro de Investigaciones Sociológicas.

UGT-Departamento de la Mujer. 1994. *Guía sindical sobre acoso sexual en el trabajo.* Madrid: UGT-Departamento de la Mujer.

16 Sexuality and work

Contrasting prostitution policies in Victoria and Queensland

Katrina Gorjanicyn

There has been a rapid expansion of the availability and consumption of commercial sexual services in Australia since the 1970s. The traditional organisation of prostitution – massage parlour and street prostitution – has been extended to include a range of other services: escort agencies, solo prostitutes trading from residential premises, fantasy telephone calls, and sex tours to Thailand and the Philippines where child prostitution is rampant. In addition to the proliferation of prostitution services there has been an escalation in the sale, production and marketing of pornographic material in Australia. These diverse prostitution and pornography services have been lumped together and deposited under the catch-all phrase of the 'sex industry'. This discursive trend has been woven into popular culture, parliamentary discourse, government reports and public policy since the 1980s, its commonplace usage representing a distinct shift in the degree of community tolerance relating to sexual transactions.

Not only does the 'sex industry' terminology signify a swing towards legitimising the formal organisation of prostitution, it is also indicative of the multiple powers with vested interests in the sex trade that have emerged to increase and control the demand and supply of sexual labour. Given that the sale of sex has become a business in Australia with its own professional category, it is clear that prostitution and pornography have become entrenched and more acceptable practices in Australian culture. Moreover, repeated reference to the 'sex industry' indicates that, politically and legally, commercial sex is being transformed into a legitimate form of work in Australia. This has been the case particularly in regard to prostitution. In recent public-policy initiatives, perceptions of problems, and solutions, pertaining to prostitution have been largely structured around, or at least as a response to, the Prostitution-as-Work discourse. In this chapter I contrast the ways in which decriminalisation of prostitution was approached by Labor governments in the states of Victoria and Queensland during the 1980s and 1990s. Two pieces of legislation are the focus of my analysis: the lead-up to and final outcome of the 1986 Prostitution Regulation Act under the Cain government in Victoria, and the formation of the 1992 Prostitution Laws Amendment Act under the Goss government in Queensland.

Victoria – the pragmatic approach

The Victorian story opens in the late 1970s but does not begin to unfold as legislation until the 1980s. Parliamentary debate throughout the 1970s concerning the spread of 'massage parlours' in inner-city Melbourne marked the first phase of the prostitution law reform process. This activity occurred under the gaze of a conservative State Liberal Government.

In response to residents' complaints about the noise of kerb crawlers and the visible aspects of prostitution, harsher penalties for street prostitution were introduced in the 1970s. With new measures to control streetwalking in place, a large portion of on-street soliciting was recast as off-street prostitution. This resulted in a proliferation of brothels, masquerading as 'massage parlours', in pockets of inner-city Melbourne. It became clear that massage-parlour prostitution posed a new set of 'problems' in public policy: massage parlours could not be forced to move on as easily as streetwalkers could be arrested and shifted from view. Policy-makers would have to think of new ways of tidying the streetscape.

As these facts came to light there was a discursive shift within political parties from the term 'massage parlours' to 'brothels'. Where the use of 'massage parlours' was seen to be more discreet and able to keep the prostitution business under wraps, reference to 'brothels' was seen as more forthright and an open acknowledgement of the existence of organised prostitution. Choice of language and its role in policy was recognised as an important facet of the prostitution debate by politicians from the Right, who argued in Parliament during the 1970s that retaining the label 'massage parlours' accorded business profiting from prostitution a more significant standing in the community than did the word 'brothels'. However, talk of 'brothels' went beyond a simple play with language; with it arrived an important change in policy direction. This started within the Victorian Liberal Party and transferred to the State Australian Labor Party (ALP).

Brian Dixon, a Liberal minister and Member of the Legislative Assembly for St Kilda – an inner-city Melbourne area renowned for prostitution – was in the midst of the prostitution 'crisis'. In the wake of gentrification of St Kilda, residents pressed Dixon to 'clean up' areas where prostitution was at its most visible. However, after researching prostitution in St Kilda, Dixon understood the 'problem' as being much more complex than the issue of residential politics and he campaigned for reforms that were based on decriminalisation in order to cease punishment of prostitutes (Dixon 1980). Dixon's push for prostitution law reform was rejected by the Liberal Party and his controversial stance saw him come close to losing his parliamentary seat. In the end, Dixon was unsuccessful in bringing his own party to accept a policy of decriminalisation, but he did open up a new discursive space in Victorian politics.

Ironically, the Victorian State ALP took over Dixon's ground. The Victorian ALP's proposals for change to prostitution laws appeared within its Status of Women's Policy Committee, which was led at this stage by the Hon. Joan Coxsedge from the radical Left, who had already achieved notoriety for her reformist stance on rape laws and peace issues. Working with a newly formed prostitute lobby group and openly pushing a strong feminist line, Coxsedge was the key figure in getting a policy of decriminalisation onto the ALP's agenda.

When the ALP came to office in 1982, it brought with it a specific prostitution policy based on decriminalisation as outlined by its Status of Women's Policy Committee. To this end, it had a distinct feminist flavour. However, from the late 1970s until the mid-1980s when the Cain government's Prostitution Regulation Bill was drafted, Coxsedge was the only sitting member of the State ALP who continually pinpointed the broader issues of gender and class inequality and discrimination, which she claimed needed to be addressed in order for a radical reform in the area of prostitution to be achieved (Victorian Parliamentary Debates). Despite Coxsedge's long-term commitment to reform in the area of prostitution and her involvement through the ALP Status of Women's Policy Committee in directing party policy, she did not participate in drafting public policy pertaining to prostitution. Nor did the newly established Women's Policy Co-ordination Unit, which sat within the Premier's Department, play any role in the formulation of prostitution policy. The task of designing prostitution policy was given to the Minister of the Department of Planning and Environment and then passed on to the Attorney-General, marking the beginning of the end of direct feminist involvement in the design of prostitution policy within the Victorian ALP.

The policy process concerning the decriminalisation of prostitution in Victoria was protracted. It involved several stages during the 1980s – none of which had a major feminist input from the State ALP. First came a working party set up in 1983 to look into the ways in which the location of brothels could be regulated. Its recommendations formed the basis of the Planning (Brothels) Act 1984, which aimed at controlling prostitution through town planning regulations. This Act removed criminal penalties for prostitution in brothels that had a planning permit to exist but left criminal laws against all other forms of prostitution intact. The decriminalisation of brothels presented the Prostitutes' Collective Victoria – a prostitute advocacy group – with an opportunity to argue for (sex) workers' rights, such as health and workplace safety, award pay, and the right to be affiliated with a union.

Further recommendations were put forward by the 1983 working party to examine the social, community welfare, public health and criminal aspects of prostitution in Victoria. The Cain government made a commitment to conduct a full inquiry into these issues and in 1984 it established the Victorian Committee of Inquiry into Prostitution. The committee released its final report in 1985 (Neave report).

The Neave report described prostitution as an exploitative business that should not be encouraged or promoted. However, criminal laws were not regarded as an appropriate means of deterring people from participating in the industry. The report recommended that criminal penalties had a place only to protect prostitutes from violence, intimidation and exploitation and to protect the community from nuisance. It proposed that prostitution be legalised through a system of licences, which would be granted to brothel operators by an independent licensing board. Brothel operators would have to apply for a licence from the board as well as obtaining a planning permit to set up their premises. The purpose of the licensing system was to block criminals from entering the prostitution industry, to protect prostitutes from exploitation and to prevent public nuisance. Under this scheme, local councils would not be able to prohibit brothels in their areas. Another key recommendation was that prostitutes working alone or in pairs outside the larger brothels would be exempt from the licensing system. The report argued that prostitutes operating alone or in pairs from their own homes were less likely to be exploited and unlikely to be a public nuisance. There was a feminist approach underlying the Neave report that put forward structural explanations of prostitution, linking it to economic, social and sexual inequalities in society (Neave 1985, vol. 1: 425). The Neave report's tacit acceptance of Prostitution-as-Work appealed to the liberal feminist ideology dominant in Australia.

The recommendations made in the Neave report were reached after a lengthy process of community consultation and a call for submissions, which allowed interest groups to air their positions on the issue. Nearly all of the recommendations in the Neave report were accepted by the government and received a favourable response from the principal interest groups. The Prostitutes' Collective of Victoria gave its support to the report on the basis that it proposed decriminalisation. Most of the Neave report's recommendations were written into the government's Prostitution Regulation Bill 1986.

However, the passage of the Prostitution Regulation Bill 1986 through Parliament was not smooth. The amendments made to the bill in the Legislative Council were accepted by the government in the Legislative Assembly (lower house) so that at least some of the minor reforms with which the opposition had not tampered could pass into law. However, the Attorney-General refused to proclaim a number of the amended provisions that undermined the essence of the Neave report, including the opposition's version of the licensing system, the power given to local councils to prohibit brothels and the revised 'living on the earnings' provisions.

Viewing the events associated with prostitution law reform in retrospect, women politicians who had been part of the Cain government revealed reservations that they harboured concerning the way in which their support – albeit low key – for decriminalisation had implied an acceptance of Prostitution-as-Work. These women politicians had personally held the belief that prostitution was degrading and exploitative for the women involved in it and they questioned the degree to which women exercised choice in entering prostitution, yet as politicians they endorsed the Prostitution-as-Work discourse that underpinned the government's proposals for reform.

Speaking seven to ten years on from the Cain government's proposals for prostitution law reform, women who had been part of that government perceived the Prostitution-as-Work framework, which had been implicit in policy, as problematic in terms of the legitimation it gave to turning female sexuality into a commodity. At the time the prostitution policies were formed, concerns regarding the concept of prostitution as ordinary waged labour were not directly raised within the feminist network that existed among women in government.

However, the Prostitution-as-Work model was privately debated by femocrats who were involved in the 1983 working party that made recommendations leading to the Planning (Brothels) Act 1984. Although women in government did not champion the Prostitution-as-Work model, they respected that it was the preferred option of the prostitute lobby group, the Prostitutes' Collective of Victoria, and saw it as a step towards eradicating criminal sanctions against women prostitutes who had traditionally been the victims of law. Furthermore, women in the Cain government favoured legal brothels on the basis that they would provide a safer workplace environment for prostitutes, who were more likely to be subjected to violence and coercion on the streets and in illegal 'massage parlours' than in legal establishments, encourage greater practice of safe sex, and see award wages and conditions implemented. It was the pragmatic element of Australian state feminism that prevailed among women in government.

Queensland – the interventionist approach

The decision to review Queensland's prostitution laws occurred in a more colourful context than that of Victoria. While in Victoria the Cain government had initiated prostitution law reform in its own time and linked it to the ALP's broader agenda of social reform, in Queensland the public exposure of police corruption that had infiltrated an illegal prostitution industry was an issue that the Goss government was forced to confront immediately it came to power. Furthermore, notions of what constituted 'solutions' to prostitution 'problems' and responses to the Prostitution-as-Work model differed markedly between the two governments: the Victorian Cain government's solution package focused on planning schemes, and implicit in its proposal to decriminalise prostitution in licensed brothels was an acceptance of Prostitution-as-Work; in Queensland, Premier Goss conceptualised problems and solutions in prostitution in terms of morality and his refusal to decriminalise brothel prostitution was based on a rejection of Prostitution-as-Work.

It was the media that first exposed the corruption that had infiltrated Queensland's brothels and escort agencies. By the late 1980s, corruption in Queensland's prostitution industry had become a fully blown scandal of headline proportions around Australia, securing it a prominent place on the policy agenda that could not be dislodged easily. These media reports were the precursor of the Fitzgerald Commission of Inquiry, which under its terms considered economic, drug, health and criminal issues relating to prostitution.

The Fitzgerald report gave formal recognition to the criminal elements that journalists had already revealed: the Licensing Branch knew that massage parlours and escort agencies were operating illegally but did not enforce laws to close them down; senior officers in the Licensing Branch were connected with prostitution industry operators and officers-in-charge were given payoffs by the prostitution industry on a regular basis in return for protection; police received money, property, alcohol and sexual favours from parlour and agency owners (Fitzgerald 1989). Senior officials in the Police Department were aware of this situation and allowed it to continue; prostitutes and operators in the industry who did not comply with police demands were charged more often than those who co-operated with them. Finally, the Fitzgerald report concluded that the law had reached too far into prostitution and highlighted that, when areas relating to morality and human behaviour are over-regulated, corruption can find an opening.

After the fall-out from the Fitzgerald report, the Goss government had a great deal of mopping up to begin in Queensland. During its first term in power the government acted on the Fitzgerald report's recommendation that a thorough investigation of prostitution and the laws pertaining to it should be conducted by an independent body before any new policies were formed. The Criminal Justice Commission (CJC) was given this task, submitting its report *Regulating Morality? An Inquiry into Prostitution in Queensland* in 1991 to the Parliamentary Criminal Justice Committee (PCJC), with recommendations for decriminalisation of some forms of prostitution. With issues of safety and health for prostitutes paramount in the CJC report, the Queensland inquiry echoed the emphasis of Victoria's Neave report. The CJC's proposals for prostitution law reform included: protecting sex workers and children from exploitation and coercion; minimising health risks among prostitutes and their clients; and introducing a regulatory model, to operate in conjunction with criminal laws, that would allow individuals to work from their own homes or in groups of up to ten prostitutes, who would work from quarters approved by government-appointed regulatory bodies. This system of regulation, which would be overseen by a Registration Board responsible to the Minister for Health and Local Authorities, would have the authority to screen prospective prostitutes and their employers in order to determine their suitability for registration, and it would be in charge of compiling a record of prostitutes licensed to work.

In spite of widespread public support for the CJC's recommendations, Premier Goss set his own personal agenda for reform that did not correspond to that of the CJC, the sex industry, the public majority view, or many members of his own government who supported decriminalisation. When the direction of the CJC report became apparent, Goss pre-empted the outcome by publicly opposing decriminalisation, partly on the basis that such an initiative would allow organised crime to continue at the same rate as previously. Goss's strongly held personal beliefs on prostitution and his reputation for clashing with the CJC, which he resented on the basis that he perceived it as trying to act as an upper house would operate in Parliament, meshed together at this point. The media, the CJC, feminist groups and the Queensland sex-worker organisation, Self-Health for Queensland Workers in the Sex Industry (SQWISI), crowned Goss a moral conservative for rejecting decriminalisation and adopting a discourse that described prostitutes as victims and prostitution as exploitative and degrading of women. Ironically, the language that Goss employed to describe the situation of women prostitutes was the same as the radical feminist discourse on prostitution that occupied a tiny space within the state's bureaucracy. Yet Goss also borrowed from a liberal feminist discourse when he spoke publicly of women's 'choice' to enter into prostitution (Sullivan 1993: 187).

The Goss government only tinkered at the edges of prostitution law reform. Under the 1992 Prostitution Laws Amendment Act, the core of previous legislation was left intact, and most prostitution-related activities still remain criminal offences, with the police continuing to enforce the laws that regulate the industry. Legislation prohibits organised prostitution such as brothel work but allows individual sex workers to operate from their own homes. This is the reverse situation to the one that was created in Victoria, where it became legal to operate a brothel if in possession of an appropriate town-planning permit but was a criminal offence to run a prostitution business from residential premises. Queensland's laws do not by any means provide the optimum set-up, according to prostitutes who have argued that working alone without another prostitute or support staff on the premises makes women much more vulnerable to violence than working in a brothel. In Queensland women in prostitution remain the target of criminal law and there is still a means for organised crime and official corruption to exist.

Although prostitution law reform in Queensland appeared on the ALP's political agenda as an issue of police corruption rather than as a feminist-driven initiative, it attracted close attention from feminists within and outside the party. However, for women in government, inserting a feminist perspective into the reform process proved a difficult task. Not all women in government were feminists, which meant that there were vast differences in how problems and solutions in prostitution policy should be interpreted.

In their first term in government, women ALP Members of Parliament shared the same disadvantage as their Victorian counterparts, whereby the parliamentary process was a foreign experience to them and difficulties that women experienced in terms of access and participation in government were a common occurrence. When the Goss government first came to power there was only one woman minister in Cabinet, Anne Warner. Warner struggled to participate in agenda-setting, and according to women who had served in the government she was perceived as being a 'ratbag feminist; a radical blunderbuss' by most of the men who held senior positions in the Goss government.

Women on the ALP's back bench operated in an environment whereby they were instructed, along with all other backbenchers in their party, to endorse policy that had been decided in Cabinet rather than create it. Goss demanded full party loyalty and to step over this mark meant risking alienation. To spend time trying to sculpt prostitution policy could be politically dangerous to women ALP politicians as they would risk being further marginalised within government.

However, while these factors mitigated against women's participation in prostitution law reform within government, it did not silence those who supported decriminalisation. At the time Goss refused to accept the CJC's recommendation for decriminalisation his view was criticised by women in government and vigorously challenged by a feminist backbencher, Judy Spence, in caucus.

A large section of Queensland's feminist movement devised multiple strategies and lobbied extensively to have a policy of decriminalisation accepted by the Labor government. Although groups of feminists worked together very closely at times, they were not without their differences. For example, some members of Labor Women were not as accepting of the Prostitution-as-Work model as were the representatives of SQWISI, whose discourse was based on rational choice in entering prostitution. However, for the sake of progressive reform based on decriminalisation, these differences were pushed aside. If creating prostitution as a standard occupation would assist in protecting prostitutes' safety and health – particularly in an era when HIV/AIDS had emerged as a major health concern – and justify the removal of criminal laws that targeted prostitute women, Labor Women members were prepared to modify their position and accept the Prostitution-as-Work model.

A small group of feminists was not so willing to follow this tide. Within the bureaucracy, there was a scattering of radical feminists. Although they lent half-hearted support to a policy of decriminalisation so that prostitutes would at least escape being victims of the law, they refused to equate prostitution with work. For these radical femocrats, prostitutes were victims; prostitution was not a voluntary choice; violence and exploitation were part and parcel of prostitution; and prostitution degraded women. Radical femocrats were accorded no significant place in formative or discursive developments in public-policy process pertaining to prostitution, and in mainstream feminist circles they were marginalised, if not ostracised, because of their views. Liberal feminists dismissed this minority as being out of touch with contemporary feminism. These fissions within the feminist movement have been deep and lasting.

Conclusions

The Victorian and Queensland case studies of prostitution law reform provide striking examples of the state developing policy to control the organisation of prostitution without directly incorporating feminist involvement. Feminists' outer position in decision-making processes relating to prostitution law reform was clearly linked to three factors: men's control of the political agenda; uncertainty among women in government concerning their exact position on how prostitution should be defined; and divisions within the feminist movement concerning the Prostitution-as-Work model.

In working for the state, women politicians and femocrats were restricted in their opportunities to steer prostitution policy. Although feminists were accorded a degree of power in Parliament and the bureaucratic arena, they were often held back from advancing policy initiatives. Interviews with women who were members of the Cain and Goss governments revealed that, as ALP party members and new Members of Parliament, women were often sidelined in decision-making processes. The development of prostitution policy is a prime example of the way in which the initiation and carriage of policy that was of direct concern to women was taken out of feminists' hands. The suppression of feminist involvement in the official production of prostitution policy occurred to a degree unsurpassed in other policy reforms in which feminists participated, such as women's health, domestic violence and education. The key point in this is that prostitution – the policy area in which women were most restricted – brought into play issues relating to the state's control of women's sexuality and men's access to women's bodies in a way that these other feminist initiatives did not.

A degree of ambiguity among some feminists concerning their personal positions on prostitution meant that women policy-makers were not in a strong position to initiate or control legislative changes relating to prostitution. Although women in the Cain government had supported party policy on decriminalisation, they were in fact still refining their interpretations of problems in prostitution. Seven to ten years on from the formation of Victoria's prostitution laws, women who had been members of the Cain government explained that they had not completely accepted the concept of prostitution as a form of waged labour that had been implicit in legislation. While women in government had perceived advantages in defining prostitution as work on the basis that this model would give prostitutes greater rights as citizens and workers, they were left to question where their concerns regarding the exploitation and degradation they associated with prostitution fitted into this approach to law reform.

A lack of consensus among feminists working in the policy process over whether prostitution should be regarded as work hindered women's participation in policy formation. In Queensland, divisions among feminists regarding the Prostitution-as-Work model were more pronounced than in Victoria. The contentious relationship that existed between the femocrats, who adhered to a radical feminist perspective on prostitution in the early stages of policy reform, and liberal feminists, who were positioned in key interest groups, caused a major rift to develop in the feminist movement. This division at the practical level served to complicate feminism's place in the prostitution law reform process.

Throughout the process of prostitution law reform in Victoria and Queensland, the role of competing discourses was central: liberal, radical and moralistic discourses, each with its own interpretation of the 'prostitution problem', vied for a place in the policy arena. Feminists were at the forefront of this struggle to shape policy agendas, devising discursive strategies that contributed to the renaming and redefinition of prostitutes and prostitution within policy systems. While feminists did not influence the public policy agenda in Victoria and Queensland by operating the machinery of government that gives access to decision-making, they did have some success in shaping the prostitution debate in a more peripheral way through the use of specific discourses that revolved around decriminalisation and Prostitution-as-Work.

However, these words that gave new meaning to prostitution in public policy were delivered by liberal feminists and were not representative of all strains of feminism. Radical feminism, although barely occupying a place in the policy process, had its own discursive construction of prostitution, which rejected the Prostitution-as-Work model. Therefore, discourse was a site of struggle as much between different ideological camps within the feminist movement as between feminists and other actors involved in the policy process. Had these divisions within feminism been less prevalent and a multiplicity of feminist voices co-existed and interacted with each other within the policy sphere, feminists might have had greater success in designing the specific details of prostitution law reform in Victoria and Queensland. However, whether Australian feminism and policy systems would allow such discursive diversity to operate is open to question.

Language and its linkage to a set of values, priorities and social capital is an important component in the construction of public policy (Considine 1994). The case studies of prostitution law reform in Victoria and Queensland show that when individuals and groups take control of language they are better placed to define 'problems' and offer 'solutions' in policy according to their ideology (see also Valiente, Chapter 15, and Outshoorn, Chapter 17 of this volume). In Victoria and Queensland, policy actors who invented and reinvented language to specify what prostitutes and prostitution should or should not be called – 'sex worker', 'prostitute', 'victims', 'exploited', 'degraded', 'massage parlour', 'brothel' – inserted values into the policy arena that had an influence on processes and outcomes. The players who succeeded in defining problems and solutions in prostitution policy, and thus became the protagonists instrumental in creating new policy agendas, were those who were able to initiate or master a language that categorised prostitution and drag this discourse into the boundaries of pre-established policy cultures. Developments in prostitution law reform under Labor governments in Victoria and Queensland provide examples of the way in which language can be used as a vehicle to shape preferences, processes and outcomes relating to issues of sexuality within policy systems.

References

Considine, M. 1994. *Public Policy: A Critical Approach*. South Melbourne: Macmillan.
Dixon, B. 1980. 'Prostitution and massage parlours'. Unpublished discussion paper. Melbourne.
Fitzgerald, G.E. 1989. *Report of a Commission of Inquiry Pursuant to Orders in Council*. 26 May 1987, 24 June 1987, 25 August 1988, 29 June 1989. Brisbane: Government Printer.
Neave, M. 1985. *Inquiry into Prostitution, Final Report, Victoria*, 2 vols. October. Melbourne: Government Printer.
Sullivan, B. 1993. 'Women and the Goss government'. In B. Stevens and J. Wanna (eds), *The Goss Government: Promise and Performance of Labor in Queensland*, pp. 174–88. South Melbourne: Macmillan.

17 Sexuality and international commerce

The traffic in women and prostitution policy in the Netherlands

Joyce Outshoorn

At an official government conference on sexual violence in The Hague in 1982, the general feeling of the meeting on prostitution and traffic in women was summarised in the proceedings of the conference in the following way:

> Tackling it [traffic in women] is stiff work, but if one demands from the government that prostitution be legalised, it stands to reason to also demand that the exploitation of prostitutes be prosecuted.
>
> (Acker and Rawie 1982: 130, my translation)

This quotation brings to light the rise of a new idea among feminists of the second wave: that prostitution might be 'a free choice' for some women and that only excesses like trafficking should be combated by governments. This novel idea is now becoming the content of official policy in the Netherlands, creating a position that is relatively rare among states, Victoria in Australia being the only other state to decriminalise some forms of prostitution (Gorjanicyn, Chapter 16 of this volume). It also demonstrates the time-honoured connection between the issues of prostitution and the traffic in women, a linkage already forged in the 1880s by feminists of the 'first wave' and their abolitionist allies, and consolidated in international law.

This chapter analyses the way in which the issue of 'traffic in women' re-emerged in the late seventies and became a matter of policy concern in the Netherlands over the past fifteen years, giving rise to these innovations. It also analyses how far the government agency charged with the improvement of women's status in the Netherlands has been able to affect debates over the issues of trafficking and prostitution and how far it succeeds in redefining these, creating access and participation for women in the policy process. This agency, the Directorate for the Co-ordination of Equality Policy (Directie Coordinatie Emancipatiezaken – DCE), is located within the national Ministry for Social Affairs and Employment, and it co-ordinates all policy on women (Outshoorn 1994, 1995).

In the first part of this analysis I shall trace the re-emergence of the political debate in the Netherlands since the 1970s up to the point when the issues reached the political agenda in 1982 as part of the women's liberation platform against sexual violence. In the following discussion I shall trace the policy lines that were followed to deal with this matter, showing how it became subject to warring definitions as other actors entered the fray and what the outcomes have been since then. In conclusion I shall return to the question of the impact of the central policy unit, the DCE, on the issues.

Re-emergence of the issue

Traffic in women is an old issue. From the beginning of this century, international law has tried to outlaw and eliminate it by various conventions to which states are party. It has always been tied up with the matter of prostitution, as the issue was defined as trafficking women for the purposes of forcing them into prostitution. Moreover, trafficking and prostitution were prominent issues in first-wave feminism in Western Europe, where feminists fought against brothels and set up networks to aid prostitutes and to prevent young girls from falling into the hands of procurers (for the Netherlands, see De Vries 1997).

The prostitution issue has been defined in numerous ways, resulting in many different policies that states have developed in order to handle the prostitution issue. If states define it as a moral offence, they will be prohibitionist, outlawing all forms of prostitution and prosecuting both prostitutes and pimps. If states see it as a problem of public order or public health, they will accordingly try to regulate it in various ways by permitting brothels or streetwalking in certain areas, devising measures to control sexually transmitted diseases, usually subjecting prostitutes (but never their clients) to medical check-ups. The United States takes a prohibitionist line, whereas Germany is the best-known case of regulation, allowing for 'Eros-centres', controlling STDs by compulsory medical check-ups of prostitutes, and requiring income-tax levies on prostitutes. The UK, France and Italy have taken up abolitionist positions, forbidding brothels but not prosecuting prostitutes.

In the nineteenth century, the Netherlands had a regulatory regime, allowing for brothels and medical control of prostitutes, but after concerted efforts by feminist and Protestant abolitionist groups, it shifted to an abolitionist position in 1911 (De Vries 1997). In the course of time, policy unofficially reverted to regulation, limiting prostitution to certain areas, with some 'window' prostitution (women sitting on view behind their windows while the punters pass by and peek) and use of private houses. The Amsterdam 'red-light district' is probably the best-known example of these practices. When the United Nations adopted the Convention for the Suppression of the Traffic in Persons and the Exploitation of the Prostitution of Others in 1949, the Netherlands did not ratify it, as the government was implicated in a brothel for the military in the Caribbean part of the Kingdom (Haveman 1995: 98). More recently, the Dutch government has accepted prostitution as a fact of life and aims at protecting women (persons) from being prostituted against their will, thus making a distinction between 'forced' and 'voluntary' prostitution. Underlying decriminalisation is a strong urge to regulate prostitution as a normal business sector. The UN

Convention embraces the abolitionist position, making no distinction between 'forced' and 'voluntary' prostitution; the Netherlands is now opposing it for this reason.

The Netherlands did sign earlier international conventions on trafficking, which has also been prohibited in the Dutch Penal Code since 1910 (art. 251ter); the clause is an elaboration of the Paris agreement of that same year. It states that traffic in women is an offence regardless of its taking place internationally or locally, whether minors are involved or not, and whether the woman has consented or not. In 1983 a Supreme Court decision maintained that traffic in women is 'any deed that has the intent of delivering a woman into prostitution for instance by undertaking travel or travelling with women to get them to a place where they will be prostituted', regardless of their being minors or not, or working as prostitutes or not, prior to being trafficked (Buijs and Verbraken 1985: 5).

In 1911, when a solid religious parliamentary majority enacted the 'Sexual Morality Laws', traffic in women, along with issues such as pornography, rape, abortion, sex with minors, homosexuality (both of men and women), the open display and advertising of contraceptives (selling these was not illegal), pimping, and running a brothel were all redefined as crimes against sexual morality. Only in the 1960s did these laws come under attack; armed with the slogan of 'the state is not a moral police', reformers held that it was not the state's business to define and police sexual morals, as these were held to be private affairs, and reformers demanded the revision of all of these clauses. To pacify these demands, a government commission was set up in 1970 (the Peters Commission – later renamed Melai, after its chairpersons). Abortion and contraception were not part of its task, but it was supposed to tackle all the other issues, including rape, prostitution and the age of consent. In 1977 it reported on prostitution (Commissie Melai 1977), coming out in favour of maintaining the ban on brothels. Such a ban was seen as providing a form of protection for prostitutes, who themselves are not liable to prosecution. The commission was opposed to so-called 'Eros-centres', the state-controlled brothels in Germany, which it saw as too large-scale for the diverse prostitution scene in the Netherlands. Maintaining the illegal status of brothels gave local government a weapon against brothel keepers; if they did not observe some minimal standards of discretion, safety and hygiene, they could be closed down. This reflects the pragmatic Dutch approach to prostitution; officially brothels are banned, but they are tolerated unless they exceed certain limits. In the dealings of the commission, traffic in women was not mentioned; very few cases seem to have occurred in the 1970s, and there was no public debate on the topic at all.

New demands for the political agenda

The 1970s saw a number of thoroughgoing changes in the prostitution business as it turned into a modern sex industry (Van Mens 1992). As sexual mores changed in the 1960s and 1970s, moving – in a relatively brief period – from a highly regulated sexual life to an unprecedented sexual liberty and openness in the Netherlands, sexual desires also underwent a transformation. With the rise of prosperity, sex tourism boomed. Sex entrepreneurs in South East Asia, who were left with a slack demand after the US army departed from Vietnam, were able to attract Western male tourists as new consumers for their services, catering for both heterosexuals and gays. Back home, sex telephone lines, sex clubs and escort services proliferated, catering to the new demands of the increasingly affluent Dutch male (heterosexual and gay). At the same time, and for the same reason (rising living standards), the supply of prostitutes in the Netherlands ran low. A rise in the number of foreign prostitutes in the Netherlands was the result. First they were recruited from the West Indies and Latin America, and later they originated from Thailand and the Philippines. At the beginning of the 1980s it was becoming apparent that women from these countries were being trafficked and that professional crime networks were involved in this business.

In contrast to the small-scale businesses of the traditional red-light districts in the big cities, which existed in relatively peaceful coexistence with their working-class neighbours, the new sex industry was neither small-scale nor peaceful. Neighbourhood protests against its activities soon gained in strength. In response to these, local governments attempted to regulate and to re-zone the sex industry, only to find that the courts struck down such legislation as contravening the Penal Code. The ensuing demand for repeal of the ban on brothels by munici-palities effectively redefined the issue from a moral matter to one of law and order.

At the same time, the women's movement rediscovered prostitution and traf-ficking of women as issues. The context in which this happened was the campaign against sexual violence, which took off in the Netherlands in the mid-1970s when rape became an issue. But whereas feminists agreed on the goal of eliminating rape and other forms of sexual violence, on prostitution there was no feminist consensus.

Usually two feminist positions can be discerned. First, there is an anti-violence position, which regards prostitution as inherently involving sexual violence against women, thus making it essential to eliminate it – the abolitionist position. Kathleen Barry, an American feminist activist whose book *Female Sexual Slavery* (1979) played an important part in reviving the issue in the late 1970s on an international level, takes this position, regarding prostitution as sexual slavery. She is in favour of pressing states into ratifying the old UN Convention of 1949, with its abolitionist intent, and more recently she has been lobbying for a new international convention against sexual exploitation (Barry 1995). In this discourse 'forced' prostitution is a pleonasm; prostitution is by definition forced, leaving no room for the notion of 'voluntary' prostitution.

Second, there is a pro-rights approach, which sees prostitution as a choice or as a strategy of survival taken by women, which one should respect. Women have the right to sexual self-determination, and thus also to work in sex and to migrate in order to do so (Bell 1994; Phetersen 1996). Therefore prostitution itself is not the problem, but the excesses are; forced prostitution and trafficking, and the stigmatisation of prostitutes (usually called sex workers in this discourse) should be combated. The difference in the two feminist positions is reflected in the existence of two international feminist anti-trafficking organisations – the abolitionist Coalition against Trafficking in Women, and the Global Alliance against the Traffic in Women, which accepts prostitution as sex work.

Underlying the difference between the two positions is a conflicting view of male and female sexuality. In the first view, male sexuality is the problem, being seen as intrinsically connected to violence and domination. In the second view, male sexuality is a non-issue; it is just there. Both views share a basically essentialist position on male sexuality and the male sexual drive, which is held to be unchangeable and ever present. As to female sexuality, in the first view it is denied – women are seen as victims of male lust; the second view contends that women can voluntarily choose prostitution, thus defining prostitutes as knowledgeable sexual agents. Not all of those adhering to this second position set prostitution in the same feminist framework. Some are radical liberals, embracing free choice and celebrating sexual variety (e.g. Bell 1994). Others retain a feminist power critique by contextualising prostitution within an unequal relationship of sexual economic exchange (Phetersen 1996).

As prostitution became a feminist issue in the Netherlands – after rape, pornography, incest and sexual harassment had been redefined in terms of sexual violence and brought into the political arena by feminists – it was initially framed in the same terms as the other issues, as a matter of power of men over women. When in 1981 a new Cabinet of Christian Democrats and Socialists came to power, the new state secretary for women's equality policy, the socialist (and feminist activist) Hedy d'Ancona, made sexual violence a core topic in her policy. She had The Hague government conference on sexual violence organised in 1982, opening a policy arena for women experts in the area of sexual violence, women police working on vice squads, women civil servants from various ministries, and feminists campaigning on sexual violence. Although there was some prior discussion as to whether prostitution could be defined as sexual violence, the matter was left open for debate in a workshop on prostitution (Acker and Rawie 1982: 124). The workshop settled on a hybrid definition of prostitution. Prostitution was seen as reflecting power relations between men and women; woman is equated with her sexuality and has to submit her sexuality to the man's. At the same time, it held that prostitution could be work. The problem is then that prostitutes are labelled whores, stigmatising them. The workshop came up with a demand to repeal the ban on brothels as a first step in regulating the sex business and for improving the working conditions of prostitutes.

During the conference, members of the Working Group against Sex Tourism, which had set out to protest against male sex tourism in the Far East and to raise the issue of the prostitution of young girls in Thailand and the Philippines, brought trafficking in women to the fore. When at the end of the conference a Cabinet paper on sexual violence was announced, acknowledging it as an inter-ministerial issue and promising subsidies for research on the various sub-issues, traffic in women was included (Acker and Rawie 1982: 166). At this stage, one can conclude that prostitution was already defined as work, but as work within unequal relations between women and men. Trafficking was explicitly linked to women and to prostitution. Three very concrete demands on trafficking were now on the political agenda, all requiring the co-operation of the Ministry of Justice. First, there was a demand for raising the maximum penalty for trafficking from five to six years' imprisonment (in offences with a sentence of more than six years, suspects can be held in remand custody). Second, there was a demand to grant victims of trafficking a residence permit while offenders were being tried, as women who reported trafficking were usually expelled from the country straight away as illegal immigrants, and thus could not testify against traffickers. Third, there was a demand for the repeal of the clause prohibiting brothels in the Penal Code. When in 1982 a new Cabinet took power, in which the Liberals replaced the Socialists as coalition partners of the Christian Democrats, trafficking and lifting the ban on brothels both remained on the political agenda.

Decision-making

After this Cabinet change, feminist civil servants at the DCE were able to prevent prostitution reverting into a moral issue. At first they were ambivalent about the sex-as-work view of prostitution, but adopted it in the longer run, partly out of conviction, partly because it went along well with the pragmatic policy style prevalent in the Netherlands. The DCE started by commissioning research on trafficking; the ensuing report confirmed that it was no longer a marginal phenomenon but had become big business, linked to professional crime and to violence and coercion in recruitment practices (Buijs and Verbraken 1985). There followed a policy paper on sexual violence (Nota 1984), which defined traffic in women as a form of sexual violence that contravened basic human rights, such as women's sexual self-determination and their right to physical and mental integrity. Lifting the ban on brothels and setting up decent business practices were formulated as policy goals in the 1985 policy paper on the status of women (Beleidsplan 1985).

As a first step in developing a policy network, the DCE set up and subsidised the Foundation against Traffic in Women, in which several members of the group against sex tourism were able to professionalise their activities. The Foundation has been able to establish contacts with an increasing number of victims of trafficking and to trace shifting 'trade routes', from the Far East to Latin America, and, since the fall of the Berlin Wall, increasingly Eastern Europe. In the following years the policy network also included the pressure group 'The Red Thread', which prostitutes had formed – with the help of a DCE subsidy – to secure their interests. Along with a civil rights group on prostitution (the Mr de Graaf Foundation) and a number of feminist lawyers, activists were able to develop an analysis of the issue in terms of a dichotomy of rich versus poor nations, and later on increasingly as a migration issue. They pointed out that sex work provided one of the very few migration options for women from developing nations, and they were careful to distinguish between forced prostitution and sex work. By subsidising these new groups, the DCE succeeded in creating its own clientele-system, but at the same time the network also challenged the monopoly held by traditional interests in the policy arena around the issues.

However, by 1986 it was becoming evident that an effective policy against trafficking in the Netherlands was hampered by several factors. The police were neither much informed about trafficking nor very active in tracing it. Victims of trafficking could only escape from their plight with great difficulty, not having passports, not speaking Dutch, often not trusting the local police, facing the risk of expulsion. Complaints from feminist activists and some more knowledgeable police officers led to the formation of a working party on traffic in women in 1987 by the five attorneys-general in the Netherlands, who formulate the policies and priorities on prosecution in the Dutch legal system. It resulted in temporary residency permits for victims of trafficking in 1988 (Vreemdelingencirculaire, in De Boer 1994: 4). The attorneys-general also came up with five new directives to facilitate prosecution of traffickers, and they produced a new definition of the crime in 1989, which became the basis of all later debate on revising the Penal Code. A person is held to be guilty when he forces another 'person' into prostitution, whether by violence or deception or misuse of authority (Staatscourant 1989).

Subsequent events have shown how hard it really is to tackle the issue. Local police forces often lack know-how and resources, and communication between them and national criminal investigation agencies is inadequate; moreover, the issue does not have high priority, despite the fact that fighting big crime is a top policy priority and that new guidelines for combating trafficking were issued in 1995 (Aanpak 1995). A small adjustment was also made in the Aliens Law in 1993, now allowing witnesses testifying in court on a trafficking charge to stay in the country for the duration of the trial (Staatscourant 1993).

Further legal changes demanded the co-operation of the Ministry of Justice, a traditionally conservative department. Faced with a successful feminist redefinition by the DCE and the women's movement of the sexual and moral issues in his territory, the Minister of Justice, Korthals Altes, a liberal of the law-and-order variety, set out to modernise the laws, while shedding feminist definitions from the mid-1980s. He proposed a parliamentary bill to repeal the brothel clause in order to be able to regulate prostitution and to prevent disturbances of the peace (*Handelingen Tweede Kamer*, 1984–85, 18202, nrs 1–3). In a second bill he proposed raising the maximum penalty for trafficking in 'persons' (instead of 'women') from five to six years, which fitted in well with increasing public sentiment in favour of higher sentences for criminals (*Handelingen Tweede Kamer*, 1988–89, 21027, nrs 1–3). The legalisation of brothels was passed by the Second Chamber in 1987, but the bill was temporarily stranded in the First Chamber. A new Cabinet of Socialists and Christian Democrats took power in 1989, and in 1992 a new Minister of Justice, the Christian Democrat Hirsch

Ballin, a militant Roman Catholic, amended the trafficking bill, introducing a surprise article on brothels.

Control over the brothels was to pass to local authorities, which would then be able to maintain the ban. The trafficking clause retained the new penalty and the gender-neutral definition of the offence, but created a difference between EU-resident and non-EU-resident women. Normally the latter need working permits to work in the Netherlands, but his bill stipulated that for work in brothels no such permits would be granted (*Handelingen Tweede Kamer*, 1992–93, 21027, nr 296). Furthermore, no distinction was made between 'forced prostitution' and 'voluntary prostitution'. Thus all women in prostitution from non-EU states were defined not only as victims of trafficking but also as illegal immigrants (Haveman en Wijers 1992: 30). The Second Chamber passed the bill, but the First Chamber was faced with a dilemma, as it cannot amend bills. If it wanted to legalise brothels, there would be no higher penalty for trafficking. By using the constitutional argument of equal treatment under the law, it had the brothel part retracted, and it managed to save the trafficking clause; the penalty was now raised from eight to ten years (*Handelingen Eerste Kamer*, 1992–93, 21027, 7–12–93). After this episode it took a new coalition government (Liberals, Socialists and D66) four years to draft a new bill on brothels. In June 1997 it was introduced in the Second Chamber, where it received its first reading in October. This bill again distinguishes between 'forced' and 'voluntary' prostitution, but will make it impossible for non-EU women to be legal prostitutes. Lifting the brothel ban does mean that prostitution can be regulated as work, but regulation also means control. Moreover, all proposals on trafficking have been framed gender-neutrally as trafficking of 'persons', while the overwhelming majority are women.

Foreign affairs and human rights

At the international level, femocrats from the DCE have formed an alliance with their colleagues from the Ministry of International Affairs. When human rights became central on the international agendas of the UN and the Council of Europe, this provided an excellent opportunity to introduce the distinction between forced and voluntary prostitution. In order to do so, the Netherlands representatives had to contest the article on trafficking of the UN Convention to Eliminate all forms of Discrimination against Women (CEDAW), which requires states to take measures against trafficking and 'the exploitation of the prostitution of women'. This can be read in an abolitionist way as being against the exploitation involved in the prostitution of women (e.g. Barry 1995), but the Netherlands interprets it to mean being against exploiting or taking advantage of prostitution as such, rather than being against it altogether. At the UN Beijing conference the Netherlands successfully pressed for sexual self-determination to be included in the final declaration, which also allows for the sexual self-determination of prostitutes (Beijing 1996). Recently, on the instigation of the DCE, the Netherlands tabled the issue within the EU, which led to the The Hague

Ministerial Declaration, in which the issue has been redefined as 'trafficking in women for purposes of sexual exploitation', holding it to be a violation of women's human rights. No stand was taken on prostitution.

Conclusions

From this analysis it can be concluded that the Dutch position on prostitution has evolved towards decriminalisation, with a strong attendant plea for eliminating trafficking and recognising prostitutes' rights, but that it is not wholly consistent. This is partly due to clashes between the prevalent pragmatic attitude to prostitution and remnants of the old moral position, and partly because of bureaucratic realities – several departments and units are involved, with diverse views and competing interests. It also emerges that the DCE has played an important role in getting the trafficking issue further up the political agenda and in reframing prostitution as sex work; it was already on the agenda through the lobbying efforts of various municipalities that wanted to repeal the ban on brothels in order to regulate the sex industry. The DCE has managed to open the policy arena for both issues to women's rights groups by funding their initiatives, an area that used to be dominated by the police, civil servants in the Ministry of Justice, and the local lobby. In alliance with sympathetic civil servants in Foreign Affairs, DCE femocrats have managed to get the issues addressed at the international level. Although in the legal battle a gender-neutral definition of trafficking is now on the books, in the international circuit the fight to maintain the older definition about women being trafficked is not lost.

Having read this article, the reader may well wonder what has happened to sexuality in the course of events. Sexuality has indeed almost vanished from the public discourse on these issues. This disappearance is the result of the fact that all actors in the debate have come to agree, more or less, with the construction of prostitution as work. They distinguish between voluntary and forced prostitution, pointing out that many prostitutes from abroad are not victims of trafficking but are (mainly illegal) immigrants. Once one subscribes to the view that prostitution is work, one does not have to discuss the nature of the interaction. In the broader definition of 'traffic in persons', the link between prostitution and trafficking has disappeared, undoing the old feminist linkage. This link helped to remind us that women are being trafficked for the sexual needs of men, exposing the fact that both issues – prostitution and trafficking – are about sexuality and sexual domination. In public debate, prostitution has become detached from this feminist framing. It is forgotten that the economic exchange of sexual services functions within unequal relationships between the sexes; the buyer wants sex but the seller needs money (Phetersen 1996).

References

Aanpak van mensenhandel. 1995. *Handleiding van de collegevergadering van de Procureurs-Generaal*, 10 May 1995.

Acker, H., and Rawie, M. 1982. *Seksueel geweld tegen vrouwen en meisjes.* Den Haag: Ministerie van Sociale Zaken en Werkgelegenheid/Directie Coordinatie Emancipatiebeleid.

Barry, K. 1979. *Female Sexual Slavery.* New York: Avon Books.

——— 1995. *The Prostitution of Sexuality.* New York: New York University Press.

Beijing nu en toekomst. 1996. Den Haag: Ministerie van Sociale Zaken en Werkgelegenheid, September.

Beleidsplan Emancipatie. 1985. *Handelingen Tweede Kamer.* Zittingsjaar 1984–85, 19052, nr 2.

Bell, S. 1994. *Reading, Writing and Rewriting the Prostitute Body.* Bloomington/Indianapolis: Indiana University Press.

Buijs, H.W.J., and Verbraken, A.M. 1985. *Vrouwenhandel. Onderzoek naar aard, globale omvang en de kanalen waarlangs vrouwenhandel in Nederland plaatsvindt.* Den Haag: Ministerie van Sociale Zaken en Werkgelegenheid.

Commissie Melai. 1977. *Derde Interimrapport: Prostitutie.* Den Haag: Staatsdrukkerij.

De Boer, M. 1994. *Vrouwenhandel: beleid in beeld. Eindrapport 'Evaluatie van de PG-richtlijnen voor de opsporing en de vervolging van vrouwenhandel'.* Utrecht: W.C. Pompe Instituut voor strafrechtwetenschappen.

De Vries, P. 1997. *Kuisheid voor mannen, vrijheid voor vrouwen. De reglementering en de bestrijding van prostitutie in Nederland in de tweede helft van de negentiende eeuw.* Hilversum: Verloren.

Handelingen Eerste Kamer. Zittingsjaar 1992–93, 21027, 7–12–93.

Handelingen Tweede Kamer. Zittingsjaar 1984–85, 18202, nrs 1–3 (Opheffing bordeelverbod).

——— Zittingsjaar 1988–89, 21027, nrs 1–3 (vrouwenhandel).

——— Zittingsjaar 1992–93, 21027, nr 296.

Haveman, R. 1995. 'Slavernij of reguliere arbeid?' *Nemesis* 11: 97–102.

Haveman, R., and Wijers, M. 1992. 'Vrouwenhandel als politiek spel.' *Nemesis* 8: 30–5.

Nota Bestrijding Seksueel Geweld. 1984. *Handelingen Tweede Kamer,* zittingsjaar 1983–84, 18542, nrs 1–2.

Outshoorn, J. 1994. 'Between movement and government: femocrats in the Netherlands'. *Schweizerisches Jahrbuch für politische Wissenschaft/Annuaire Suisse de science politique,* 141–65. Bern/Stuttgart/Wien: Haupt.

——— 1995. 'Administrative accommodation in the Netherlands: the Directorate for the Coordination of Equality Policy'. In D. McBride Stetson, and A. Mazur (eds), *Comparative State Feminism,* pp. 168–86. Thousand Oaks/London/New Delhi: Sage.

Phetersen, G. 1996. *The Prostitution Prism.* Amsterdam: Amsterdam University Press.

Staatscourant. 1989. *Richtlijnen voor de opsporing en vervolging van vrouwenhandel,* 24 May 1989, nr 100.

——— 1993. *Aanpassing Vreemdelingencirculaire B22,* 19 April 1993.

Van Mens, L. 1992. *Prostitutie in bedrijf: organisatie, management en arbeidsverhoudingen in seksclubs and privehuizen.* Delft: Eburon.

Index